APR 19	DATE DUE		
JUL 14			

The Operative

F
Jeno

The Operative

A NOVEL

JERRY B. JENKINS

1817

Harper & Row, Publishers, San Francisco

New York, Cambridge, Philadelphia, St. Louis
London, Singapore, Sydney, Tokyo

FIRST HARPER & ROW PAPERBACK EDITION PUBLISHED IN 1989.

Library of Congress Cataloging-in-Publication Data

Jenkins, Jerry B.
  The operative.

  I. Title.
PS3560.E48506   1987   813'.54   87-45179
ISBN 0-06-250410-X

88   89   90   91   92   MAPLE   10   9   8   7   6   5   4   3   2   1

For my father—

To have half his character
is my loftiest dream.

The Operative

One

Just before dark, Jordan Kettering arrived at the tacky Coachlight Hotel, six hundred thirty steps from the underground at Piccadilly Circus. He had come a day's journey by train and ferry from West Germany, carrying the burden of the secret he had learned in Frankfurt. Now he registered as P. Gaston Blanc of Le Havre, France, and using an accent that would have fooled all but a Frenchman, he ordered a double room with private W.C. "My wife will be joining me later."

Jordan was on his own, off duty, in London on pleasure. Yet after his assignment in Germany, he couldn't relax. In nearly twenty years of intelligence service, he had never used his own name outside the United States. Jordan had a gift for blending into any background. To be visible was to be vulnerable, and in Jordan's profession, vulnerability was a mortal sin. Remaining invisible was at least good practice, even when unnecessary. But now it was necessary.

He climbed the stairway to room 312, then walked past the room and around one corner to a window at the end of the hall. None of the four rooms in that wing appeared occupied, so Jordan carefully set his trunk in the middle of the wood floor and moved back for a quick look down the other hall. There was no one.

He returned to the window and located the drain pipe outside that led to the alley below. The window lock, buried under dust and grime, was stuck rock solid. Jordan traced a circle around the lock with his finger, then pushed the greasy soil around and between the metal parts.

1

He spread his legs and pressed his thighs against the sill, using both hands on the lock. When it broke free, he gripped the handles at the bottom of the frame, filled his lungs, and held his breath. His veins bulged and blood rushed to his face as he began a slow, steady pull. At last, the frame cracked free of the years of paint that had sealed it shut.

Jordan raised the window, lowered it again, and looked up. Above his head, two ceiling bulbs gave off a dim light. The one nearest the window hung bare; the other had a glass globe fixture. He headed back out to the corner for another peek. Confident he was still alone, he moved his trunk under the light farther from the window. Without a sound, he leaped atop the trunk and removed the glass globe. Within another minute, he had moved his trunk to reach the other light and unscrewed the bulb just enough for it to go out. He put the globe over it to discourage a lazy maintenance man. The window sill was now in nearly total darkness, and Jordan's way of escape, should he ever need it, was prepared. He figured he could be out of his room, through the window, down the drain pipe, through the alley to the street, and into the traffic at Piccadilly in less than a minute and a half.

In his room he hoisted his trunk onto the squeaky bed and removed from it three spring-loaded, wooden pistols. Each pistol contained so little metal that it could elude x-ray detection, yet was so powerful that it was worthless after its second shot. The only time he had tried to coax a third firing from one, the gun had disintegrated in his right hand. The resulting injury had left a rubbery scar in his palm. Jordan slipped one loaded pistol between the mattress and springs, taped another under the lid of the tank behind the toilet, and wrapped the third pistol in the top of his sweat suit on the dresser.

From deep in one corner of his trunk, he pulled a gray, metal box that looked like a clock radio with suction cups on the back. It was only about six inches square, but weighed more than ten pounds. Jordan removed the suction cups and applied them directly to the wall beside the door, using drops of hydraulic fluid and miniature vise tighteners. He then screwed the heavy box to them and, from the side of the box, pulled a woven wire cable with a loop at its end.

The cable loop he slipped around the handle of his closed door. He then opened the door a half inch until the cable grew taut. Jordan grasped the door handle with both hands and planted both feet on the wall beneath the box.

With his hands and feet just inches apart and his body suspended at doorknob height, he pulled on the handle and pushed with his legs, using all his strength and 165 pounds to test the security system. Neither the box nor the suction cups gave way. When he felt the wall creak under his feet, he slowly released his grip and stepped down. Anyone who tried to get through that door with the box and cable in place would do better to blast through the hinged side.

Jordan hung four days' worth of clothes in the closet, put his toiletries in the bathroom, and crawled on the floor to wedge his makeup kit between the tub and the wall. He secured the trunk not only with its normal locks, but also with a dead-bolt system that required a screw driver and pliers. The trunk was too large to hide, so he shoved it as deep into the closet as he could.

He changed into his hooded sweat suit, stretched arms, legs, and back, and did forty fingertip push-ups. Jordan glanced at his watch. Rosemary's plane from the States would touch down in exactly four hours. A hard four-mile run would leave him time for a warm-down, his makeup, a leisurely stroll to the Tube, and the ride to Heathrow.

He made sure his wooden pistol was loaded, but uncocked, before he slipped it and his room key into the deepest part of the pocket that extended across his sweat shirt at the abdomen. He'd come close to seriously injuring himself a few years earlier when he took a tumble in a dark tunnel while jogging in Quantico, Virginia. His gun had discharged, and the bullet had ripped through his sweat pants at the crotch, miraculously missing his body. The equipment manager smiled when he surveyed the damage and issued the new sweats. "Almost a .22-caliber vasectomy."

Jordan stepped out into the hallway and pulled the door shut to within a hand's width before he reached in deftly to slip the security cable around the inside knob. He gave the cable a slight tug to trip the mechanism, much like that on a standard sun shade, which pulled the heavy wire taut.

At home in the United States, Jordan would have pulled his hood up over his ears and begun his run inside the hotel, bounding down the stairs and past the desk, reaching cruising speed by the time he burst through the front door. But such behavior would have been considered noisy and offensive in London, even in a dive like the Coachlight. So Jordan maintained a casual walk as he dropped off his key and exited the lobby, nodding to the clerk who merely returned his gaze. Under a street light, he set the reverse stopwatch on his wrist for twenty-one minutes.

He stepped across the street and rolled from a slow trot to a full, striding, elbows-out gallop that quickly settled into a five-minute-mile pace. To the uninitiated, his run might have looked like a sprint. Jordan liked to give the impression that he was doing more than jogging. He had a purpose, a goal, a destination. He was on his way somewhere and he had to be there soon.

In fact his only destination was wherever he found himself when his watch said he'd run for half of however much time he had allotted. Figuring that he was stronger when he started, the challenge was to make it back to his starting point before the rest of the time was gone.

He resisted the temptation to sandbag the first half of his run to make the second half easier. While his lungs were strong and fresh and his lactic acid and oxygen were in full supply, he made himself run straight up, breathing only through his nose, keeping his gait and the swing of his arms strong and fluid.

At the five-minute mark, he could no longer keep his mouth closed, but he was careful to breathe through both mouth and nose. When he felt his arms dropping, he shook them out and quickened his pace. Evening was coming on. The exclusive shops on Bond and Regent streets were closed. A few still had lights on in their display windows, and Jordan took passing notice of the heavy, woolen women's apparel that Rosemary would love.

When he reached ten and a half minutes not far from a cross street to Saint James, he pulled his hood down and ran back almost the whole way in and around the traffic from the clubs, some noisy, some posh, some both. The brisk October air hit his sweaty head like a splash of water and invigorated him. He was held up only once at an alley corner where a taxi pulled in to turn around. When Jordan ran around the car, the cabbie backed up. Jordan yelled. The cabbie swore. Jordan waved him on. The cabbie waved, too, but not with his entire hand.

The stall annoyed Jordan, but the extra adrenalin gave him a second wind, and he felt he'd made up for the lost time. He avoided looking at his watch until he was within two long blocks of the Coachlight. Thirty-five seconds were left. He sprinted all out.

As Jordan pulled up under his street light, he stopped the watch. It showed minus fourteen seconds. The second leg had been slower. He was irritated with himself.

He kicked at the pavement as he neared the front door and stubbed his toe.

With his foot still smarting, Jordan gingerly climbed the stairs to his room, thinking that a bona fide limp wouldn't hurt his disguise. He used both hands to unscrew the trigger of the gun in his pocket. When he had unlocked and opened his door an inch or two, he slid the tiny trigger into the box on the wall and disengaged the cable.

Safe inside, he pulled his hood up again and sat on the edge of the bed with his head down and his arms folded, hands in his armpits. Roasting in his own body heat after a strenuous run was one of Jordan's favorite half-dozen physical pleasures. The radiator on the wall knocked and hissed, and he sat there sweating until the moisture dripped from the end of his nose.

Frankfurt. Had he been there only last night? It seemed a career ago. Somehow he had never been directed there before. And when he arrived, the assignment—though it called for a disguise—consisted of little more than information gathering.

At first, Jordan thought the whole idea strange. Why would the agency take a senior operative out of Washington just days before his vacation and assign him an essentially menial task? But when the assignment was over and he asked a secretary at Joint Operations Support Activity Frankfurt (JOSAF) to book a flight for him to London, he found she had already been given other instructions.

"Chief Stuart would like to see you, sir."

"Stu's here? I didn't even know that!"

She ushered him in to Stanley Stuart, a beefy, jowly man of bushy brow. Jordan greeted him warmly, having not seen him for more than fifteen years, but the elder exhibited no interest in bringing Jordan up to date on his career. He got to the point quickly.

"I'm sorry to have had to bring you all the way over

here to JOSAF, but the man I trust most in the agency once told me that you were honest to a fault. Is that still true?"

Jordan was stunned. How does one answer a question like that? He shrugged, choosing not to get into his fundamentalist, midwestern upbringing. A sound whipping for lying at age eight contributed to an overdeveloped conscience that had made him rather black and white in that area, it was true.

Stuart, eyes dark and face somber, didn't accept the response. "True or not, Kettering? Harley Rollins told me you wouldn't so much as tell a white lie unless it was in the line of duty."

"I guess it's true, sir." There was something ominous about the conversation, and Jordan wasn't sure he wanted to know—just before his vacation—what it was.

"Jordan, I'm sixty-six years old. I retire this year."

"Oh, sir, I hope you're not looking for a successor, because I—."

Stuart shook his head and glared. "No, Kettering. We don't pick our own replacements. And I certainly wouldn't wish *this* job on anyone, least of all you. I just need to know: can I trust you or not? Rollins told me if I ever needed someone with the bedrock trustworthiness of a Sunday school teacher, it was you. Has the job gotten to you after all these years and eroded your character as much as it had to erode your attitude?"

It was an excellent question. Was Jordan still idealistic? Did he still serve his country for the same reasons as when he started? Had he become cynical? The answers were no, no, and yes. But the question on the table now was whether his integrity had been compromised.

"The answer is no, Mr. Stuart. I have the same attitude problem as anyone who's been in this business this long, but you can trust me. If I was worthy of that comment from Harley Rollins years ago, it still holds."

Jordan hoped that this assurance would pull from the

older man whatever news it was he felt compelled to share, but no. He would have to wait.

"You know Altstadt, Jordan?"

"Old Town? Sure. Bordering the river."

Stuart nodded. "In the medieval section where the tradesmen and craftsmen have their shops is one called *Jurgen Glaswerks*. I'll see you there tonight at eight. In the back."

Stanley Stuart stood quickly and pulled on his coat and hat. Jordan felt stupid, still sitting back in his chair with his legs crossed. He rose awkwardly, but before he could produce any departing amenities, Stuart was gone.

In London nearly thirty hours later, Jordan shuddered when his body temperature peaked and he began coming down the other side. He removed the pistol, shedded the sweats, and stretched back onto the bed in his underwear. There was fatigue from the run, but no drowsiness. He had been on such a disciplined sleeping pattern for two decades that he was able to regulate his alertness in any time zone.

With three hours left until Rosemary's plane landed, Jordan turned over in his mind the events of the previous evening. Finding the *Jurgen Glaswerks* had been easy. He was greeted in broken English by the owner, who thrust out his hand and announced himself loudly. "Jurgen Hasse! You are welcome, sir."

With barely a moment to notice the beautiful blownglass objects gracing the shelves, Jordan followed Herr Hasse to the back. There his host left him alone with Stanley Stuart. Stuart was even more direct and laconic than he had been a few hours before. He sat stiffly with his hands thrust deeply into his pockets, his hat still on. The room was cold, despite a few remaining glowing coals from the central furnace where the craftsmen plied their trade by day. So Jordan left on his coat, too. He held his hat in his hands.

Without a word of greeting, Stuart nodded toward the departing Hasse. "An old, old trusted friend. I wish he had your gifts."

Jordan fought a smile. "What you wish is that you knew me and trusted me as well as you do him."

Stuart was not amused. "True enough." He changed the subject. "The place is not bugged. Hasse has never heard of or seen either of us. We can talk."

Jordan wanted to say, "So, talk," but he said nothing. If ol' Stu Stuart needed to be cajoled into revealing what was on his mind, it was probably more frivolous than not. Anyway, Jordan knew he couldn't convince Harley Rollins's old friend of his trustworthiness by just talking about it.

Stuart rose wearily and dragged his heavy, wood chair next to Jordan's. "Wife died four years back."

"I heard. Sorry."

Stuart waved off the tardy sentiment. "Funny thing. Lost the drive after that. Never gave her enough time. Never loved her as much as the agency, she always said. Probably right. But when she was gone, I knew I'd been showin' off for her all those years. That was what kept me goin'. The change in my performance showed, Jordan. And quick. I was reassigned here so fast, I'm still gettin' over the jet lag."

Jordan wanted to chuckle, but Stuart was so subdued, so melancholy, he knew the old man wasn't trying to be humorous. "I guess I lost track of you, sir. Didn't really know you were here."

It was as if the older man hadn't heard him. He stared deep into Jordan's eyes, as if searching for confirmation that he was doing the right thing. His voice came thick and labored. "I can't even tell Harley this, Jordan. And there's no one else I trust anywhere."

Jordan felt burdened already, and he hadn't even heard the news. "Why can't you tell Harley, Stu? You know you can trust him. You can trust me, too, but it's clear you're not as comfortable with me."

"He trusts you. That'll have to be good enough for me."

"But it's not. I can tell. Why don't you tell Harley? He can bring me into it if he wants."

Jordan knew how that must sound to Stuart, and the JOSAF chief *had* brought him to West Germany for this conversation alone. He tried to communicate with his expression a willingness he had not exhibited in words.

Stuart glowered. "Rollins is not in a position to do any good. And this is big, Jordan, bigger than anything I've been involved with. Ever. I've been offered money."

"For what?"

The older man leaned over and looked to the front of the stop. It was dark. There was no sound from the alley in back. He dug deep into a breast pocket and pulled out a fat manila envelope that had been folded vertically. Stuart carefully pressed the package flat against his thigh, then opened it.

He produced three eight-by-ten, black-and-white photographs. The first showed a rolling hillside with a huge dark opening cut into one end. Stuart pointed to that dark opening with his thumb. "That's maybe two hundred feet across." Jordan nodded.

The second photo showed two corrugated metal doors recessed beneath the earthen overhang of the hill, set in about thirty feet.

"What's that look like to you, Jordan?"

"A Quonset hut?"

"Bigger. Remember the relative size of all this. What's a huge Quonset hut?"

"A hangar?"

"Exactly."

The third photo had been taken inside the hangar. Jordan pursed his lips.

"MiGs?" he asked.

Stuart nodded.

Jordan held the photograph up to the dim light. "Apparently, Russian MiG-23s, but no markings. I don't get it."

Stuart reached for the picture and placed it atop the others. He picked up the stack and held it gently, as if he had been perusing family photos.

"Pure white. The naked eye can hardly find them in the sky on a clear day. And this photo shows only a handful. Actually, there are nearly two dozen in that one double hangar built into the hillside."

"Cuba?"

"Don't get ahead of me now, Jordan."

"Sorry."

"It's just that now that I've shown you these, I have to tell you, and you have to believe me. I'm not a crazy old man, though you'll be tempted to think so. Your job, your life, will never be the same."

The older man stood and paced the cold room. The last ember had died, and the only light came from a couple of weak bulbs.

"The hangar is not in Cuba, my friend, though the planes came from there, yes. Actually, they came from the Soviet Union first, of course."

Jordan squinted at him. "Stu, we've known of Soviet MiGs in Cuba for years."

Stuart held up a hand and continued. "These are not *in* Cuba, Jordan. That's what I'm trying to say to you. They are *from* Cuba. This hangar is set back into the earth, invisible from the sky, but it lies in the middle of four other hangars that hold crop-dusting planes. Radar or aerial photography merely confirms the existence of crop dusters and a small landing strip in the middle of thousands of acres of farm country." Jordan was afraid to ask where. Stuart continued. "You're well aware of our radar gap along the southern border of the United States?"

Jordan nodded. "Biggest headache is drug traffic, right?"

"Until now. These MiGs were shipped from Cuba to Central America, trucked north into Mexico, and then flown—get this, *flown* into the United States between El Paso and Laredo, Texas, or through the Yucatán Passage via the Gulf of Mexico."

Jordan felt the blood drain from his face. "You're telling me these Soviet MiGs are hangared in the States?"

"Alabama."

Jordan stood. "I don't believe it."

"That's a big help."

"What evidence do we have that they have nuclear capability?"

"That's next."

"What do you mean, that's next?"

"The next step is equipping them for nuclear warfare."

"Says who?"

"My contact."

"Which is who?"

"Jordan! If I knew that, I wouldn't be talking to you. But I do know this: the source is *very* highly placed in our agency."

"How do you know that?"

"How long have I been around, kid? This guy knows too much."

"Soviet counter intelligence?"

"Nah. A newcomer. In it for the dough."

"And how does he contact you?"

"Through a local mouthpiece. I've been sitting on this for a month, Jordan, trying to decide whom to tell."

"A month! Stu, those MiGs could be nuclear equipped by now!"

"You think I don't know that? Who was I supposed to tell? I could go to the top, but what if it's him?"

"Don't be silly."

"Silly! Whoever this is knows all about me, Jordan. Things no one but an insider would know."

"Are you being blackmailed?"

"Of course I'm not, but who do I go to? I had to tell somebody who can check it out before making any moves. Harley can't do that anymore."

"So, the deal is what?"

"If I help, big dollars. If I don't, I'm dead meat."

Jordan closed his eyes. "You've been threatened before, Stu. We all have. And you've risked your life a dozen times in defense of the United States."

"Of course I have! But the message goes like this: The source says I've got what—fifteen, twenty more years max on this earth? So what's it matter who's in power if I'm taken care of, and very handsomely?"

"That's ridiculous."

"Of course it is! It makes me sick, and don't even imply otherwise."

"But why you?"

"Why not me? This inside man says he knows I have to hate the agency for reassigning me after my wife's death. I don't, but if that's what he wants to think, maybe that's all right for now. I'm just glad he started with me instead of with somebody who might have been tempted."

"And what are you going to do?"

"I'm doing it, Jordan. Right here. Right now. I'm telling you about it. There's nothing more I *can* do. Knowing what *I* know, where would *you* start? Somebody big is helping Cuba and Mexico put Soviet planes right in our backyard. And if I forget that at least one of our own people is involved and just send the defense department in shooting, how do I know there isn't a nuclear warhead in there that'll touch off World War III?"

Two

Jordan rose from his creaky London hotel bed to shower and shave. He was glad he had never had to shave more than once every two days. His face in the mirror seemed younger than his forty-one years. Not even a crow's foot wrinkle had begun around the eyes yet, and for that he was grateful. He did nothing except stay in top physical condition to be able to pass for as young as his early twenties. Even his doctor was impressed. "The body is one thing, Jordan. But the face, that's a gift."

His feathery, blond hair was a gift, too, for it had not begun to gray yet, even after many dyeings and washings. Only occasionally had he risked a temporary dye. A sudden rain or having to go several days without a touch-up would have given him away.

For the Frankfurt assignment, he had dyed the hair dark brown, including eyelashes and eyebrows. Rosemary didn't know. There had been times early in their marriage when it had been disconcerting to her to not know what Jordan would look like when she picked him up at Dulles International. He might have left her a golden-haired, hazel-eyed young man and returned weeks later a gray-haired, dark-eyed man in his early fifties.

The only characteristic that got in the way of his disguises was the broad neck of the football player he had never been. He had never even tried out. But the weight training and the neck bridging that football players found so crucial, Jordan needed as well. It added a core of power unusual to his five-foot, nine-inch frame, but it was hard to hide at times.

Jordan was so good at the disguises, became so immersed in them that until his normal hair grew back out and he removed the contact lenses (which were only for color because his vision was still perfect), he often forgot to drop the voice or carriage that went with the ruse.

Rosemary had even accused him of faking that now and then, but she knew better. She could only guess at the tension, the deep-down, drop-dead terror of being found out that made him concentrate so fully on every bogus nuance.

She would never forget the day she called him to the dining room for Sunday dinner and he awoke from dozing before the television. His hair was white from a recent assignment, and not until he was at the table and was fully awake did he remember to drop the feeble voice, the bent posture, and the halting gait.

It had scared her, made her wonder if he had somehow become trapped in one of his many personae. He apologized and found the incident troubling, but better he err in his own home than in the face of a mortal enemy.

In Frankfurt, he had passed for a thirty-year-old with his own eye color and dark hair. Now he would use the same hair color, but try to look like an undergraduate student. As he knelt to retrieve his makeup kit, he despised the whole idea.

For once, he wished he had a break, a reason not to look over his shoulder at every corner. He was looking forward to spending three weeks with his wife in Europe; it was a dream they had shared since he began traveling the continent so many years before. He was to have flown with her to London this very night, but then the emergency arose in Germany and he had come ahead of her by ten days. He had hoped that maybe when they had been together a week and the pace slackened, he would

15

tell her about it. And maybe about some of the other assignments, too.

But now, he was still compelled to use an alias, secure his room, and prepare his escape route. These precautions would allow him to sleep. Just because he was on vacation didn't mean that those whose responsibility it was to keep tabs on him were napping on the job.

He guessed that at least four agencies and as many individuals knew he had booked several flights to various locations out of Frankfurt. And maybe all of them knew he had actually boarded a train to London. How many knew he was to be on the flight from America with his wife? He had never cancelled the reservation.

As he combed his eyebrows in toward his nose and snipped them carefully, he hoped his wife wouldn't be offended. Just once he wished one of his disguises could be only for fun. She would wonder, he knew, why he couldn't just forget the job for these three weeks they had been looking forward to for years. She would wonder why he didn't just dye his hair blond until his natural color came back.

He had planned it that way, but now—since Frankfurt—it was impossible. Since Frankfurt. That thought, he feared, would follow him to his grave. Rosemary couldn't know. Not yet. And since he had to stay underground anyway, he would introduce himself even to her as Gaston Blanc, hoping to pass as a European undergraduate student. He would ask if she was Mrs. Jordan Kettering and then inform her that her husband had asked him to escort her to the hotel.

It wouldn't be long before she would recognize him from his height or his eyes—even with the dark brown lenses—or his hands. She said she would recognize his hands anywhere. Perhaps he would walk with his hands thrust deep in his pants pockets. Still he was betting he couldn't fool her more than a full minute.

Under other circumstances, the ruse might even be fun. Perhaps she would assume this lighter side of him was evidence that he was indeed putting the job out of his mind for the brief time they would enjoy together. For as long as possible, he would pretend it was just for her benefit. The only storm in their marriage had arisen over his obsession with the work, but she had reconciled herself to it.

He had been careful, of course, to force the job out of his mind as much as possible when he was home in Maryland. But he and Rosemary had talked of the day when their son and daughter would be in college and she could travel with him the first time. That time was now, and while Europe had long since lost its novelty for Jordan, he planned to make the most of it for Rosemary's sake. She had looked forward to this trip the way she looked forward to Christmas. Or heaven.

His face was smooth, his dark lenses were in, his hair was dark and longish. He spread a light latex film over his teeth to give them the not-repugnant, but distinctive look of the casual European hygienist. That would brush off easily.

At worst, Rosemary would be hurt that he would even think she would be amused by a disguise. At best, she would be impressed, but then she would assume he could forget all vestiges of the deceit that for him was everyday reality. But, since Frankfurt. . . .

He slipped on worn, tan, rubber-soled hush puppies over thin, light green socks, and dark brown, corduroy trousers that rode low on his hips under a thin belt. A shiny, medium brown shirt with a pointy collar was mostly hidden under a horizontally striped, deep purple sweater vest, and the whole ensemble was topped by a waist-length jacket of indeterminate origin. All his clothing carried labels from France. All were mass produced. For good measure he added a pair of gold, wire-rim glasses

17

with round lenses and a fabric fisherman's cap with a short bill. There was the hint of a young John Lennon, but with a wood pistol in the right jacket pocket.

Over his shoulder Jordan/Gaston slung a worn, leather pouch with school books, wallet, and forged papers. On his way to Heathrow, he spoke either in French or with a thick French accent to ticket sellers and conductors. He arrived at the airport an hour early and paced the corridors, his left foot with the jaunty step of a young collegian, his right with the tender flinch of a limping jogger who had taken out a disappointing performance on an innocent toe.

Heathrow didn't slow to a crawl near midnight the way O'Hare or Dallas-Fort Worth did. Though the late afternoon and early evening peak was past, several international flights were scheduled to arrive around the same time, and crowds began to build again after 11:00 P.M.

The closed-circuit monitors told Jordan that Rosemary's flight would arrive in Terminal Two, which surprised him. It was the same terminal in which one of his decoy flights from Frankfurt had arrived, and it was generally limited to European traffic.

On his way to the customs area, he noticed a Scotland Yard antiterrorist commander he'd worked with two years before. He and Huck Williamsby knew each other well. To test himself, he stepped up to the husky, freckly, red-eyed detective.

"*S'il vous plaît.* Vy vould American flight arrive in Terminal Two?"

"I dunno. Security, I suspect. Wouldn't make too much of it."

"*Merci.*"

Williamsby had not shown the slightest suspicion. Jordan felt a tingle at the base of his spine. He wished he could enjoy this.

He was among the first at the thick, Plexiglas window

that separated the waiting from the arriving foreign passengers at the international gate in Terminal Two. The customs desks had been hastily assembled as if the arrival were an unscheduled late change. The glass partition, however, was permanent.

As midnight neared, Jordan felt the heat and heard the murmuring of the crowd stacked several deep behind him at the glass wall. The line of more than four hundred that had emerged from the Boeing 747 was quickly divided into eight rows, and the tedious customs process began.

Jordan felt a worrisome nagging in the pit of his stomach. Was it only coincidence that he had run into Williamsby, and that the overseas flight was arriving at Terminal Two, and that the customs officers had apparently been instructed to search all hand luggage?

The process would take more than an hour, and it simply wasn't standard. After about twenty minutes, Rosemary appeared in the line directly in front of Jordan and about forty feet away.

Her line was moving particularly slowly, but she appeared in good spirits. Jordan thought she looked youthful and radiant, and he more than ever regretted the necessity of his charade. If only he could take off the glasses and the hat and wave at her, smiling in a way that she would recognize.

But she had apparently already studied the crowd behind the glass and decided he wasn't there yet. She struck up a conversation with the passenger behind her, a well-dressed man of average height and blond hair. When they noticed lightning from the north windows facing Bath Road, he joked and she laughed. From her huge shoulder bag, she dug out a pair of rubber boots.

The man extended his hand to help her balance on one foot as she struggled with the boots. Jordan was impressed that the stranger was not forward. His hand was there if she needed it and could be ignored without embarrassment. She used it and thanked him, and when her boots were on, she studied the crowd behind the glass again.

Opening lines ran through Jordan's mind as he fixed his eyes on his wife. If she could recognize him before he spoke, then good for her. No harm done. She looked at him, behind him, next to him, and at him again. He made no attempt to hide or look the other way. She looked through him as if he wasn't there. To her, he was a young European of inconsequential description.

Suddenly, from just above Jordan's head to his right and behind him about four feet came rapid-fire explosions that drove everyone, including Jordan, to the floor. Even as he went down his trained ear told him that the weapon tearing into the Plexiglas—weakening it, cracking it, shattering it, then cutting down the passengers as they scattered, screaming—was an American-made M-16.

Jordan instinctively reached for the wooden pistol in his pocket and tried to turn to see the gunman. But a thick, middle-aged woman had tumbled onto his legs and an infant had been dropped on his back. As the others behind the now-fragmented glass moaned and wailed and hid their faces, Jordan knew the attacker was long gone. Slowly he drew himself up to his knees, his hands empty, careful to let the baby slide gently to the fake marble floor.

From his position, Jordan could see the damage. Apparently the M-16 had carried a thirty-shot magazine that was spent in one burst of nearly two and a half seconds. The first dozen shots had obliterated the Plexiglas except for a three-foot, mountain-shaped shard that could now be pushed over with a finger.

Once the glass barrier had been eliminated, the next twenty or so rounds had been sprayed back and forth over a fifteen-foot area, leveling customs agents, shattering their portable wood partitions, and dropping passengers from forty feet with 5.56-millimeter ammunition that had kill-power from 500 yards.

Uniformed police and military men appeared from all directions, shouting instructions, securing doors and corridors. Plain-clothes men, including Huck Williamsby, arrived seconds later, producing badges from inside their suit jackets and displaying them from breast pockets.

Passengers who had miraculously survived the attack huddled behind their hand baggage, terrified of the weapons they saw in several hands. Directly in front of Jordan a customs agent was bleeding from the head and neck. He had turned at the first sound of the gunfire against the normally bullet-proof Flexiglas and, wide-eyed, took two rounds before he knew what was happening.

Now he crawled, expressionless, eyes vacant, toward Jordan, but his nervous system surrendered, his elbows quit, and his forehead thudded lifeless to the floor. Beyond him and his splintered work station Jordan saw the central target of the shooting, the line in which his wife had been standing, bantering with a stranger after pulling on her boots.

The man behind her had taken at least four bullets and had flipped backward, his metal attaché case sent sliding. Rosemary's shoulder bag had been ripped from her by the fusillade, dropping in front of her and providing a macabre cushion for her petite body after she had spun in a circle, ankles crossing and tripping her.

She had landed with her back on the bag, her head hanging over it, facing Jordan. Not sixty seconds had passed since the first shattering noise, and now Jordan cursed himself for his disguise. Bile rose in his throat as he fought the emotion that threatened to jeopardize the level-headedness that had always been his in the face of carnage.

He whipped off his hat and glasses and squinted hard as he pressed fingers to his eyelids, popping out the dark lenses. He stared into his wife's unblinking eyes, willing her to see him, to recognize him despite the dark coloring of his hair, brows, and lashes, showing her his teeth in a half-sobbing smile, praying she would recognize him.

Jordan knelt transfixed before the image of her there. As officials scurried among the dead and the dying, he caught and lost and caught again the clear view of her face. There was no expression. No response. One of the first bullets not deflected by the plexiglass had entered her neck from the left side, nicked a jugular vein, destroyed a carotid artery, pierced a parathyroid gland, and severed the spinal cord on its way toward the heart of the man behind her.

Rosemary Kettering had been dead before she hit the floor.

Three

During the ghastly silence between the thirty shots and the shrieking that still carried on, Jordan realized, though he wasn't ready for the full absorption of it, that his beloved was gone. Still, he stared at her and wanted to go to her, to pull her from her awkward repose on the shoulder bag.

With his contact lenses in his left hand and his hat and glasses in his right, he slowly stood. Law enforcement officers tried to calm the surviving passengers and those who had been waiting. People all around him were trying to tell the police what had happened. They imagined that the gunfire had come from all angles, the noise had been so deafening. They concocted stories of a band of men and women terrorists with grenades and pistols.

Jordan was tempted to break his cover, to tell the authorities that all the bullets had come from the same weapon, from the same gunman. However, he knew that this would be determined soon enough by ballistics experts and a simple study of the angles of the damage. He knew also that if everyone in the terminal were searched, he would get his chance to tell what he thought had happened. For some reason, the weapon seemed to have been trained on his wife and her companion, and the deadly arc of coverage had not expanded until the two of them, and many in front of and behind them, lay twisted in death.

His breath came short as he and others were herded to the south wall of the terminal. He strained to keep his wife in his vision. His thoughts were jumbled. He was oblivious to the pain in his toe, though he wondered about the stiffness and soreness in his legs, a strange, unique feeling to a daily jogger. He decided the sensation was a result of his having dropped so quickly to the floor.

He tried to focus on his loss, but it wouldn't penetrate his mind. He was aware of the wooden pistol in his pocket and that the odds were terrible he would be able to ditch it or get it out of there undetected. For some strange, elusive reason, he was grateful that Huck Williamsby was there.

Physicians and paramedics descended on the scene, ignoring their sophisticated equipment for the moment and relying instead on their most rudimentary instincts and techniques. Their first grisly task was to determine who was beyond help. Williamsby and an assistant directed them to begin in the middle, in the line where the most damage seemed to have been done. With index fingers and thumbs pressed deep under the jaws of the victims to check for pulses, they began realigning the bodies.

When it was determined that he was dead, the man behind Rosemary Kettering was quickly outlined in charcoal marker on the light-colored floor. One of Williamsby's men also withdrew identifying papers from the body and scribbled on a note pad to cross-reference the papers with the proper corpse. The dead man was then gently laid on his back, feet drawn together at the ankles, hands draped across his midsection. A small, metallic-looking covering, like a survival blanket, was pulled up over his head. In a few minutes, a second wave of medical personnel would lift him, head and feet, onto a stretcher and transport him to the makeshift morgue on the opposite wall under the windows where someone would be required to make identification.

Occasionally, as death was being determined, as a

body was traced and identification secured by these legal pickpockets, someone from the grieving line across the room would cry out:

"There's my husband!"

"That's Mildred!"

"Oh!"

Now it seemed there were more uniformed policemen than passengers and relatives, most of them busy holding back the grieving from disturbing the scene of terror. They spoke softly, trying unsuccessfully to soothe the mourners, but succeeding in keeping the area uncontaminated. "You must understand. You are safe, and we are doing everything possible."

Jordan was stricken with a feeling of violation, of invaded privacy of the most intimate sort, when his own wife was examined by a young paramedic. She was so obviously dead that the check for a pulse was cursory. Rather than shake his head or drop his gaze or shrug, the medic merely pointed to the officer who traced her, fished through her bag for identification, and wrote on his note pad.

It was all Jordan could do to suppress a whimper as a man and woman gently lifted Rosemary so the bag could be moved from under her. He wanted to run to her, to embrace her, to comfort her, to speak to her. Now they laid her flat, uncrossed her ankles, and covered her. When her face was no longer visible, Jordan felt as if his own breath had been stolen. He knew the same procedure was being performed on a dozen others, but his eyes were riveted to her until someone came with a stretcher and moved her away. Her life's blood, which had poured from several wounds, already looked as black as the tracing of her body on the floor.

Jordan felt guilty that he had the presence of mind to insert his contact lenses again and put on his glasses and cap. The pistol would give him away, he knew, but unless Williamsby recognized him or someone searched him, he was going to pose under his alias.

He knew his ruse was futile, senseless even. He would be asked why he was in the terminals, for whom he was waiting, and what his business was. It would be easier for him to state his real name and tell of his relationship to one of the slain passengers, but how would he explain the bogus identification papers? And what would he say he did for a living? He tried to think what he should do, but he was so stunned, so shaken that he could only react from instinct. And his instinct was to mislead, as his job had been for years. For now he was Gaston Blanc, a university student from La Havre. He might be arrested on suspicion of terrorism, of being an accomplice to murder, but as long as he kept Williamsby in sight, he would have an ally.

Certainly there were occasions when it was permissible to break the code of silence, to fully identify oneself. And surely this was one of those occasions. However, nothing Jordan had heard or read in the intense preparation for his assignment had ever had anything to do with losing one's wife before one's very eyes. Could he be forgiven for dropping his guard, for identifying himself and his business? He didn't know and, in a way, he didn't care. Who could fault him? His reserves were gone and when he looked deep inside himself for the strength and the courage to do what was right, all he found were the automatic reactions that had been drilled into him.

He would keep his head, keep his emotions intact, use panic as a signal to trigger calmness. What scared him was that his conditioned responses were confusing him. He had never daydreamed this situation the way he had preformulated so many other crises. Had he been attacked or kidnapped, he would have responded in an instant with the immediate, logical, life-preserving action. He'd have been prepared.

26

For the first time, Jordan resented his own training, because it dominated his thinking. He envied the others their grief and fear. Such open, honest, human emotions, unchecked. Why couldn't he cry out, "That's Rosemary! That's my wife! Oh, God, how could You let this happen to her? To me?"

But in his orderly, disciplined mind, he traced over-lapping thought patterns that wouldn't untangle, wouldn't focus, wouldn't free him to pray, to cry, to shout, to fear, to show anger, to grieve. Second after second, minute after minute, hour after hour, day after day, week after week, month after month, year after year with every repetition of every physical exercise, every jogged step, every idle moment, he had followed the advice of his first mentor. He had trained his mind to react the opposite of its natural inclinations.

The results of that training had stunned his wife, who noticed the difference in him first at home. She had suffered the usual battles against anger and sometimes found herself shouting at the children when they were preschoolers and incorrigible. At first she thought Jordan had simply not been around enough for them to get on his nerves. Later she saw he didn't fail even when he had been home all day every day for a couple of weeks and even when the children were at their most irritating. One of them would do something so inciting, so spiteful, so worthy of an angry response, that she felt certain he would explode. Yet he did the opposite. In perfect calm-ness and dignity, he firmly and clearly disciplined the child.

He tried to educate Rosemary in the art of the disci-plined mind, the science he called opposite triggers, but it wasn't an avenue for everyone. Even in Jordan's profes-sion, only a handful of operatives had mastered the tech-nique the way he had. It was more refined than the tranquility of Eastern mystics who claimed to have found peace by becoming one with the cosmos. Jordan found those types pliable in the face of death, neither rational nor able to defend themselves.

His success at the training had often saved his life, but now he hated the result. His natural mind wanted to panic, to fall apart, to break down, to unravel. Yet the automatic response, the signal that triggers the opposite, told him to separate himself from the trauma, to become bored with it. His disciplined mind wanted him to take deep breaths, to relax, to look away, to concentrate on the confrontation ahead.

If only God would let him be a human being, able to vent some normal reaction, even if that meant anger directed at God Himself. As he tried to force his natural mind to override his trained response mechanism, he felt he might go mad. That seemed sweet relief. He prayed silently, "Yes, let me go crazy, right here, right now."

Jordan knew he was suffering from sensory overload. Everything he thought and said, even silently, acted as a trigger. He felt he was wavering between rationality and insanity, and even that pushed him to a heightened awareness of details around him.

From what he could determine, it appeared that at least eleven passengers and customs agents had been killed. Four others had been wounded, three seriously. The savage power of the weapon was all too apparent. It didn't maim, as a rule. If it got you, you were dead. That confirmed his M-16 theory. It also convinced him that not even the second five shots, which had been instrumental in eliminating the Plexiglas barrier, had been slowed enough to diminish their killing force. Murdering people from forty feet with a weapon that powerful was like raising a tricycle with a hydraulic jack.

Indeed, as he looked to the far west end of the terminal, his suspicion was confirmed. More than a dozen deep, black pock marks marred the white wall. So, of the thirty rounds fired in two and a half seconds, maybe five had damaged only Plexiglas. The rest had wounded and killed and passed through bodies and still carried hundreds of feet before they lodged in the concrete block walls.

And why should I care about that? His wife lay dead, her blood spilled and the form of her body traced in charcoal by a cop who never knew her. Yet Jordan couldn't break out of character long enough to face this reality. He wondered why he had never prepared for such an eventuality, and then he chastised himself for even considering it.

A very shaken, very frightened, uniformed young woman from the airline hurried in with a computerized printout of the passenger list. It was all she could do to keep her eyes averted from the horror. Jordan was close enough to hear Williamsby instruct one of his aides to first match the names of the deceased with the passenger list, then the wounded, then the unhurt.

"Be in touch with the airline about any discrepancies, any cancellations. Let me know immediately of anyone missing. About a hundred have already passed through customs."

The young woman said the airline preferred that the waiting people be sequestered and questioned elsewhere. Williamsby looked at her sharply and moved close until his nose was within inches of hers. "I will make those decisions. Do you understand?"

Her lip quivered and she nodded.

"No one is going anywhere until everyone has been questioned and searched and we have determined their reason for being here. Is that clear?"

She nodded again and hurried away.

Jordan wondered if Williamsby had decided yet whether the gunman had worked alone or even whether there had been only one weapon. The study of the bullets would prove they all had spiraled from the same barrel, but it would be hours before that came to light.

As the waiting group was finally funneled into single file, Jordan found himself seventh in line to be questioned. The first woman, who spoke English with an Italian accent, was the one who had tumbled onto him at the first sound of gunfire. When she gave her name, she tearfully asked if her husband was lying by the wall.

She knew he was, of course, but until it was official, she apparently held out some irrational hope. Her identification was checked and she was teamed with a priest and a medical worker. She collapsed as her husband's face was revealed to her.

By the time Jordan's turn came and he was asked to sit across from a Scotland Yard agent, he was nearly exploding with conflicting emotions. He wanted to be with his wife, to care for her body, to know what they would do with her, where they would take her, how she would be transported back to the States. He wanted to call his children, to break the news, to cry with them over the phone. He wanted to fly to them, to let them comfort him and each other. But as he sat down, he heard himself say in a perfectly calm voice, with a definitely French accent, "A horrible mess, isn't it?"

He casually pulled his identification out of his shoulder bag. "Gaston Blanc, La Havre, France," he said. "Actually, I vas lost. I vas meeting another plane, a friend from Paris. Wrong terminal. I thought this vas vere European flights came in."

It was good. He was convincing. The agent's grim expression softened. "It usually is." He put Jordan's phony, dog-eared papers back together, tapped them on the table top to straighten them, and handed them across to Jordan. But Gaston Blanc reached for them a little too quickly, a little too jerkily, and in a way, Jordan was strangely relieved that he was not perfect in the face of this crisis. Indeed, the loss of a wife could affect even the best trained mind.

The agent stared deeply into his eyes, and through two phony pairs of lenses, Jordan returned the look. Just before he stood to leave, Huck Williamsby approached. "Get him hooked up with a passenger, did you?"

The agent scratched his cheek. "No, sir, he was in the wrong terminal. French student. Wrong plane."

Williamsby looked at Jordan without turning his head away from the agent. "Search him."

"Sir?"

"You heard me. I saw him earlier asking about this very flight. He knew good and well which plane was coming in. And you, Inspector, know that anyone who cannot be linked to a passenger on this list is a suspect and must be searched."

"This way, Mr. Blanc."

Jordan stood facing the wall and leaned against it, palms out, surprising the agent. "Been through this before, have we?"

"Not from this angle, Inspector." The agent started at the ankles and patted him up and under the jacket all the way to the armpits. Then he backed down to the bottom of the jacket and started up again, nearly jumping when he encountered the bulge in the right pocket.

"Commander! Believe we have a weapon here, sir." Williamsby hurried over and felt for himself.

"Call Reynolds over, and don't make a scene." The agent left. "Do we indeed have a pistol here, Mr. Blanc?" Williamsby said. "And how did we get it past security?"

Jordan didn't answer.

"We'll see soon enough. I hope for your sake you're not involved in this."

Reynolds, a forensic expert, arrived with a small plastic bag and a long metal rod about a quarter inch in diameter. He felt the pocket himself, then used both hands to nearly turn it inside out. The original agent gave a low whistle when the wooden handle appeared, and Reynolds dug into the pocket with the rod, snagging the trigger ring and working the entire pistol out.

He let the gun slide into the plastic bag, without making a show, and ceremoniously handed the bag to Commander Williamsby. "You need any more help?"

Williamsby shook his head. "I can handle this." And he signaled them both back to work with a nod. But Reynolds and the agent were slow to turn away; they watched their boss and Jordan head out of the terminal.

Fifty feet down the corridor, Williamsby unlocked a door and ushered Jordan into a small room. The two men sat opposite one another at a gray metal table. The commander sighed deeply as he studied the young Frenchman. "Do I know you?"

Jordan nodded.

"Who are you with?"

Jordan dropped the accent. "The United States."

"CIA?"

Jordan shook his head.

"Who else has this kind of weapon? Oh, don't tell me. The National Security Agency. CIA's thorn in the flesh." The relief Jordan felt as he realized he could stop his playacting opened the floodgates of emotion. He nearly burst into tears. Williamsby continued. "So, who are you? Where do I know you from, and how did your people know Lister was here?"

Lister! Jordan couldn't believe it. An American-born international terrorist, Richard Lister was nothing more than a gun for hire, a specialist in political hit jobs that paid big money. Jordan's voice was unsteady. "Who was the target?"

"Seems to me *I* have an unanswered question on the table, friend."

Jordan took off his glasses and popped out the contact

lenses. He pulled the latex off his teeth, dragged the cap off his head, and pointed to his hair. "Think yellow."

"Kettering?" The older man was incredulous. "What are you on this one for?"

"I'm not, Huck. My wife was on that plane."

"Oh, Jordan, there was a Kettering on the, uh, list of—."

"I know." And he finally broke down.

Williamsby ran a hand over his mouth and looked away. "I'm bloody sorry, man. What a horrible coincidence! We got a call about ten-thirty from one of our guys out here. Said he saw a tall man wearing all brown, seemed to fit the description of Lister without his beard. We got right over. Couldn't put it together. Diverted as much international traffic as we could into Terminal Two, but then we lost him. Thought we had him covered, but for some reason it seemed he might be up to something with a plane coming in from Algiers. Had that one scheduled in Terminal One. I was heading there when I ran into you the first time. You got me good, man. I never gave you a second thought till I saw you in line."

Jordan slammed both fists on the table, startling Williamsby and breaking free of his own captive mind. "What in the world was Lister doing here and why would he kill my *wife?*"

"We don't know yet, Jordan, but he's dead, if that makes you feel any better."

"He's dead?"

Williamsby nodded. "We got him. He went racing out and we were close behind. When he saw us, he tried to reload. That's when we opened fire."

"Was he alone?"

"Appeared to be but couldn't have been. Had to have had a driver at least, wouldn't you think? But there was no time to set up road blocks. If he had an accomplice, he's gone."

Jordan trembled uncontrollably. "I still don't get it."

"I don't either, but I have to ask you: were you booked on that flight?"

Jordan nodded.

"You know what that means."

He nodded again.

"The question, then, is not why Lister would kill your wife. It's why he would kill you."

Jordan stood and paced. "And how are we supposed to determine that now, with him dead?"

"You sound as if you're not pleased."

"The death of a hired gun doesn't avenge my wife's death, Huck. My only consolation is that whoever was behind this will soon learn that Lister blew it. Then I might get to face him."

"Or, more likely, just another hit man."

Jordan nodded, but disagreed in a whisper. "I'll get to the main guy somehow." He dropped his head and his shoulders heaved. "I'm going to have to quit."

"This is the worst time to be making any decisions, Jordan. You need friends right now."

"I need to be alone. Can you get me a ride back to my hotel after I find out what they're going to do with Rosemary?"

"You have to make an I.D. I'm sorry. Then the airline will do whatever you ask."

"I want her flown back as soon as possible."

"Whatever you want."

"I don't even want to wait for her to be embalmed or anything before that."

"Talk to them, Jordan. I'm sure they'll want to oblige. We'll have to do an autopsy, of course. But that will be done before dawn."

The airline was as accommodating as Williamsby had predicted, but by the time Jordan had identified the body and filled out all the forms, he was so bone-weary he could hardly walk to the Scotland Yard car.

None of the three agents spoke during most of the drive back into London proper, except occasionally to each other in low tones. Jordan sat in the back seat on the left side and rested his chin in his hand, staring out the window into the night. The rain had stopped, but the lights glistened in the dampness. It was the kind of a night that Rosemary would have enjoyed on the East Coast. What would she have thought of it in London? Perhaps she discussed that with the kind stranger, the man who just happened to be blond and of average height and weight and to have had the misfortune of being in the wrong place at the worst possible time.

Jordan shook his head, but didn't speak. As the car pulled up in front of the Coachlight, the driver spoke. "Would you like us to book you in a little more comfortable place for tonight, sir?"

"I won't be sleeping much, I imagine. Thanks, anyway."

Jordan was moved when the other two young agents stepped out of the car with him. Nothing was said. They simply walked him into the lobby, waited until he got his key, then flanked him on both sides as he trudged up the stairs. They weren't protecting him necessarily, not staking out the hotel. They were just accompanying him on a long, painful journey. They waited in silence as he opened his door and glanced at each other as he disengaged the security system. As he stepped inside, they spoke in unison. "Good night, sir." He turned to face them, weeping softly, unable to speak. He just nodded, tight-lipped, shut the door, and collapsed on the bed.

He knew he should call his daughter and son. Judith was a sophomore in prelaw at Brandeis University in Waltham, Maryland. Kenneth was in California, a freshman on a tennis scholarship at Stanford. It was the middle of the evening in Maryland and three hours earlier on the West Coast. But he couldn't call them right then.

He just couldn't. He'd do it before take-off the next afternoon, try to reach them before they left for class.

He rolled over and buried his sobs in the pillow. He was consumed with Rosemary, unable to think of anything else. Flirting at the periphery were thoughts of his future without her, the bankruptcy of his spiritual life, and his resolve to quit the agency, to spare his family the danger that had never even come close to them before but which now had devoured his wife her first time in Europe. And having soviet planes in the United States was like knowing there was a murderer under your bed and not knowing which side to look under first.

Fitful sleep finally came near dawn, but lasted less than an hour. Jordan stood in the shower like a zombie, scrubbing his hair in a futile attempt to erase the permanent, dark brown dye he would hate until it grew out.

He threw things haphazardly into the trunk, something he had never done before, then dropped his makeup kit into the garbage. He didn't know why, but on his way out, he detoured to his unused escape route and put everything back the way he'd found it.

Limping and lurching down the stairs on his bad toe and with his heavy trunk, he thought about running that day. He had a lot of reasons not to. In fact, he had a lot of reasons to quit running altogether. He wondered what would happen to his body, and he decided right then to find out. He had temporarily wrenched himself free of opposite trigger thinking, and while he wasn't too high on himself just then, the cynical freedom felt good in its own painful way. It was as if he deserved the luxury.

When Jordan reached the lobby, he was surprised to see a familiar form dozing in an overstuffed chair by the door. Could it be? He paid his bill quietly, ignoring the morning clerk's banter about shortening his stay, and tiptoed to the sleeping man. The lanky, swarthy fifty-year-old with the generous lips and the shock of black hair was Felix Granger, a good old boy from Hattiesburg, Mississippi, and now deputy director of the NSA's BRUSA, the British-U.S. Agreement.

Jordan was impressed that Felix had come. He put a hand on the big man's shoulder. Felix jumped. "Oh, Jordie! Do I have bad news for you." His drawl hadn't been affected by six years in the United Kingdom, and he was nearly in tears.

Jordan settled onto his trunk next to Granger. "You think I don't know?"

"You don't know this." The tall man straightened up and pulled his coat tighter around his neck. "Our man at JOSAF was found dead at his home in Oberursel this morning. Stanley Stuart. You knew him, didn't you?"

Four

Jordan was speechless. He had not, until that instant, entertained the idea that the airport shooting was in any way linked to his clandestine meeting with Stanley Stuart.

His first impulse was to burst forth with the fact that he had just been with him. He fought the urge and his voice came in a whisper. "I met him several years ago. Friend of Harley's. How'd it happen?"

"Suicide, I'm afraid. Never got over the death of his wife, ya know. That's why he was reassigned administrative, they say. I didn't really know the man. Met him a coupla times. Understand he was a heck of a nice guy. Pity."

Jordan hung his head. Now he could empathize with Stu. Who could he tell? Who would believe it wasn't a suicide? And what if Jordan told the wrong person? Would he too wind up mysteriously committing suicide in his despondence?

"Jordan, I'm sorry. That news coulda waited. I didn't mean to be insensitive. Forgive me. Listen, headquarters has informed your kids. Ken is flyin' in from the coast, so they'll both be there when you get back. You wanna call 'em, or you wanna just get home?"

Jordan, the man of action, Jordan, the decisive, started to speak several times and gave up, shrugging.

Felix Granger was an incessant talker. The mere mention of his name generally elicited raised eyebrows from Jordan's colleagues in the National Security Agency. But Jordan had always been fascinated by Felix, a child prodigy who had graduated from high school at fourteen and become the youngest code man inside the NSA. Jordan had always enjoyed talking with the man, but he never appreciated him more than now. Felix told Jordan without blinking that he just happened to have been called back to the home headquarters and would be able to accompany Jordan on the flight to the States. "If that would be all right with you. If it is, then my advice is to forget calling and just fly home."

In fact, Jordan was nearly staggered by the offer of companionship on the journey. Down deep he knew it was only an attempt by his bosses to get his mind off leaving the agency. He wished their reasons for trying to stall his resignation were because they truly cared for him or because he was so good they couldn't function without him. However, while there was an element of truth to both those ideas, the fact was he had been with them too long. He knew too much. He was a walking time bomb of information, a target for too many international low-lifes to be allowed to resign.

Only ten years his senior, Felix fathered Jordan until they boarded the plane and then promised to leave him alone during the trip. Jordan knew Felix couldn't remain silent that long, and he didn't want him to anyway. The veteran had begun by lugging Jordan's heavy trunk to his car, the first of many burdens he would bear over the next several hours.

At the airport he insisted that Jordan not wait for him in the terminal while he parked, but stay instead in the car while he checked the baggage through. He hurried back and parked, and together they walked to the terminal. "Nothin's goin' out of Two today, as you can imagine. Our office has already cleared us through British intelligence, so there won't be any unnecessary delays."

That proved an understatement. Jordan soon found himself waiting outside the entrance to the classified cargo section. Granger leaned close and spoke in his homiest lilt, "You just tell me what you want. If you want to see her again, we can have that arranged. If you want to give them any special instructions, just let me know. In fact, if you would rather a gub'ment plane come over here and git her and you and me, we can do it. You understand what I'm sayin'?"

Jordan assured him he did, but he declined all the suggestions. "I just want to get on that plane and know that she's in the cargo hold, Felix."

"Good enough. You wanna board early?"

"Don't mind if I do."

Felix arranged to get them on the wide-bodied craft nearly an hour before anyone else. The flight was full except for the seat between Felix and Jordan. "I coulda got you four seats in a row in the middle with me on the end if you wanted to stretch out."

Jordan shook his head, but even though he knew there were probably dozens in the terminal wishing for the vacancy next to him, he didn't try to talk Felix out of that one. "It ain't for you anyway," the older man said. "It's for me." Jordan couldn't smile, but he nodded in appreciation at Felix's attempt to humor him.

The BRUSA deputy director tried to settle in with a newspaper, but it was clear he wasn't reading it. He gazed at one page for several minutes, then engaged in a complicated folding operation to expose another section to his blank stare. Finally he leaned across the empty seat. Jordan, who had been daydreaming with his arms folded, cocked his head toward Felix.

"I'm sorry to bother you, I really am. I know I promised I'd leave you be, but I feel I gotta express myself. I learned a long time ago that there's nothin' anyone can say at a time like this and that the best thing to do is to say nothin' and let your actions do the talking. I been trying to do that, but Jordie, I just feel so rotten for you, I want to tell you how awful sorry I am. You know, I

40

never knew Rosemary very well, but I never heard you say a thing about her that wasn't special, and I just know she was a wonderful woman and a good wife. I hope you don't mind my saying that."

Jordan's eyes filled. He couldn't look at Felix, but he nodded and thrust out his hand when he noticed Felix had extended his. He found himself on the receiving end of a down-home pumper and was reminded that the Mississippian could never shake hands without talking throughout the exercise.

"I'm gonna offer all the help we can in London to find out who was behind this, Jordie, 'cause I know as well as you and Williamsby do that you were the target. Fact is, I'll be workin' on it during the flight, makin' some notes, trying some theories, but don't feel obligated to be involved. You know they won't let you in on this one anyway, and I know you got other things on your mind."

The things on Jordan's mind might have surprised Felix. As the plane started to fill and the temperature to rise, Jordan was finally able to let drowsiness take over. Sitting straight up, unable to really sleep, he closed his eyes, and let his mind take him back to high school, even before he met Rosemary Holub.

During the summer of 1962, just before Jordan's senior year, he had joined a dozen other high school and college students from his church in a short-term missionary trip into Southeast Asia. The focal point was a missionary air base in Sentani on the Irian Jaya-Papua, New Guinea border in the eastern portion of Indonesia. The group's instructions were to consider the internal strife of the country irrelevant and to concentrate on the assistance the students were to give to the pilots and missionaries of the area. In fact, they were to consciously avoid discussing politics. The Christian endeavor in the country was tenuous at best, and those responsible for it didn't want to alienate either Sukarno's forces or those who would attempt to overthrow him.

But Jordan had been fascinated by the political situation and was thrilled when the return trip to the United States was delayed in Jakarta. While most of the others were shopping and sightseeing, he went off by himself to explore the unusual sights and smells and sounds of the noisy capital city. He even hired an interpreter and interviewed locals about their views of the government.

On the last day of the trip, six days after the students had been scheduled to leave, two American men in business suits showed up at the mission guest house where the group and their sponsor had been staying. The men wanted to see Jordan.

The sponsor was protective. "May I ask why?"

They responded by flashing U.S. government business cards, identifying themselves as Stanley Stuart and Harley Rollins, agents of the National Security Agency. Until that moment, Jordan had never heard of the NSA. The agents told him privately that they had been investigating the CIA's involvement in Indonesia and charges that the CIA had attempted to enlist Peace Corps and missionary personnel in its activities.

It hadn't taken long for a very nervous young Jordan to convince the investigators that he had not been approached by anyone from the CIA. The agent who did most of the talking was Harley Rollins, a black-haired, brush-cut, stocky, military type. He gave Jordan his card and a clear instruction: "Show this to no one. If anyone asks what we wanted, tell them you can't say. If they ask if we were CIA, tell them you can't say. If they mention NSA, tell them you can't say, but call me when you get home and let me know."

"And if no one mentions NSA, I shouldn't call you at all?"

Rollins started to nod, but hesitated. "Tell me

something. You run everyday like you did this morning, no matter where you are?"

"Yes, sir."

"Any particular reason?"

"I'm on the track and cross-country teams at Muskegon Central."

"You any good?"

"Yes, sir."

"How good?"

"Twelfth in the state in cross country. Fourth in the four-forty."

"No kidding. What's your best time in the quarter?"

"Fifty flat."

"Flat?"

Jordan nodded.

Rollins smiled wryly. "That bothers you, doesn't it? Not to be able to sneak into the forty-nines, I mean."

"Like everything."

"Any other sports or activities?"

"I play basketball."

"Guard?"

"Uh-huh."

"You start?"

Jordan nodded.

"Average?"

"Eleven something."

"What else?"

"Class officer."

"President?"

"No, vice."

Rollins studied the young man. "Would you call yourself a patriot?"

"I guess. Sure. Yeah."

"Not good enough."

"What do you mean?"

"We're a little gung ho, that's all. We see ourselves as

throwbacks to the old days, when people said things like, 'Give me liberty or give me death' and 'I regret only that I have but one life to give for my country.' Can you identify with that?"

Jordan nodded slowly. "My dad was wounded in World War II. Got enough shrapnel in his leg that he wouldn't have had to work another day the rest of his life. But he wouldn't take any money. No charity. Been working twenty years. And he always said stuff like you just did. Said he would have given an arm and a leg to be able to raise his boys as free men. I don't know what I'd do if a commie stuck a machine gun up to my head, but yeah, I guess I'm a throwback, too."

Rollins glanced at Stuart, the fleshier of the two, who was sweating and uncomfortable, yet smiling. Brush Cut turned back to Jordan. "Tell you what, Kettering. I want you to call me on Christmas Day."

"Even if no one mentions NSA?"

"If they do that, you call me right away. But they won't. Nobody knows us. You call me Christmas if you've run every day from now to then, if you finish in the top five in the state in cross country this fall, and if you're averaging over fifteen points a game in basketball."

"What for?"

"You'll see. You don't have to if you don't want to. And there's one other condition. Only call me if you've kept our confidence. You show no one the card and tell no one about our conversation."

"Even my parents?"

"No one."

"My brothers?"

Rollins shook his head. "Let's see what you're made of."

Nearly dozing, Jordan felt the knuckly hand of Felix Granger on his arm. "Don't open your eyes, partner. Just tell me if you want a drink or not. Juice or a Coke or somethin'?" Grateful to not have to speak, Jordan shook his head. Felix patted his arm. "All right, then."

Jordan nodded and, within seconds, he was back to his senior year of high school. He had finished eighth in the state cross-country meet and was averaging almost seventeen points a game in basketball. He had been named Most Valuable Player in an early tournament, and he had run every day, even twice with colds. Christmas approached. His team would be in another tournament in Detroit over the holidays, much to the disappointment of his parents. There was a family squabble over it, the outcome being that Jordan's parents refused to come and watch. Jordan was angry enough not to care. Except for his finish in the cross-country meet, he had satisfied every condition Harley Rollins had laid out.

The phone call, however, had been deflating.

"You've run every day?" Rollins sounded cold.

"Yes."

"But you finished eighth in cross country."

"How did you know?"

"Why did you call? Am I to understand that you didn't mention to anyone your contact with me?"

"Yes, and my average this season is—."

"Seventeen-one, and so you thought that made up for the eighth place."

"Eighth in the state isn't bad, you know."

"You going to get straight A's this year?"

"I think so."

"You're getting a B in Sociology."

"What else do you know?"

"I know you're only seventeen."

"Anything wrong with that?"

"Only that I can't talk to you about what I wanted to talk to you about until you're eighteen."

"Great."

"Call me on April 14, when you're eighteen." He didn't wait for a response. "But only call me if you're still running, if you make all-conference in basketball, get straight A's, score in the high twenties on the ACTs and over 650 on both ends of the SAT."

"We don't take the ACTs."

"Find a place to take them. And I want to see that quarter mile under 49.5 before the state meet."

"The only time I was under fifty-one was at the state meet last year."

"I know. Because of adrenalin. Get it down there in advance this year and maybe you can win it."

"And I still can't tell anyone what this is all about?"

"Nope."

"And you still want me to call, even though you'll know everything already?"

"The one thing I won't know until you call is whether or not you'll call." ·

Jordan was startled by the gentle touch of his colleague. Felix was almost remorseful. "I should let you sleep, Jordan. I'm sorry."

Jordan's throat was thick. "It's all right. I wasn't really asleep." But he felt as if he had been.

"Just wondered if you wanted some dinner. You ought to eat something. You can get dehydrated real quick on these flights. Well, hey, you know that well enough."

The flight attendant brought their meals. Jordan only picked at his food, but drank some juice, a cup of decaffeinated coffee, and some water. He had collapsed once with heart attack symptoms on a flight to the Middle East, only to discover he hadn't stayed sufficiently lubricated.

Felix ate quickly, keeping a wary eye on his charge. "You up to talking?"

Jordan shook his head apologetically.

"That's all right. I got nothin' important to say. You all right?"

Jordon nodded. "Just thinking."

"I understand. Can you sleep?"

"Doubt it."

"Good to rest your eyes, anyway. Some hectic days comin'."

Jordan nodded again. When the dishes were cleared and his tray table was back up, he lifted the arm rest and drew his right leg up underneath him. Felix signaled the flight attendant for a pillow and asked if he wanted a blanket. "No, thanks." Soon he was alone with his memories.

Of course, in April of 1963, Jordan had called Harley Rollins. This time the agent was much warmer.

"Okay, we've got a twenty-seven on the ACTs, a 670 and a 688 on the SAT, third in the state in the quarter with a 49.9 but you had a 49.6 in the districts. All-conference, straight A's, class officer, and everything else still in order. You called on the right date, so you're still curious. You applied to Central Michigan. How serious are you about that?"

"It's a free ride."

"But other than that?"

"I don't know. What's the option?"

"If you're open to talking about putting off college for a year and then letting us put you through International in Washington, I'll come visit you."

"International University?"

"In history and poly sci."

"Wow."

"Is that high schoolese for 'Come and see me'?"

"Yes."

The meeting with Harley Rollins at a Win Schuler's Restaurant on Interstate 94 would change Jordan's life.

He was to tell no one—not his parents, none of his many girl friends, none of his few buddies, and neither of his brothers, each of whom he had been glad to see leave home during the previous two years.

The assignment, if he wanted it, was to work undercover for the National Security Agency as a Peace Corps volunteer in Indonesia. "You find out if the CIA makes any forays into corps personnel and keep us posted. If you do a good job, we look for something full time for you, put you through school, and go from there."

"I'd be working *for* my government *against* my government?"

Rollins carefully dabbed at his mouth with a napkin. "It isn't always pleasant. But then, it's the checks and balances that keep a great country great."

"I thought you had to be a college grad to be in the Peace Corps."

"I can arrange whatever history is necessary, Jordan. It may be many years before you fully realize the resources at our disposal. One of the things I want to do soon is to get you to Washington to see the facilities. They're breaking ground on a new building in June."

"Why me?"

"You don't know?"

Jordan shook his head.

"I was impressed with you when I met you. Stu and I both were. I asked you to call me to give me time to get back to the States and check you out. The more I learned the more I liked what I saw. The Eagle Scout background, the church, the civic service. The grades. Of course, the physical stuff. Most of all, you're a bit of a loner and you can keep a confidence. You've got a temper we can work on, but the same thing that gives you the temper is what will make you a highly motivated achiever."

"*You* know what gives me my temper?"

"Don't *you*, Jordan?"

"I wish I did."

"It's your place in the family. Youngest of three. Third son in thirty-five months. Lots of competition. Strong father, passive mother, highly religious home. You need challenges, you're disciplined. At least, you think you are. You'll find out what discipline is if you join us."

"Somehow this doesn't wash. I can't believe a secret government agency would recruit someone my age."

"A legitimate doubt. But we can't grow all of our people through the armed forces. They get in a mindset in military intelligence, and often they have a militarist bearing, an age about them. We're looking for a long-term man we can groom and cultivate slowly. Each of the four of us in recruitment agreed to find a beginner and personally nurture him. I wasn't going to start looking till I got back to the States, but I saw something in you in Indonesia. It's a long shot. Maybe you're not the guy."

"Do I get paid for this year of work?"

"Just expenses. The reward is college."

"My parents will never go for it. They want me to work over the summer and go to Central Michigan."

"I can phony up a scholarship to International that starts next year, if that would help."

"I don't know. Maybe. I don't lie to them. Probably I'll just have to go against their will. I've been waiting to do that for years."

"I'd hate to see you do that."

"Well, unless you let me ask them outright, I may have to."

"Oh, you can't do that. No. The first time classified information leaks out and is traced to you, whether it be through you or your family or whatever, you're finished in this business."

"I'm going to have to think about this."

"Of course you are. But tell me how it hits you at first blush."

Jordan leaned forward and rested both elbows on the table. "It hits me like a dream, like something I was made for. The order, the structure, the responsibility. I do my job; you take care of me. I don't think I'd ever forgive myself if I passed it up, or if I let my parents forbid it."

"I'm glad to hear you say that before I tell you one of the other benefits, or drawbacks, depending on how you look at it. When you get back from Indonesia, you'll be working directly with me while you're at International."

"How do you mean, working with you?"

"Just what it sounds like. I'll tutor you, work out with you, check in on you. I'll be stationed in Washington during those three years."

"*Three* years?"

"You think we'd let you have summers off when we're footing the bill? And let me say this, too: Very, very few people even within the NSA will know about you, because if it works out, much of what you do in the course of your work will involve surveillance of U.S. agencies."

"My role would be something new then?"

"Entirely. It might even include surveillance within the NSA itself. But I'll tell you this. How you do on your training assignment will make you or break you. Think it over and let me know."

That year became the most difficult in Jordan's young life. He told his parents he was joining the Peace Corps and would think about college later. They never asked about the college requirement, and they did indeed forbid him to go. His decision cost him their blessing, and in his family, that was no small issue.

His father had come home late, as usual, from the paper mill, smelling of the place. Loretta Kettering was already crying. "Raymond, Jordan has something he wants to tell you."

"It isn't something I want to tell you. It's something I want to talk with you about."

Raymond Kettering was pushing fifty. He was tired and in no mood to argue. He put his lunch box atop the refrigerator and pulled out a chair from the kitchen table. "I'm hungry, but I'm listening. What now?"

Jordan stood and shook his head. "What am I supposed to say when you talk to me like that?"

"Oh, sit down. I come home to a crying wife and you think I'm gonna be easy to talk to." He crossed his bad leg over his good one and began carefully untying the thick-soled work shoes.

"I want to join the Peace Corps, that's all."

Raymond Kettering let his shoe drop to the floor and ignored the other one. "That's all, is it? What about college?"

"I can always go to college."

"You think those scholarships will just be sitting there waiting for you? How long is the Peace Corps?"

"Normal term is two years."

"Two years!"

"I think I can get out after one."

"So then you'll be a quitter. You know Raymie may not have been the hot-shot athlete you are, and Walter may not have had your brains, but those boys were never quitters. If they'd had the chance you have to go to college, you can bet they would have taken it."

"Does that mean I have to?"

"You ought to. Where do you think you wanna go in the Peace corps? Are those people Christians or just a bunch of bleeding-heart left-wingers?"

"There are plenty of Christians in the Corps. And I liked Indonesia when I was over there. I want to go back."

Mr. Kettering shook his head, and just when Jordan thought he would quit, he shook it some more. "Now either my memory's gone bad or you're lyin', 'cause all I remember you sayin' when you got back was that the place was a smelly hole and you didn't care if you ever went there again. You didn't like the people, the smell, the traffic, anything."

Jordan's guilt hit him before the second lie was even out of his mouth. He knew he would hate himself for it, but he was losing ground and he needed a stopper. "Maybe God did a work in my heart about the people over there."

He couldn't look at his father. He knew he'd hit home, pierced his armor. He'd never tried to use his father's bedrock faith against him, but now it was out. Mr. Kettering stared at him until Jordan was forced to peek up at him. "Is that it then? You feel that's where God wants you?"

Jordan nodded.

"You don't seem too sure."

"I'm sure."

"You've prayed about it?"

Jordan reddened. And nodded.

"I don't think you have."

"I don't care what you think! I'm going and that's it."

His father slammed his fist on the table. "Well, when you come back, don't come here!"

His mother flushed. "Raymond!" But the old man stormed out of the kitchen.

When Jordan opened his eyes, he realized that he had indeed been sleeping some. The cockpit was dark and a foreign movie was showing. Felix had earphones on, but was sound asleep. And Rosemary was gone. Sweet, innocent, lovely Rosemary, Jordan's lifelong love. He wanted to think about her, but in a way it was as difficult to think of her as it was to avoid thinking of her. He knew his melancholy memories were racing headlong toward their first meeting and realized that he had been protecting himself from the pain by thinking of things pre-Rosemary. Now, he wondered, when there was nothing more to think about, when he had exhausted his early memories, should he skip ahead to the children?

The children. What had he done to them, letting them hear the awful news from bureaucrats? Did they know the whole story? Would they want to hear it or not want to hear it? And what about Rosemary's parents? And his own mother? Who would be there? Surely not his brothers. Both worked at the mills in Indiana and barely scratched out a living.

Confusion and fatigue were doing one good piece of work on Jordan Kettering. He fought two painful memories from his abbreviated second stay in Indonesia, memories he was not able to deal with just then, memories that had transported a ton of adolescent guilt into present-day reality. In trying, through his exhaustion and grief, to relive his beginnings with the NSA and to imagine how things would be when he landed, he was able to skirt temporarily the two issues he had never really faced.

The trouble was, nothing in his mind was working correctly. And those two issues were lying in wait ahead of him. Something may have told him that if he pushed from his mind the Indonesian trip, he would find even the bittersweet memories of Rosemary more agreeable. But when he tried, he wished he hadn't.

Five

In the fall of 1964, Jordan had been standing in line during freshman registration at International University in Washington, listening to an amusing conversation behind him. Apparently, the Reverend George T. Holub was the only parent in the line, and his daughter was more than a little embarrassed.

"I'll be all right, Daddy, now please. I know what I want to take, and I have the check, and I love you and appreciate you and need you to go now."

"Well, what will you do if one of your classes is full?"

"Then I'll either flirt with the registrar or choose another one."

"Rosemary!"

"Oh, Daddy, it isn't like I'm going off to camp."

Rosemary finally coaxed her father into leaving, and Jordan casually turned around to get a peek at the coed. He almost missed her. She was a head shorter than he was. But not skinny. She was pretty, with dark hair, dark eyes and full, rosy cheeks. Rosemary was still smiling and shaking her head as her rotund father headed for the door. Jordan pretended to not have overheard.

"That your dad?"

She nodded. "He forgets I'll see him this afternoon. I'm living at home."

Jordan laughed and introduced himself. She impressed him as well bred, unpretentious, smart, refined, at peace with herself. "You're from around here, then?"

She told him her father was a Presbyterian pastor and

that she was an only child. They chatted for the next several minutes, but Jordan carefully avoided the issue of his own church background. In fact, he really said little about himself. Only that International University had not been his first choice.

"I didn't know you could get in at the last minute."

"Yeah, well, I was fortunate it worked out. I was going to go to Central Michigan, only because it was cheap and close to home."

"Which is?"

"Which *was* Muskegon, Michigan. Heart of the boring Midwest."

"Oh, don't say that. I visited Chicago once. It was fascinating."

"I was a long way from Chicago. I was even a long way from Detroit."

Rosemary was an unusual girl, exuding optimism and excitement. She smiled at Jordan and responded to his every dark comment with something cheery. She wasn't afraid to disagree with him and almost scold him for his negativism. "How does one go about getting you out of a cynical mood?"

"Ah, I sound cynical, do I? I thought I was being pleasant enough."

She was still smiling, but her comments found their mark. "Pleasant enough for Attila the Hun. But that's not your name."

He flinched. "Just had a tough year, that's all. Spent some time overseas, lost my father, that kind of stuff." Much as he wanted to impress this girl, maybe she was right: everything he said *was* coming down on the negative side. He felt trapped in his mood.

She appeared sympathetic. "I'm sorry I said anything. Forgive me. Of course I didn't know about your father, and if I had—."

Impulsively he reached out and gently touched her

shoulder, then took his hand away. "No, I'm sorry. You're right. I'm not usually like this."

"Of course you're not. And I was just teasing you. You know that, don't you?"

He nodded. What a strange, revealing conversation to have upon first meeting, he thought. As they parted and wished each other luck, Jordan detected sadness in her eyes. He hoped it wasn't pity for him because of his loss. Because there was more to his father's death than he could ever have told a stranger. In fact, the timing of his father's death and the circumstances surrounding the woman he was in love with then were something he never fully revealed to Rosemary even during two decades of marriage.

The young Jordan Kettering had his own tiny apartment in Washington, and he was lonely. The capital was a strange place in 1964. John F. Kennedy had not been in the grave a full year. Lyndon Johnson seemed a shoo-in not only in the upcoming election against Barry Goldwater, but also in 1968—whoever the fragmented Republicans chose to throw at him. There was little to debate, little to talk about. Except for the shift to a huge Democratic majority, some already saw similarities between the Eisenhower years and what could become the Johnson years. There was little controversy—just one political party taking advantage of the mood of the country and trying to entrench itself again as it had during the Roosevelt and Truman administrations.

Besides being bored with the political situation in the capital and the country, Jordan was particularly lonely because he had only one real acquaintance in Washington. Admittedly, his entire future was linked to the man, but he had been sworn to secrecy about having ever even met him.

He wondered what Harley Rollins would think of his preoccupation with Rosemary. It wasn't like Jordan to have missed her last name. He was normally good with such details. But since no whistles or bells had gone off during his chat with the young woman, he wasn't concerned that he remembered only the first initial of the last name. The conversation, except for that look of pity he detected, had not really affected Jordan until two or three days later, after he had sat through a few history and political science classes and spent the rest of his time studying, working out, eating, and sleeping.

Harley came over every few evenings to check on Jordan's studies, his prescribed menu, and his conditioning. Jordan found his visits inspiring, and their Saturday and Sunday afternoon workouts invigorating, but Harley never stayed long enough.

Jordan wanted, needed, someone to talk to, to share his life with. He knew that was why the girl in the registration line kept invading his thoughts. He was irritated when no one in the admissions office could come up with her name in the records. All he wanted to know was what she was studying so he could hang around the right building and run into her again. Maybe something more would come of it this time. He didn't know. If it didn't, then it didn't.

When his search resulted in his thinking, mistakenly, that he saw her three different times in one day, he knew he had it bad. On Tuesday he went back to admissions and asked for "any sane person, maybe someone who's been here a while." That sufficiently offended the woman who'd tried to help him before and won him the assistance of a stern, middle-aged supervisor.

"All I'm looking for is the correct name of a freshman I met the other day. The first name is Rosemary and the last name is Holcomb or Holden or Hughes or something like that. It just seems to me there wouldn't be that many freshmen named Rosemary H. and that it wouldn't take too terribly long to look her up for me. If she's already dropped out or something, her name would still be around, wouldn't it?"

The supervisor gave him a bored look. "On campus or off?"

"Off."

The first woman, who had been sitting with her back to them and pretending not to listen, swiveled in her chair. "You never told me that!"

All Jordan could get out of the supervisor was a last name. She was not, she said, at liberty to provide addresses or phone numbers. But he remembered that Rosemary's father was a pastor, so finding the phone number was simple.

He dialed.

"I'm the one you met in line the other day."

"Oh, yes, hi, um—."

"Jordan. Jordan Kettering."

"Yes, hi, Jordan."

"I was wondering if I could see you?"

"See me?"

"Yeah, I mean, like for dinner or something."

"Dinners aren't really the best for my schedule."

"Oh. Well, maybe some other—."

"Would a lunch be all right, Jordan? Maybe at the university or close by?"

"Yeah, sure! Tomorrow?"

"Oh, uh, no, not tomorrow. Maybe early next week?"

"Monday?"

"How's Tuesday?"

"Great, Rosemary. I'll see you then."

"Jordan?"

"Yeah?"

"Where?"

"Oh, yeah. Um, same place we met. At noon. Okay?"

Only after he hung up did he realize that she had managed the conversation. She had dissuaded him from a dinner date and guided him toward something less committal and more informal. She had backed him off his pushiness for the next day or even the first day of the next week. In fact, she had delayed their meeting a full week, and he hadn't even remembered to ask her what she was studying so he could watch for her before that.

During the next week, Jordan looked for Rosemary everywhere, but the campus was so huge and there were so many students that he failed again. The woman had been craftier than she knew. By the time the weekend arrived and Harley showed up for their discussions and workouts, Jordan was in a frenzy about seeing Rosemary. He was up, enthusiastic, energetic. Harley had never seen him run a mile on the beach—barefoot in the sand—in less than five minutes.

After they'd endured a hard, ten-minute swim out and about a seven-and-a-half-minute swim back, they cooled off in Jordan's government-paid apartment with tall glasses of fresh-squeezed orange juice. Usually Jordan stretched out on the floor while Harley took to the couch, but now Jordan either paced or sat on the edge of a living-room chair.

Finally Harley sat up and looked at him. He ran both hands through his own crew cut. "What is it with you today, anyway? You worked out like you actually want this job."

"I've always wanted it."

"Yeah, but c'mon kid! You were unconscious today. Tell me."

Jordan shrugged. "Got a date Tuesday, that's all." He smiled. Harley didn't.

"Hm." Harley rolled onto his back again and covered his eyes with his forearm. "Wives don't mix with this business, you know. Not at this level."

"I said it was a date! I'm not marrying anybody. I hardly know the girl."

"Who is she? I want to check her out."

"You have to check out even my acquaintances?"

"Don't give me that! You don't date your acquaintances."

"Rosemary Holub."

"From?"

"Washington."

"Father?"

"The Reverend George T."

"Thanks."

"When do I know if she qualifies?"

"Wednesday."

"I told you I was seeing her Tuesday."

"Okay, I'll shoot for the end of the day, but don't—."

"*Noon*, Tuesday."

"Don't be cute, Jordan. That doesn't give me enough time."

"I don't care! You can't totally mess up my private life."

Harley studied him with a soft, closed-mouth smile. "If you want this job, I can."

"Then maybe I'd better think about it some more."

Harley sat up quickly again, glaring stonily. "Have I misjudged you, or do we just call it quits right here?"

Jordan looked at the floor and shook his head. "Just call me Tuesday as early as you can."

Now it was Harley's turn to stand. He was clearly agitated, bothered about something, and it wasn't Jordan's new acquaintance. "While we're talking about women, I've got to ask you about Cydya LeMonde."

Jordan's eyes popped open in disbelief. Felix put a hand on his shoulder. "You're sweating, pal. You okay?" Jordan nodded, but burst into tears. He leaned forward and hid his face in his hands, sobbing. Felix leaned over and massaged his back. "That's all right, partner. Let it out."

But it wasn't just grief over Rosemary. It wasn't the sudden realization of his loss. It wasn't the lack of sleep or the anxiety over the reactions of his children. No, it was the memory of Cydya defiling his grief. How could he think of her at a time like this?

And how many times had he asked himself that same question over the years? Memories of Cydya had teased him early in his marriage whenever he had been away from home for weeks. That he could rationalize and understand. But today? Now? Something told him he'd made at least a subconscious effort to avoid thinking of her when he'd tried to skip past the memories of the second Indonesian trip. But there she was.

Was there any hope in trying to push her from his mind? The effort was futile, he knew. But if only he could postpone his memories. Even thinking of Cydya seemed like an act of unfaithfulness to Rosemary. Which was worse, he wondered, thinking of Cydya with his wife asleep beside him or with Rosemary's body in the cargo hold, riddled with bullets?

He knew if he allowed himself to, he would think of little other than their first meeting, his and Cydya's, and their few brief months together. He had long since quit denying that she was his first true love.

There had been the usual high school romances. He had been athlete, an honor student, a class officer. So there had been cheerleaders and homecoming queens. He'd even gone steady twice. Thought he was in love many times. Until he met Cydya.

Then he knew what love was all about. Love was more than a faster pulse, more than just wanting to be with someone all the time, more than spending so much time on the phone that your parents threatened to make you pay for your own line.

He blamed the place. The setting. The weather. The heat. The humidity. The thousands of miles between Jakarta and Muskegon. The fact that Cydya was of French extraction. But, ultimately, he didn't care what the reasons were. He had loved her so deeply that she had burned her image on his soul.

He didn't want to think about her now! He forced himself to open his eyes, to smile at Felix so the older man would quit rubbing his back. "I'm okay, thanks. Just need a little shut-eye."

Felix squinted at him. Jordan lowered his head to his chest and put his hand over his eyes, pretending to sleep. He felt like a schoolboy, with his eyes still open, surveying as much as his limited vision would allow.

In the aisle next to him a woman removed her shoes and dragged a travel bag closer so she could rest her feet on it. A flight attendant walked by. There was grime on the plastic twist-lock holding Jordan's tray table. He didn't want to think; he just wanted to look.

If his mind had been empty, save for thoughts of his wife, he'd have shut his eyes again. If he could sleep without dreaming. . . . Could he peek at his watch without Felix noticing? Why did he care? Anything, anything to occupy his mind. Could he push Cydya from his thoughts until after the funeral?

He chastised himself. *You will face your children and your in-laws in a matter of hours, and already you're planning what to think about after the funeral! Your wife's funeral!* He found it hard to believe.

Jordan felt Felix flinch. He glanced to his right, his hand still covering his eyes. Through the sliver between his fingers, he saw Felix wave at a fly. His legs were crossed, left over right, his bony knee pressing against the back of the seat in front of him. *Must be uncomfortable,* Jordan decided. *And impossible to disguise. No wonder he's in administration.*

Anything for a distraction. Jordan continued to spy

on Felix, letting the full irony of that play on his tortured mind. He pressed his fingers harder to his forehead, as if he could somehow slow the thoughts, the emotions, rattling around in there. Guilt. Vengeance. Rabid curiosity. Dread. Fear. Remorse. Love. And a memory he couldn't, wouldn't face, until it beat down his every last defense.

Felix fumbled for a button in the arm rest and Jordan heard the loud tone. Had he mistakenly buzzed the attendant? One arrived.

"Yes, sir?"

"Could I get a coffee with one packet of sugar, honey?"

"Certainly."

Felix flexed his thumb and middle finger in a way that reminded Jordan of how he shot marbles as a child. Jordan felt like a child right then, excited by the knowledge that Felix didn't know he was watching and wondering why in all the world he was limbering up his marble-shooting finger.

When his coffee came, Felix lowered the tray table from the seat between the two men and ignored the coffee. He tore open the sugar packet, licked his finger, and dipped it into the granules. He rubbed the sticky substance between his finger and thumb and wiped it on his left knee.

When all the sticky stuff was off his finger and on his knee, he rested the heel of his hand near it and resumed the cocked, marble-shooting gesture. Within seconds, the fly landed on the sugar. Jordan's eyes widened.

Amazingly, Felix didn't immediately flick at the fly. Jordan decided that he must have some knowledge of when a sugar-sucking fly is most vulnerable. Perhaps when it's rubbing those appendages against each other like a wino near a trash-can fire.

When Felix finally pulled the trigger and the fly caromed off the seat ahead of him, Jordan jumped. The fly landed, stunned, in Felix's lap. It staggered in circles before Felix closed a loose fist around it. With his other hand, he snagged the fly by one wing under his fingernail.

First, he removed the right wing with a quick motion. Then the left. The fly crawled quickly around his hand. He transferred the insect to his left palm and got his right hand ready to shoot again. When the fly stopped, Felix flicked it against the seat once more, caught it between his thumb and finger, and crushed it.

Casually he deposited the creature in his napkin, guzzled the coffee without a breath, and dropped the napkin into the cup. He turned off his light and folded his hands in his lap, his head on his chest.

Jordan was sick. The trick had not been unimpressive, he thought, but Felix had clearly not done it for effect. This simply wasn't something one did for the benefit of the bereaved.

Jordan sat forward and rested his head in his hands, elbows on his knees. Within seconds, he might as well have been sound asleep, dreaming. For the picture in his mind was as clear and three-dimensional as life, and it wiped all other reality from his senses.

The sounds of the plane, his revulsion at Felix's execution of the fly, the stewardess who leaned over Jordan to retrieve the coffee cup and replace the tray, Jordan's fatigue, his longing to be with his children, even his festering, angry grief faded into some insulated, subconscious pocket while the image of Cydya LeMonde dominated his mind's eye.

To Jordan, she never aged. Forever locked in his memory as an almost-twenty-two-year-old, she fit every description he had ever heard in sappy love songs. A green-eyed goddess. A blonde vision. A gift from heaven. Perfect.

The day he met her, he was overwhelmed. He had flown from Muskegon to Los Angeles, and from Los Angeles thirty-six hours through South Pacific islands and Australia before landing in Jakarta in the middle of the night.

The flight had seemed endless. He had been told there would be one stop in Hawaii and the next stop would be Jakarta. The six layovers ranged from forty-five minutes to five hours, yet no one was given the opportunity to shave or shower. And Jordan had not thought to bring a change of clothes in his carry-on bag.

Besides feeling gamy, Jordan was already homesick. His fear of the unknown vied with his remorse over a difficult farewell with his parents. And he doubted his own ability to carry out the assignment.

All that, combined with his three-day growth of beard, made him feel like a sight when he finally reached Indonesia. He stood in a customs line like a zombie for more than half an hour, staring blankly out the window until something caught his eye. In the window of a tiny, white Japanese station wagon was a handlettered message: "Welcome, Jordan! We've only been waiting since nine!"

Even in his exhaustion, the sign worked on him. He scanned the area around the car and found two women waving at him. One was thick, open faced, and friendly looking with a jaunty cap, a terrycloth top, and khaki shorts to her knees. She wore thongs and had a key ring around her finger. Jordan guessed she was about forty.

Next to her was a girl who looked half that age. She wore sandals, faded, blue denim short-shorts, and a sleeveless pink, pullover blouse. Her sun-streaked hair was pulled back behind her ears. Jordan wondered if he could sneak a splash of Old Spice before they met him.

He waved back tentatively. In a way, he wished they hadn't seen him. It would be impossible now to gaze at the lithe, leggy one. Could she be a Peace Corps volunteer? How would anyone get any work done? He felt even grimier than he was.

When he finally made his way through customs and got his baggage, he left the security area and was immediately met by the older woman. She was a talker. "I'm Michelle." She grabbed his largest suitcase. "But I hate that name, so call me Mickey like everyone else does. This is Cydya, and we know who you are, Jordan."

"Thank you." He realized he hadn't spoken for hours. He set down his other suitcase and extended his hand. "Cindy?"

Mickey shook it. "That's what everybody says when they meet Cydya. You wanna give him your stock line?"

Cydya winked at him and he felt short of breath. She spelled her name for him. "C-Y-D-Y-A. You can remember how to pronounce it by thinking of the word *insidious*. Take off the first syllable and the last letter, and that's me."

He repeated the name aloud. Up close she was almost too much to bear. Her huge eyes were pale green. She wore no makeup, not even lipstick or nail polish, and she didn't look as if she would ever need to. Her deeply tanned arms and legs had the everpresent shine of perspiration common to everyone in that climate, but it made Cydya look luminescent.

They filled the back of the wagon with his things. "I'm sorry I'm so grundy."

The women laughed. Mickey looked at Cydya. "Michigan, right? Every region, every state has its own word for the way its natives look when they finally get here." She cackled and turned to Jordan. "Don't worry about how you look, smell, or sound. Believe me, we understand."

Mickey drove, Jordan sat next to her, and Cydya sat behind them. To be polite, he kept telling himself, he turned sideways in the seat so he could speak to both of them at once. It was small talk—welcome to Indonesia, a shower is waiting at the guest house (cold, you know; he knew), and all that—but it afforded Jordan several opportunities to glance at Cydya. Each time, it was all he could do to look away.

He wondered if she would look as good in the light of day, after he'd had a good night's sleep. Maybe Mickey, who was plain, made Cydya look better than she was. Maybe it was his fatigue.

He asked about assignments. Mickey chortled. "You're wondering how we got stuck with escort duty tonight."

"No, it's not that. I—."

"I'm a group leader, and the newcomer's group leader gets to pick him up at the airport. We always travel in twos, and Cydya drew the short straw tonight because she's going to train you. You're replacing her."

Jordan was amazed at how deeply disappointing he found that after having just met Cydya. He knew what he felt was a crush, that he was merely enamored by her beauty. He tried to tell himself anyone who looked that good had to be dumb or lazy or cantankerous. But he didn't believe it for a minute, and none of his excuses consoled him in what he already considered his loss. He asked where she was going.

Her voice was at once throaty and melodic, and as she spoke she seemed to be suppressing a smile. "France." It was almost an announcement. "My parents are French, so I'm fluent in French. I studied Spanish in high school, so I'm sort of fluent in that. And I was raised in the States, so English is my mother tongue."

Jordan smiled at her. "So why France? Why not Spain?" He wanted to add, "Why not Michigan?" but he let it slide.

She smiled back. "Interpol."

"The international police thing?"

"The International Police Organization. I've wanted to work there for as long as I can remember. The three languages I know are the three languages of Interpol."

"Did you do that on purpose?"

"Well, I didn't have much choice about the French and English, but yes, I studied Spanish so I'd know all three."

"What will you do there?"

"I'll start at the bottom. After that, who knows? I can hardly wait."

"You've already been hired?"

"Yes. I begin next spring."

Jordan nearly sighed aloud. She'd still be around more than six months. "It takes that long to train a replacement?"

"Not really. I involve the children in sports and games, while Mickey and the rest of the group involve the parents in farming and building projects."

Jordan nodded. "The Peace Corps' loss will be Interpol's gain," he said, then felt silly.

Cydya must have thought his statement was mere platitude. She turned and stared out the window.

Six

Just before touchdown at Dulles International, Jordan was gently shaken by Felix Granger. He pulled a business-sized, NSA envelope from his trouser pocket. It showed the punishment inflicted by a trans-Atlantic flight in a big man's pants. Inside was a cable: THE SECRE-TARY HEARD THE KITTY TELL THE RIVER, "NOW I KNOW MY ABC'S."

Jordan shook his head and blinked slowly, amazed that anyone, especially the ranking intelligence community in the free world, thought anyone else would be fooled by the simplistic code. Felix interpreted. "Secretary is the airport because Dulles was—."

"Secretary of State, I know."

"I'm the kitty, Felix the—."

"Yeah, I know."

"And you're—."

"The river, Jordan. Clever."

"And where does that ABCs line come in the song?"

Jordan sighed. "At the end, so we have to get off the plane last."

"So you do get it. What was I 'splainin' it for?"

Jordan rubbed his eyes. "Too simple."

"Yeah, well. I thought it was good."

"So, why do we have to get off last?"

Felix looked surprised. "You think Lister was workin' alone and now that he's dead, you're safe?"

"Are you telling me I'm going to have NSA guys hovering all over the place?"

"For a while, I s'pose. Till they're sure no one followed you over."

Jordan was nearly overcome with longing to see someone who loved him. His knees were weak. His back ached. He had the dull headache afforded by hours of cabin pressure. But that cable was clear evidence that anyone who might have planned to meet him at the plane had already been hustled off to somewhere else. He would have to deal with NSA red tape first. And that made him angry.

At the entrance to the terminal, Felix gently took his arm and quickened his pace. They passed families in tearful embrace. Jordan was jealous, wondering what had gotten into him. Couldn't he handle this? Already he was turning into some weird combination of softy and cynic.

He wanted someone to rush to him, to hold him, to let him cry. He appreciated Felix. He would never forget his kindness. But Felix wasn't family. The big man steered him through the terminal to the Red Carpet room and straight into a tiny alcove.

The place seemed full. Jordan sensed family somewhere, but the first face he recognized was Blake Bauer, deputy director for Field Management and Evaluation. Jordan shot Felix a double take. "I didn't expect him."

The stocky, baby-faced exec wore a heavy, wool overcoat buttoned all the way up, and his dark, razor-cut hair was sprayed into place. Bureaucrats like Bauer were among Jordan's pet aggravations. They always assumed the men on the front line wanted their jobs and would compete if they had the chance. In fact, Jordan had been offered Blake Bauer's job more than once. He'd rather pump gas.

There were days when he wished more people in administration had spent some time in the trenches the way he and Harley and Felix and Stan Stuart had. The mere thought of Stu made Jordan wince. If only he could talk to Harley, tell him Soviet MiGs were on U.S. soil! What were the odds that Harley or anyone else could find the photos Stu had shown him? And would they mean anything to whoever found them? Jordan knew Harley would agree there had been no suicide in West Germany last night, but even if they could convince someone of the crisis, NSA brass would be as concerned with protecting the public's confidence in the defense community as with dealing forthrightly with the Soviets and their MiGs.

Bauer extended a manicured hand, and when Jordan grasped it, the deputy awkwardly tried to embrace him. Jordan stiffened. "Not necessary, Blake. Is my family here?"

Bauer was surrounded by young clones. He had worked his face into a look of deepest sympathy. "You may have a few moments with them and then we must talk."

Jordan pursed his lips. "I'll take as much time with them as I want. And we can talk next week, can't we?"

"I'm afraid not. A few details. In fact, give Mathews here the funeral arrangements and he'll see to the, ah, disposition of, uh—."

Jordan scribbled the name of the funeral home on a card and Mathews jogged off. Bauer squeezed Jordan's shoulder. "Just a few details from the director when you get a minute." Jordan was already pulling away as Bauer whispered, "I'm terribly sorry, Kettering."

When he was finally past the cadre of young NSA headquarter types, Jordan saw his in-laws, and his son and daughter. He wanted to drink in the sight. Ken looked good, tanned, robust, older than his eighteen years. His sandy hair and dark eyes set off a handsomeness Jordan had never possessed. But Ken didn't approach him. He had stood when Jordan appeared, but made no move to greet his father.

As the others awkwardly welcomed Jordan with only

their eyes at first, Judith broke through to him and hugged him, sobbing. Her long, black hair covered his hands as he embraced her. He wanted to see her olive face with the clear eyes and the high cheek bones she'd inherited from her mother. She felt tiny and frail in his arms. Jordan fought to keep his composure, though he hated himself for it.

"Your boss has been so wonderful," his orange-haired mother-in-law whispered, a sob in her voice. "He paid for Kenny's flight from California, and he offered us a car, but of course we have one. Judy has your car." She burst into tears.

Jordan's father-in-law, the Reverend Holub, now bald and bigger than ever, whispered huskily. "They have also offered to fly in your mother and someone to accompany her."

Jordan tried to appear grateful, but he was suspicious of every kindness on the part of his employers. They must know his work meant nothing to him now, that he would blame his profession for the loss of his wife. He spoke softly, "I'll just be a minute."

Bauer was waiting, hands in his pockets. He had learned to speak first when dealing with Jordan. "The funeral is Tuesday, day after tomorrow. We'll be there, but not in the way. You'll get one more day after that with your family, then you should plan on three days with us."

"What for?"

"Debriefing and testing. We'll be in the medical center first, then the basement of S Building." He noted Jordan's angry look. "It's security, Kettering. We have your best interests in mind, you know that."

Jordan wasn't so sure. He'd always been repulsed by the behind-the-scenes guys, especially Bauer and his boss, Kurt Erhard, the director of the National Security Agency.

Bauer clapped him on the shoulder. "Spend time with

your family. Granger will pick you up Thursday morning at seven."

"Seven?"

"You may go now."

"Oh, I may? Thank you so much, Blake."

The sarcasm was lost on Bauer. He smiled benignly. "You're welcome, Jordan. Take care."

Less than an hour later, Jordan sat in the living room of his suburban split-level trying to explain what had happened. His son still had said nothing. His daughter sat sniffling. His father-in-law told him what they had been told. "We were informed by your office that there had been a terrorist attack on the passengers in London."

Jordan was hoarse. "There's not much else to say, I'm afraid."

His son glared at him. "Were you there?"

"I saw it happen."

His mother-in-law gasped. "We don't want to go through the ordeal again, but not knowing is worse."

Jordan nodded. "She, ah—I take comfort in the fact, and you can, too, that she, uh—I don't think she ever knew what hit her." Mrs. Holub pressed her lips together, but couldn't stifle a whimper. Jordan went on. "A gunman, a, uh, terrorist, just opened fire. You probably read about it. Just broke the glass, sprayed the crowd."

Kenneth still glared. "And you were right there?"

"I was there."

"Nothing you could do?"

"Nothing."

"Were you armed?"

"Armed?"

"C'mon, Dad! You think any of us still believe you're a diplomat? Were you armed?"

"Not really, no." Jordan winced. Why had he said it that way? He knew he should have rationalized that a wooden device was not technically an *arm* and simply said no. Did they *all* know he wasn't a diplomat? They looked uncomfortable and concerned with Ken's behavior, but no one had recoiled at his assertion.

His son stood. "Not really! What does *that* mean? Have you ever killed somebody?"

"Ken, I—."

"Have you?"

"Ken, if you'd like to talk about this—."

"I want to know! You killed somebody, didn't you? You carry a weapon and you go overseas and you kill people for the CIA. And someone you killed sent someone else to kill you. That's why that guy was in the airport. He was trying for you and he got Mom!"

Jordan pleaded with his eyes. "That's not true." Ken stormed from the room and Jordan turned to the remaining three. "It's not true."

Reverend Holub raised a meaty hand. "We know it isn't, Jordan. Is there anything more we should know about Rose's death?" His wife covered her face.

Jordan stared at the floor, wishing he could die. "She was among the first hit. We can be grateful for that. I don't believe she experienced the terror of those who realized what was happening and knew they would be next." Mrs. Holub still had her head bowed, eyes covered. Suddenly Jordan's breathing grew shallow. "Mom Holub, I loved Rosemary."

"I know you did."

"I loved her with everything in me."

"We know that."

Jordan knew he was shocking them. He'd never been overly expressive. "I don't care about anything else anymore."

"Don't say that."

"I don't. I don't care if I ever work again. All I'll ever care about is my family, my loved ones. All of you."

He couldn't speak further. His professional mind argued that he had shown weakness, that he shouldn't have broken down. But he didn't care. He was going to quit the NSA, and the first thing on his agenda was to reverse all their mind training. It had served him well for a long time. It had saved his life more than once. Yet how could he argue with Ken?

If he had indeed been the diplomat the neighbors thought he was, would this have happened? He hated his own cynicism. His life, his work had made him tough and uncompromising. Realistic. But he'd never been jaded. He stood shakily. The hours of immobility on the plane had done nothing to relax him. He hoped he could sleep. There were brief flashes when he could think about something other than his loss, but nothing could blot out the realization that his son was blaming him. And he had no defense.

The funeral was more of an ordeal than Jordan could have imagined. Neighbors, friends from church, several co-workers, and family on both sides were kind enough not to pester him with questions. But their inane attempts to console him did no more than teach him a valuable lesson. Never again would he say anything to anyone who had lost a loved one. Just being there said ten times more, and there simply wasn't anything appropriate to say.

His mother, now senile, kept calling him by his brothers' names and asking for his wife. "Where is she, anyway? Is she late? When is she getting here?" Fortunately, her brother, Jordan's uncle, had accompanied her, and he made everything short of Rosemary's death worth the trip.

Uncle Dexter Lee was a white-haired, weather-worn, retired furniture magnate who had been Jordan's counselor and confidant since he was a child. He looked like a truck driver, but dressed like an executive. Jordan wept in his embrace. The big man then stood at the casket with his arm around Jordan and cried with him. "Ray, Jr., and Walt wanted to come, but they just couldn't swing it. They send their love."

Besides that, he said nothing. Nothing. He could have told Jordan how good Rosemary looked and what a wonderful woman she had been and how he had always liked and respected and admired her. He could have promised to do "anything I can." But he didn't say anything. He was just there. A most unlikely angel of support and comfort.

At the airport early Wednesday afternoon, Uncle Dexter finally spoke. "Jordie, you know where I am. You say the word, and I'm on the next plane. You need a day or more with me like we used to do, you've got it. You want to come to Muskegon, just let me know."

Jordan wanted to board with him and be fathered. "I wish we could talk about Ken. He hates me."

Dexter Lee put one hand behind Jordan's head and clapped a cupped palm to his cheek. "He doesn't hate you. He just blames you. He wants to punish you."

"Maybe I should let him. Uncle Dex, he has a right. And I feel like I owe him some answers. But you know there are a lot of things I can't tell him."

"I know." And he said no more. Dexter always knew when to quit. "You call me, hear?"

Jordan nodded.

Back at home, Judy had dispatched the last of the visitors and was ready for a nap. "You all right, Daddy?"

"Yeah. I need to do something, though. I was going to quit running, but now I feel like I'm going to explode."

"Ken said he was going for a run this afternoon. It's nippy out there."

"Never stopped us before. Where is he?"

She pointed upstairs. Jordan went up to change. Ken was already on his way down with his sweats on. "Mind if I join you, Ken?"

76

His son shrugged. "Suit yourself."

"Where you running?"

"Morningside."

"Our two-mile course? Perfect."

Ken drove, stony and cool. Jordan quickly gave up trying to chat, hoping their running together again for the first time in months would begin a thaw. He suggested a game Harley Rollins had taught him years before: run a mile at whatever speed you think you can duplicate for the second mile. Ken shed his sweats. "I think I can do two sixes."

Jordan took a deep breath. "I've been away from running for a few days. But I'll beat that by thirty seconds on both ends."

He hoped for a smile, some hint of the old Kenny. But his son's eyes darkened. "You won't win either one." And he took off, much faster than he should have.

Jordan settled into an easy pace, having run for enough years to know precisely how to turn a five-thirty mile. He wasn't sure he could run two in a row at that speed after a layoff, but he would try. If Ken beat him, so much the better. Maybe that would help.

A half mile out, Jordan caught Ken and could have passed him easily. Instead he slowed and ran with him for several hundred yards. Jordan sensed he was angering his son. He didn't want to. Maybe he should just pull away and beat him. He tried. Ken accelerated, panting. At the end of the first mile, Ken surged ahead angrily and collapsed as he finished.

Jordan followed and ran in place. "That's one. You done?" He turned to repeat the course. Ken was on his back, grimacing, his knees raised. Jordan checked his watch. "You ran your six. But I can do it again. Can you?"

Ken didn't respond. He just rolled over on his stomach, buried his face in the crook of his elbow, and sobbed.

Jordan approached him cautiously. He knelt and put a hand on his son's back. Ken pulled away, but quit crying. He looked up at his father, his face red, eyes swollen. "You're in intelligence, aren't you?"

"I'm not with the CIA."

"Don't play games with me, Dad! You're in intelligence."

Jordan nodded. "If I told you I was leaving the profession for good, would you let me keep all the confidences I've been sworn to keep?"

"Sworn to keep even from your wife?"

"Some, yes."

"Just some?"

"Most."

"More than that, I'll bet."

"Your mother was a wonderful woman, Ken. She didn't pressure me to tell her things I wasn't supposed to."

"So you couldn't even tell her she was walking into one of your cases? You couldn't tell her she would be ambushed while you watched?"

Jordan hung his head. "You can't think I knew, Ken. You can't. I would have sacrificed my own life before I let someone kill her." Saying so made him believe it all the more, and he suddenly felt strangely angry at his son. "I know you have a right to these questions, and you're upset. But how dare you accuse me of being responsible for your mother's death? You couldn't know how much I loved her."

"I sure couldn't! You weren't around very much!"

That hurt deeply. But they'd been through it before. They'd discussed it for hours. "Failing you by not being around enough is one thing. Being responsible for my wife's death is another."

Ken stared at his father. He snorted in an attempt to keep from crying again. He managed a whisper. "I want to hit you."

"What?"

"I want to hit you. I want to punch you in the face."

"What's the matter with you?"

Ken got to his feet. "I don't know! I just want to, that's all! Somebody already killed whoever was after you. Who else can I be angry at?"

"You want to take your anger out on me?"

"I can't help it! I think you're responsible."

Jordan was weary. How many times as a child had he wanted to punch his own father? How many times would he have loved to tell him what he thought of his self-righteousness, his rigidity? He'd never had the guts to even tell him. Of course, he'd never raised a hand toward his father. And here was Ken, coming right out with it, as if asking permission.

Was this the way the new generation behaved? Had he failed as a father? Jordan didn't think so. He thought what was happening between them now said more about the character of his son than about his own failings as a father.

"Do you really want to, Ken?"

Ken nodded.

"You want to slug me as hard as you can? Would it make you feel better?"

"I don't know. I just know I want to."

"You want me to fight you?"

"What do you mean?"

Jordan stood. "I want to know what you want from me. You want a shot or two at me without retaliation? Or will it make you feel better if I put up a fight?"

"What, and beat me up? Is that it?"

"You tell me, Ken. This is your therapy, not mine."

Jordan hadn't meant to anger him further. Ken moved directly in front of him and punched him hard on the left cheek. Jordan felt tissue give way from bone and his head rock to the side. He spread both hands on the ground as his knees buckled.

He squinted up at Ken and straightened to face him again. The boy slashed at him with a backhand right, catching him beside the right eye, and Jordan knew it would blacken. Now he was on his knees with his hands at his sides.

But when Ken took a step back, Jordan saw the boy wasn't through. He saw the raging passion in his son's face as he fired an uppercut toward Jordan's nose with all the power in his fabled serving arm.

Jordan calculated the leverage, the force, the speed. Taking one straight to the face while on his knees before a standing opponent would break his nose, possibly drive cartilage fragments into his skull, maybe even his brain. At best, he would be knocked unconscious. At worst, his muscled neck would be broken.

His good deed had already been done. He'd taken his punishment, and he expected to feel as good about it later as Ken had felt in administering it. But he couldn't allow this third blow. He snatched Ken's fist out of the air with both hands, his left on the wrist, his right over the back of the hand.

Simultaneously, he stepped on Ken's right foot, stood and yanked the arm toward himself. As Ken fell forward, Jordan drew the arm all the way around Ken's back. Then he muscled the boy to the cool ground, his knee at the back of Ken's neck. He cupped his right hand under Ken's chin.

"Son, I did that for two reasons. One, you could have killed me. And two, I wanted you to know that I could have killed you rather than let you hit me twice. If I drive my knee down and pull your chin up, you're dead."

"I hate you!"

"No, you don't."

"Let me up!"

Jordan freed him. Ken looked small somehow, struggling to his feet. "You've killed people just like that, haven't you?" Jordan shook his head. Soon they would have to talk.

"Are you all right, Ken?"

His son scowled at him. "I'm glad I hit you."

So was Jordan.

Seven

Jordan, his eye purple and his cheek fiery red, surprised his daughter by phoning her faculty adviser and finding out exactly how she was doing and where she was in her curriculum. "There's no way you're staying here after the weekend, Judy."

"But, Daddy, you need me. You just won't admit it."

She was so right on both counts that Jordan almost gave in. But when he learned that his daughter was one of the most promising students of either sex to come along in years, he was determined to send her back to college. "I don't need a nanny, and much as I love having you around, I won't keep you home during a very critical period in your schooling."

Judith brooded a while, then tried a different tack. "You know, maybe I need the break. This isn't any easier for me than it is for you."

"I know." He was lying. He had to admit to himself that he hadn't even considered the possibility. He knew she was shocked, hurt, sad, grieving. But apparently she was as affected by Rosemary's death as he was.

No one could know the depth of his bonding with his wife. His was a faithfulness and a loyalty that drew him to Rosemary over the years and the miles, that checked him every time he entertained the thought of looking up his old acquaintance "just out of curiosity."

The truth was, he was more than curious about Cydya, and there were weeks, months sometimes, when the memory of her haunted him, plagued him, forced him to try to think of Rosemary. The excitement, the passion, the magic had never been as intense in his marriage as it had been with Cydya in Indonesia, yet he couldn't imagine a better wife than his own.

He had loved Rosemary deeply and completely and forever. He had chosen her, dedicated himself to her, committed himself, promised himself. And the same loyalty and singleness of mind and purpose that shot his score off the charts on personality and preference profile tests and made him the ideal intelligence operative, those same qualities made him a good husband under nearly impossible circumstances.

The divorce rate was high in his business. Unhappy wives were the norm. Much of the credit for his and Rosemary's success, he knew, had to go to her. She had been a remarkable, sweet, selfless person, the type that people find hard to believe. Another secret to their success, though, Jordan was certain, was his resolve to never tell her about Cydya.

She had told him of her previous boyfriends. One had wanted to marry her, but he cared nothing for God and she had to break his heart. She told the story carefully and seemed to watch intently for any sign of jealousy or discomfort. Those feelings were there, but Jordan hid them for the sake of hearing more. How he wished she had a story like his own. Then maybe he would have felt free to share what had happened to him.

But she didn't. And when she teased him about his past, he admitted only the usual high school romances. He was amazed now that he could have loved two women for two decades, one he hadn't seen for that entire time. Finally he passed off his infatuation as just that: he decided he was enamored with the memory of Cydya's beauty.

Was it lust? Certainly it had been at the beginning. And what about his thoughts of her on dark, cold nights in lonely undercover outposts thousands of miles from home? No, those weren't always pure either. In fact, even his wholesome, otherwise innocent memories of her as a beautiful, engaging girl from his youth were never without their guilt.

He found himself wondering how he would feel if he knew his wife was thinking of a long-lost love that way. He knew he would hate it, and he considered himself unfaithful for even allowing Cydya into his consciousness. He had so often prayed that he could forget her that he wound up doing little but thinking of her. Worst of all, she had never aged in his mind. How could she? For twenty years, she had been there as she had been in Jakarta—tanned, firm, youthful.

How much easier it might have been if Rosemary had become a shrew. But she was a good mother, interesting and articulate because she passed the weeks of their frequent separations with voracious reading. When his tenuous faith was tested by the lack of anyone who seemed to live a genuine life of servanthood, there stood Rosemary as a beacon.

And she was loyal. Jordan couldn't deny he enjoyed the attention she showed him in public, but it was her consuming interest in him in private that continually amazed him. There was a time, early in their marriage, when she passionately discussed the dichotomy between her natural curiosity and her contentment with things as they were.

"I've always wanted to know everything," she would tell him. "It drove me crazy when something was going on at our house and I was the only one left in the dark. That's one of the reasons I read so much, Jordan. But for some reason, I don't even want to ask you anything you wouldn't volunteer to tell me.

"I know you. I trust you. I love you. To my knowledge, you've never told me a shred of classified information. I hope that's because you're told not to and not because you don't want me to worry. Because I worry anyway. And I pray."

She knew he worked for the National Security Agency, that he was in intelligence, and that he was anonymous even to many in the NSA. She was aware how difficult and demanding his job was, and also how much he loved it. From the beginning, when she had gone through several sessions with Harley Rollins, she knew her life would be abnormal if she married Jordan.

For years Jordan assured her that he had never been forced to use a weapon in the course of duty. On the pistol range, yes. In training, of course. But after a little more than ten years in the agency, he quit saying that. And she had never raised the subject.

United States policy prohibits political assassination or murder. However, in Cuba, Jordan had been forced to "eliminate an opponent for the purpose of preservation of one's own viability"—agency language for justifiable homicide. In fact, the incident had been a ghastly scene, caused by Jordan's own error.

He had ignored a hunch, the type of thing he should have relied on, based on Harley's counsel. "Always follow your hunch if it leads you to be cautious; never follow a hunch to take a risk." Something told him to wait. He didn't wait. Then he was jumped. A Luger pressed cold and ugly against his neck.

His assailant disarmed him and should have killed him where he stood. Instead, Jordan was forced to a wall and made to lean against it for several minutes while the Cuban agent taunted him and waited for a companion.

Jordan sagged against the wall, letting his head drop to his chest so he could see behind himself with peripheral vision. He prepared his body and mind for a technique Harley had taught him during his years as a student in Washington. Feigning fatigue, fear, and exhaustion, he tricked his adrenal gland into high gear by imagining his own death.

When his body was sufficiently charged, he leaped into the air, driving his feet off the wall and screaming as he turned around in midflight, hurtling toward the Cuban. It was kill or be killed. If you miss the gun hand, go for the neck. He missed the gun hand. It wound up under his arm, pointing toward the wall.

He clamped down on the gunman's arm with his elbow and drove him to the floor. He could release the pressure on the gun hand, provided he could break the man's neck more quickly than the man could turn the barrel and shoot.

The gun was in his ribs at his back when he felt the man's neck give way. And when the Cuban's partner burst in, Jordan had to kill him with the Luger. Rollins and other NSA brass were concerned over how the incident affected Jordan. They and his Uncle Dexter were the only people, outside the dead men, who knew what he had done.

The killings were legal. A matter of self-defense. Yet they plagued him, more than any of the serious injuries he had inflicted before. Those had been a different story. But to kill a man, to feel and see him die, to see the terror in the eyes, then the vacant stare. . . .

Though he tried to hide his feelings, he sensed that Rosemary knew. The event changed him, but it didn't make him want to leave the NSA the way the death of his wife did. Telling his bosses was going to be an ordeal. They'd dealt with burnt-out operatives before. He wouldn't say anything they hadn't heard.

Meanwhile, he had to talk Judy into getting back to Brandeis. "You'll be close by if I need you. And anyway, I have to be in the office for three days."

"But you'll be home for dinner."

"No, I won't. I'm staying right there, overnight and

everything. There'll be nothing for you to do here. Ken's heading back to California. What's the sense of staying here if I'm not going to be here anyway?"

"Ken's going back? Do you think you should let him before you—you know, get things, ah, straight?"

"We almost have. I'll be taking him to the airport, so say your good-byes here. We had a good talk, and we'll finish out there."

Judy looked at her father as if she knew him better than he knew himself. "I hate the idea that your bosses think you're up to being debriefed or whatever they call it. When will they let you mourn?"

"They can't stop me from that, honey."

Her lips quivered and her eyes filled. "But you need time to think, to remember, to cry."

He held her and whispered to her, fighting his own tears. "You're a special lady. And just for you, when I get back from headquarters, I'll take the time to rest."

"Promise?"

"I'm quitting, Judy."

"Quitting your job?"

He nodded.

"What will you do?"

"I don't know yet. I just know it's over, that's all. I've lost my drive."

"It'll come back."

"No! It won't!"

Judy flinched at his anger. "All right."

"I'm sorry, Judy. It's just that I know myself. This isn't a phase I'm going through, something caused by my grief. I don't want to get over it."

She pulled away and sat down facing him. She appeared to be deep in thought.

"Dad, do you feel guilty?"

"Guilty?"

"About Mom. Her death. Do you feel responsible?"

Jordan looked everywhere but at his daughter. "Should I?"

Her tears began again. "Oh, Dad. Kenny was right, wasn't he?"

Jordan's mind was still not right. He fought to be himself, yet he felt the conflicting patterns of his training rising to his defense. He could be lucid and evasive, even with his own daughter, if he wasn't grieving, if he was in shape. But he didn't want to be in shape. He didn't want to mislead her. He didn't want to quit grieving.

"Get your brother, and we'll all talk about it."

Then he told his son and daughter he wanted them to know the truth about their mother's death. "But I don't want you to ask me anything. If I don't volunteer it, don't ask." They nodded, and he went on: "I do feel responsible for what happened. I *am* responsible. I don't know why. You make a lot of enemies in my business, but what all worked together to cause the attack, I don't know. It's clear that I was the target and that the gunman died thinking he had succeeded."

Ken leaned forward. "What reason did he have for wanting to kill you, or is that something I'm not supposed to ask?"

Jordan's mind raced. He rationalized that he didn't know for sure that the Stuart meeting in Frankfurt had anything to do with it. "If I knew his reason, I might not be able to tell you, Ken. But I really don't know. He was a hired killer, and until I find out who hired him, I won't know the reason. It could be any one of a number of things."

Judy looked at her brother, then at Jordan. "Until *you* find out who hired him? You didn't mean to say that, did you?"

Jordan forced himself to speak evenly, though all the rage that had been building, all the grief and guilt and sorrow threatened to overflow.

"Yes, I did, and I have two reasons." His eyes burned into her. "Revenge and self-preservation."

Judy stood and walked to the window, her back to him. He could hardly hear her. "Mom would want you to leave vengeance to God, you know."

He shrugged, catching Ken's eye. "I know. That sounds good in theory. But if vengeance is God's, I want to be His instrument."

Judy whirled around. "Don't mock."

"I'm dead serious."

Ken looked puzzled. "You'll be on the case? Officially, I mean?"

"Of course not. I told you, I'm quitting. But do you think anyone else will be as interested in finding out who hired that assassin? If I don't do it, and my people lose interest, I could be the next victim. Or you." He couldn't, he wouldn't tell them that he trusted only one, maybe two others in the agency. If Stuart's information was good, Jordan's would-be assassin and Stu's own killer could have been hired by someone within the NSA.

Judy sat back down next to Ken. "That's why you want us both out of here by the time you get back. You think someone might come looking for you here and find us in the wrong place at the wrong time, just like Mom?"

Jordan caught the first glimmer of realization in their eyes. "I will not have my family living in fear the rest of their lives," he said.

Ken lowered his head and peeked up at his father. "I'm not scared."

Judy looked first at Ken, then at her father. "Me either."

Jordan knew he had to say it. "I am."

Judy tried a smile. "I thought you weren't afraid of anything."

"You did, huh? Did I ever say that?" She shook her head. "Did I act that way?" They both nodded.

"Well, there *is* something I'm terribly afraid of, besides your safety and my own. I'm afraid you'll never forgive me for costing you your mother."

They embraced him.

Jordan thought he had been tired before. The seven hours of sleep he got that Wednesday night put a mere dent in the fatigue caused not only by his grief and fear, but also by his anxiety over how to inform his superiors of his plans.

Felix was quiet on the way to the NSA compound. He had not attended the funeral, something Jordan hadn't even noticed until he mentioned it. "Real sorry I couldn't make it. You know how they tie you up when you get back from anywhere."

"How well I know. Like today. This is the longest I've ever been back without being debriefed already."

Within an hour, Felix had driven north on the Baltimore-Washington Parkway to a place just about equidistant from both cities. Noting Felix's mood, or at least his lack of compunction to chat so early in the morning, Jordan tried to relax and enjoy the scenery. He found Maryland countryside consisted of miles of trees he had never taken the time to look at before.

Felix turned right on Savage Road, bringing into view the nine-story NSA headquarters building, surrounded by the three-story complex that had preceded it. The very sight of that innocent-looking building threw Jordan back to his early days in Washington when Harley Rollins had driven this very route to show it to him while it was going up.

The three-story facility had been bulging at the seams, Harley had told him. The hope was that the new building would be adequate. The plan was that the place not look like what it was: headquarters for the world's largest secret code-deciphering plant. In those days, the NSA had no operatives who worked in the manner that Jordan Kettering would—like a misplaced CIA man. Now, twenty years later, he told himself, after this last debriefing there would be none left.

He had visited the headquarters at least twice a year since he had joined the NSA. He always hated it. The three fences surrounding the grounds, the electrically charged wires, the barbed wire, the guard dogs, and the television monitors were necessary, but there were days when all that security seemed so Mickey Mouse. Today was one such day.

No matter who you were or what your business was, you went through security here just like everyone else, including the director. As they mounted the dozen steps to the glassed-in entrance to Gatehouse One, Jordan wondered aloud if he would be seeing Erhard. Felix grunted. "Count on it."

A Federal Protective Service guard matched Felix's face with the photo on the employee security badge hanging around his neck. Then he stopped Jordan.

"You, ain't you a employee, too?"

Jordan nodded apologetically. "Forgot my badge."

Felix tried to wave off the guard. "He's with me."

"You know that ain't good enough, sir. If he ain't got his badge, you got to sponsor him just like he was a visitor. Sorry."

Felix swore and dragged Jordan off through another set of doors to the reception area where he was processed like anyone else without security clearance. Felix had to sign a promise that Jordan would be accompanied at all times. A striped, one-day badge was pinned on Jordan, and for a moment he really felt like an outsider. *Not soon enough, I will be.*

On the way down the long corridor to the lobby, Felix

chuckled. "That receptionist woulda had a fit if she'd known y'all was gonna be here three days on a one-day badge." Jordan didn't see the humor. In the mural on the wall, which purports to show the various activities of the NSA, he saw agency employees engaged in listening, writing, and collecting signals. He didn't see anyone killing anyone else or watching his wife die.

At the end of the hall was the gaudy seal he'd passed so many times, its gleaming eagle protecting the NSA. He and Felix took a left and headed toward the elevators in the lobby, past the portraits of former NSA directors and another armed guard.

The bored guard noted their badges and nodded. Felix pushed the up button while glancing at his watch. "You should see some of the new computers in the basement. But we don't have time." When they stepped into the car, he pushed the button for the top floor, nine.

Jordan had been in Room 9A197 before, the office of the director of the National Security Agency. The secretary ushered them into the empty office and pointed to two leather chairs facing a coffee table and a matching couch. As soon as she left, an edgy Jordan stood and looked out the window, then idly twirled the huge globe.

Felix sat like a gangly junior high basketball player on the bench. "Lots to do today," he said. Jordan didn't answer.

Kurt Erhard breezed in, tall and pale with dark wavy hair, brown eyes, thin lips, and hurry-up in his voice. "Good morning, gentlemen." Felix stood and Erhard shook their hands. "Don't sit down, Felix. I think you may be excused now."

Erhard unbuttoned his suit coat as he sat on the couch, swinging both legs up to his side. Settled in, he stared long and hard at Jordan. "Tough, tough thing for you, Kettering. A lovely service, though. Happy to be there. Beautiful family. Enjoyed getting to meet your mother. Is she well?" Jordan shook his head. "And your father?"

"Dead, sir."

"But the old gentleman—."

"Her brother, my uncle."

"Ah. Nice. Good he could come. You're okay?"

"Hardly."

"Well, of course not. I can imagine. Sorry we have to jump right into things. You could use more time, no doubt."

"No doubt."

"But such is life. Tough, tough thing. Is there anything at all I can do for you, Jordan?"

It was an idle statement, one he had heard many times during the past two days. But here was a man with resources. "Two things."

Erhard looked surprised. "Anything."

"I'd like to see Harley Rollins."

"He's coming! Didn't you know?" Jordan shook his head. Erhard nodded. "Oh, yes. We knew he was very instrumental in your career. He's coming. Absolutely. Up from Florida. In fact, he'll be involved in some of your debriefing and counseling."

"Counseling?"

"You said there were *two* things I could help you with?"

"But, sir, please, you said counseling?"

Erhard gestured before he spoke, as if coaxing the words from his throat. "In, uh, situations like this, we like to, you know, do a variety of diagnostic and evaluative things, run some tests. There is some counseling involved, mostly as interrogative inventory."

Jordan loved the double-talk. "You mean a shrink is going to ask me if I'm suicidal."

Erhard swung his legs down off the couch and planted his feet in front of him. He put a hand on each knee and leaned forward. "I understand you are one of our top men in the world, Kettering, and I can see why. I know you're unique, and I also know we'll have to fight to keep you around here." Jordan was stunned. He thought at first that Erhard had been tipped off about his decision to leave. "The CIA is always on our case to lend you to them. Same with military intelligence. Anyway, I appreciate your subjecting yourself to this. Tough—."

Jordan nodded and parroted him. "Tough thing."

"You did say there was something else I could do for you."

"Well, I was going to ask you to get me out of this, but it's apparent I'm the highlight of the week around here."

Erhard studied him and smiled. "I'm impressed you can keep a sense of humor after what you've been through. Listen, I understand how you feel. I sympathize. I pledge we'll keep things moving, and the earliest we can get you out of here on Saturday, the happier we'll be. You know this gives us time to be certain of your security and start working on a suitable new assignment for you. And the more you cooperate, the quicker it'll go."

So, there it was. A plum position. Whatever and wherever he wanted. Resignation was not in their thinking. Neither was bitterness or cynicism or lack of cooperation. Get in line, stay in line, be loyal, and we'll take care of you. The problem was, Jordan wasn't in the mood. It all seemed like such a waste.

Erhard stood but motioned for Jordan to stay seated. "Two things I want you to know before you head over to Medical. First, you're the boss. Your next assignment is up to you. You want to go to Florida and work with Rollins in administration? Okay. You want to learn a new area? Decoding? Management? You tell us. The other thing I want you to know is this: we're fully aware that you were the target in London. You will be under constant surveillance for your protection, and we will be tracking down the perpetrator with every resource available to us."

"Except me."

"Pardon?"

"Every resource except me."

"We'll use you, Jordan. That's part of what this three-day session is all about. We must comb through all your activities for any leads."

Jordan sighed. "How far back?"

"All the way back. But first, a physical. Then a psychological. Then a debriefing on the Germany assignment. Then a history search, an inventory of your contacts."

"For twenty years?"

"If necessary."

Jordan had not been easy to talk to. He had not been kind to Erhard. The director would pass that off as bitterness or grief, but Jordan knew the truth: he had come to the end of his patience with the work. He wasn't saying what the NSA did wasn't valid or necessary. He just knew the organization was too big, too cumbersome, too corporate, too bureaucratic. And, since he'd quit working for Harley Rollins, it was too lonely. Besides, he couldn't imagine any possibility of confirming Stan Stuart's secret from the inside.

Erhard extended his hand, as if to help him up. Jordan ignored the assistance. He wasn't old and weak, just tired and heartbroken. "I'll walk you over myself." Erhard knew Jordan had to be accompanied, but he could have assigned a secretary. Apparently it made Erhard feel important to condescend to such a task.

They went back down through the lobby and into the hallway connecting the headquarters tower to the three-story operations building. Getting through the most secure doors required Erhard to reach inside a box and depress the right buttons. At other passageways he slid a magnetic card into a slot. Jordan had been on the second and third floors of the operations building, where each new wing was color-coded for level of clearance. There were some not even the director could enter without advance permission.

Corridor C at the center of the complex was nearly a thousand feet long, the longest clear hallway in the United States. Jordan felt fortunate he didn't have to walk all the way to the other end. Erhard delivered him to a physician, Dr. Luschel Bradley, a freckle-faced redhead who, except for the fact that he was Jordan's age, could have modeled in children's commercials.

He ran Jordan through five hours of the second most rigorous physical examination he had ever had. The first had been his initial exam for the NSA before he enrolled at the International University. Harley Rollins had prepared him for that one. "No sense educating you if you're going to fall apart on us."

If anything, Jordan was in better shape now than he had been then. The doctor asked a lot of personal questions Jordan would have expected more from a psychiatrist, but that was coming next. The redhead smiled and thanked him when it was over, extending his hand. "Couple of test results will be back later, but meanwhile, all things considered, you're a thoroughbred."

Did *everybody* know what he was going through? He began to resent his macabre celebrity. The doctor put a hand on his shoulder. "I get to walk you to Dr. Fazio. You know who he is, I assume."

Jordan certainly did.

Tall and thin, wearing moccasins and his shirt open at the collar, the fiftyish Dr. Fazio was bald with a rim of hair over his ears. He wore glasses he seemed fonder of chewing than using, and rather than employ a couch or even a chair, he preferred walking interviews.

Very early in their first conversation, Dr. Fazio stopped at the corner of two hallways.

"Could you briefly tell me of your religious background, Jordan?"

"How briefly?"

"Three words."

"I'm not too devout now. Having trouble, uh, praying. My wife was—."

The doctor shook his head. "Background. Training. Upbringing. Briefly."

"Ah, Protestant. Fundamentalist. Um—."

The doctor sighed. "Two's enough." He rubbed his forehead. "Oh, boy."

Eight

By the time Dr. Fazio and Jordan had walked the length of corridor C, including a brief stop for a snack, each had formed conclusions about the other. The doctor, it was clear, had decided that Jordan would hide his true grief in the belief that God knew what was best, cared personally about him, and was watching over him.

"My fear, young man, is that you will soon turn the blame on God, still assuming that He takes a personal interest in each of His charges, and wonder why He has done this to you."

Jordan shrugged. "I'll survive. I'm not suicidal. I'm still in shock, or is that too pedestrian for what you're after? You know, five days ago I saw my wife alive one minute and dead the next. Is it all right with you if that traumatizes me a little?"

The doctor sniffed. "No need to be testy. I'm just trying to determine how deeply ingrained your belief is in a personal God."

"For what purpose?"

"I'm not supposed to say why and run the risk of affecting your answers, but you're a reasonably intelligent man, Mr. Kettering. Unfortunately, some of these childish, excuse me, childhood myths can be difficult to overcome. In limbo they are harmless, but when employed to assuage grief, well—."

"Well, what?"

"To a, shall we say, more simplistic mind, the notion of a personal deity can be comforting. To someone such as yourself, the sudden realization of a lack of validity or, uh, substance there could set you back. In other words, if everything is not all right and God is not in His heaven, what then?"

Jordan shaped his hand in the form of a gun and held it to his head. The doctor flinched. "That does not amuse me."

"And you don't amuse me, doctor. My fundamentalist background gave me some solid beliefs, but I don't think I have to be some sort of a weirdo to be a Christian."

"But you do believe God exists as a real person?"

"Yes."

The doctor raised both hands. "I find you otherwise mentally healthy."

"Are you going to put that in your report?"

"That you're mentally healthy? Yes. I don't worry terribly about you. I'd like to check on the condition of your faith in about six months, however."

"I'll look forward to it. But I want to know if you're going to make note of my faith as some sort of a psychological aberration."

The doctor leaned against the wall. "If that would trouble you, I will leave it out."

"I'd appreciate that."

"Don't deceive yourself, however. It's not as if they don't already know. Why do you think I asked you about your religious background?"

"I know they know. Harley Rollins discovered me with a church missionary group, for pete's sake. I've never hidden it."

"Then what's your trouble with my recording it?"

"I'm talking about your recording it as a problem."

"Oh, I rarely record my personal opinions."

Jordan sincerely doubted that. Still, he found the psychiatrist a reasonable man, interesting to talk to. It was time for dinner when they finally finished. "Who'll be working with me tomorrow?"

The doctor raised his eyebrows. "You don't know? You rate top brass."

"Not the director. He would have told me."

"No, but the deputy. Bauer himself, along with some aides."

"Oh, joy."

"Plus they're bringing in one of the old timers from out of state."

"Yeah, Rollins. The one I mentioned."

The doctor nodded. It was clear to Jordan that he didn't care. He wasn't counseling; he was interrogating. There would be no comfort, no condolences, no suggestions on how to work through the dark times, the teary times.

Jordan was surprised when Dr. Bradley, the M.D., joined them for dinner. "If you don't mind, I've been assigned to go through the line with you and prescribe your dinner."

"Prescribe?"

The redhead smiled. "You are going to sleep tonight, Mr. Kettering. Like you've never slept before."

"I could use that. And you're going to pull it off with food choices?"

"Partly. Also this." He held out a plastic packet containing two capsules. "Good for hours of solid, and I mean uninterrupted, sleep."

While the doctor pointed to high-protein, high-fiber vegetables and a small chicken dish, no dessert, no dairy products, Jordan examined the capsules. "No label. No ingredients."

"You mean no ingredients listed." They sat again with Dr. Fazio. Bradley borrowed back the packet and showed the psychiatrist. Fazio nodded and smiled. "Take it when you're finished eating, but find out where you're bedding down first so you can tell whoever scrapes you up off the floor."

Jordan fingered the packet again. "I'm not a big chemical man. I stay away from aspirin as long as I can. So, what's in here?"

"Ever hear of sodium pentothal?"

"Of course. For major surgery. Surely you're not—."

The doctor stopped him with a wave. "Of course not. The key ingredient in sodium pentothal is phenobarbital." He switched into a bad W. C. Fields impersonation. "A white, odorless, crystalline powder."

Dr. Fazio broke in. "Five cc's of which will kill a twelve-hundred-pound race horse in thirty seconds. You know how much five cc's is?"

Jordan remembered, from somewhere, that thirty cc's made an ounce. "A sixth of an ounce." The doctors looked at each other, impressed. Jordan dug his fork into a bite of broccoli. "I won't take it."

Dr. Bradley sat back from his plate. "No one will force you, of course. Let me encourage you, however. You've been through a difficult ordeal. Tomorrow and Saturday could be painful as well. You should be in bed by seven tonight. Within twenty-five minutes of taking those capsules, which I assure you are potent, but not dangerous— I blended them myself with just a minuscule amount of the good stuff—you will sleep up to twelve hours without dreaming. In fact, you will sleep without moving. Be sure to eliminate before you retire."

Doctors were always so delicate, Jordan decided. Directed to a comfortable but not fancy room, he wearily sat on the bed and disrobed to his shorts. Someone would be by in the morning to escort him to S Building. That was hard to figure. Surely he, and those working with him, would be in the way in the bronze-colored home of the agency's Communications Security Organization.

Jordan padded around arranging his room, hanging up things, turning off the lights. After brushing his teeth, he stared at the haggard face in the mirror. He felt old and looked older. It wouldn't be long before his natural color would begin peeking out at the roots of his dyed hair. He wouldn't be surprised if it came in gray this time. Stranger things had happened.

Did he feel like sleeping? He wasn't sure. There was no question about his exhaustion. The only question was whether he was too wired to be able to relax from so much happening so fast. He went to the closet and searched for the pills in his pants pocket.

When he slid between the cold sheets, he decided to try to stay awake until the pills took effect, just for the experience. Unfortunately, that gave him time to think. He stared at the ceiling in the darkness, reliving his meeting with Stanley Stuart and the icy feeling in the pit of his stomach at the very thought of the enemy on American soil. He experienced anew the shooting, the trip home, Felix's compassion, Bauer's prissiness, Ken's anger, Judy's sweetness.

His mother had declined. That was clear. When would she have to be institutionalized? And when would he be jetting back for her funeral? Uncle Dex had been his usual, rare self. Jordan felt fortunate to have had him over the years.

He found himself weeping as he lay there on his back, legs crossed at the ankles, fingers entwined over his chest. The tears rolled over his ears, but he didn't move to wipe them away.

He knew when his eyelids grew heavy that he was past the point of no return. A warm glow radiated through his muscles and joints, leaving a floating numbness. He felt giddy, then drowsy, then incoherent, even in his thinking. Hallucinations teased him and he tried to think, to remember. Hadn't that doctor said no dreams? Nonsense. No sense. But which doctor? Witch doctor? He saw Bradley with a bone through his nose. In London. On the floor, next to his wife. Or was that Cydya? Whoever it was, she was dead. A train pulled slowly away from him as he ran leaden-legged along the platform. He ran and ran, waving, but all he could see through the windows were Russian MiG-23s. At the end of the platform he stopped at a huge corrugated steel door, but the train kept moving.

As these thoughts faded, so did all consciousness.

When Jordan's eyes popped open, it was still dark. He still lay in the same position. *Didn't even work. Probably didn't put enough stuff in them. Shoot! For a few minutes I was gone. Completely gone.* He rolled over and reached for his watch, feeling groggy. He squinted at the luminous hands. Five fifteen. Couldn't be.

He raised the shade. Still dark. Where was another clock? In the hall? He peeked out the door. The sound echoed through the corridor. He heard footsteps and moved back in, keeping the door slightly ajar. When the footsteps came closer he peeked out again. It was a guard.

"Help you, sir?"

"Just wonderin' what time it is." Jordan sounded drunk.

"Almost five twenty, Mr. Kettering. Need anything?" Jordan shook his head.

The doctor had said he would sleep without moving or dreaming. He didn't say anything about losing even his subconscious awareness of time passing. He sat on the edge of the bed, trying to convince himself he had slept more than ten hours. It didn't register. He had known he would feel better, a little rested. But it was as if he had lain down, thought awhile, drifted off a minute, and then woke up. Ten hours later. He wished he could think of a cute line for all the times he would be asked, "Sleep well?"

As life returned to his limbs, he worked out. He ran in place, did push-ups, sit-ups, leg-stretching exercises. After he had showered and shaved, he felt like a hard four-mile run. But they'd never let him do it in that complex.

After breakfast, Jordan met in the basement of S Building with Blake Bauer and two of his clerical assistants. They were to take notes and look up records. Bauer insisted Jordan make himself comfortable in the room, which was much too large for the few sticks of furniture and the file cabinets that had been brought in for the occasion.

The chair of honor was a dilapidated green vinyl job with sagging springs and spindly legs. Jordan got as comfortable as he could. Blake sat facing him in a hardwood, Bank of England chair that caused him to squirm all morning. The aides were behind him in secretary's chairs, on rollers, near the file cabinets. They shared a small table.

Bauer smiled at Jordan as if he relished his assignment. If anything, Jordan thought his case should be considered grunt duty for someone at Bauer's level, but apparently the deputy enjoyed such activity. "Mr. Rollins is expected after lunch. Meanwhile, let's get better acquainted."

"We know each other, Blake. And please, let's not talk in agency language all day."

"Pardon?" Jordan waved him off, knowing the request was moot. "As you recall, Kettering, I joined the NSA from the military some five years after you had already been on board. The fact is, I was unaware of you for almost a decade. I had no reason to be aware of you in my climb, or my, uh, progress through the ranks, as it were, to the level or the area of responsibility which is now mine, or which I now hold."

Good grief! "Now you're important enough to know about one of the only remaining CIA types within the NSA."

"I wouldn't express it quite that way, but you have described yourself well. You know, when Mr. Rollins received permission for this highly unusual undertaking—that is, developing clandestine operations with anonymous recruits such as yourself, bringing them along, training them individually—most thought it would fail."

Jordan straightened up in his chair. "And it did fail, didn't it? I've heard this pitch before."

Bauer cocked his head and looked hurt. "Please don't call it a pitch, Jordan. We have a job to do here."

"And do you realize that I don't know yet what the job is? Would you mind telling me what we're trying to accomplish here while whoever had my wife hit is still looking for me?"

Bauer was suddenly serious. "Don't be naive. That's one of the reasons you're here."

"I can't stay here forever. And if you're just protecting me, what are we doing down here with the files?"

"Your files have never really been open to the administration. For so long, your role was one of investigation, even inside the agency. I think we all realize how important that function was, but our handicap now is that so few people inside were aware of your activity and sphere of influence that we hardly know where to begin to look for leads on your pursuer."

Jordan thought he detected something. "I'm in the way, now that I'm in trouble, aren't I?"

" 'In the way' is not the right word for it."

"Not the right word, but the right idea. You people wish that I had been either more visible or less effective."

Bauer shook his head, smiling. "There are those, I'll concede—though I'm not one of them—who are, shall we say, less than comfortable with having had one of our own keeping us under surveillance for a time."

"A very short time. Most of my time was spent watching other federal agencies."

"For which we are grateful."

"Oh, you're grateful that someone is watching *them*, as long as no one is watching *us!*"

Bauer stood, his face red. "Enough people are watching us from the other agencies, Jordan. Can't you understand that? We don't need to watch ourselves!"

Jordan smiled at him, letting his own statement ring in his ears. "Is that what you meant to say, Blake?"

"Well, of course, we keep an eye on our people. That's part of any manager's job. But we're talking here about a band of a dozen or so young people, some just out of high school—yourself included—who were somehow brought in by Rollins when he was a maverick, and—."

"He's not still a maverick?"

"He's less a maverick. He's a company man, Jordan, and always has been. Anyway, he and some long-since-departed associates got this scheme passed through the former director—heaven knows how—and frankly, for a decade or so, it ran amuck." Bauer looked at Jordan as if waiting for acknowledgment, a nod of agreement, something, anything. It was not forthcoming. "Well, do you or do you not agree?"

"We did our jobs, Blake. We were totally committed. It was an unusual group. You know, don't you, that for a couple of years we weren't even aware of each other? It was an experiment."

"I heard something about that. See how long each big brother, or whatever Rollins and his cohorts called themselves, could keep his man working and effective without anyone knowing who he was. Didn't work too well, I understand."

"Worked very well. Made the director and your predecessor very nervous. They knew us on paper, but they didn't see photos or know names. For a while, we were their best people, and they had no idea if they'd ever seen us or ever would. Finally called us in."

"It wasn't quite that simple."

Now it was Jordan's turn to stand, only he wasn't upset. Just cramped. "There were a few failures, sure. Some of the guys were found out. Some were lured away by other agencies. Some were bad choices, couldn't hack the work."

"One failed miserably. Stanley Stuart's selection, I recall."

"Granted, but the failure was in the choosing itself. He wasn't studied the way Harley studied me."

"Stuart suffered for it, too. He was not allowed to select another man. He was just reassigned."

Jordan smirked. "At least he still had an interesting job. He wasn't kicked upstairs until fifteen years later when his wife died."

Bauer looked hurt. "Your idea of a raise and a promotion to administration is getting kicked upstairs?"

"My apologies. But I didn't get the impression Stu was happy about it."

Bauer was obviously distressed. "You can't blame his suicide on his job!"

Jordan was tempted to tell Bauer what he really thought about the alleged suicide, but his survival instinct took over.

"What do you think caused it, Blake?"

The deputy stared at the ceiling. "Grief. Depression."

"Four years after he lost his wife? C'mon!"

"Well, who knows, Jordan? Did you get a chance to see him when you were there? He requested you, but you worked independently there, didn't you?"

"Right."

"So you didn't see him?"

Jordan hesitated and hated himself for it. "Not really, no."

"What's that mean? You ought to be a better liar than that after all these years. A routine check of his day to see if anything specific might have triggered his demise revealed that you spent five minutes with him in the afternoon and that he went home early, right after your meeting."

"If you knew, why'd you ask?"

"To see if you'd deny seeing him."

"I didn't exactly deny it."

"You didn't exactly do anything, did you? You didn't exactly see him, and you didn't exactly deny seeing him. Which is it?"

"Is that what we're here for? To see if I caused Stanley Stuart's death?"

"Just answer the question."

"I said I didn't exactly see him because I hadn't planned to see him. And we just greeted each other. I hadn't even known he was there."

"Get serious. You know where everyone is, especially your old acquaintances."

"I knew he'd been reassigned in Europe, but I didn't know he was at JOSAF. You can ask his secretary."

Bauer picked through some documents before him. "True enough. She said you expressed surprise that Mr. Stuart was there. So what did he want?"

"Five minutes for old time's sake. Nothing of consequence."

"He seem depressed?"

"Tired maybe. Showed his age. Mentioned retirement."

"That's it?" Bauer stared at Jordan.

The second meeting with Stuart had been private and personal, away from the JOSAF office. And Stu had only assumed the man behind the local mouthpiece was an NSA man because he had information only an insider would know.

"That's it." Jordan stared back, silent and unmoving as if his life depended on it.

Bauer walked to the file cabinets. "Pull me the Rollins file on Jordan, would you? It's time to get back on track."

He sat in his chair and waited for the delivery of four inches of manila. "There's something missing here, Jordan."

"I'll bite."

"I'm not being cute. I've been over this and over this, and I'm still puzzled. Rollins carefully documents how he ran into you, how he baited you, how he tested you to see if you wanted the position. He's clear on some of your shortcomings and how you worked to improve. But what I don't get is how he made that step from seeing an admittedly impressive high school resumè to somehow knowing that you were sincere."

"Sincere?"

"Don't be coy, Jordan. The reason you lasted, the reason you're the only survivor of this crazy twenty-year-old plan, is because you had the ideals for it."

Jordan was shocked. Was Bauer serious? Had he seen that for himself? "Do you really think so?"

Bauer slammed his fist on the table. "That's just it, Jordan! I don't know! Maybe, yes. But how do we know? With inside men, you have military records and then years of climbing the corporate ladder. With you, we've got what? You were a Boy Scout and a church-going Christian. So what? Most of us were. How did Rollins know you were also a true patriot, a loyal American, totally honest, and for the right motives?"

Jordan fought a smile, tempted to ask why it was so hard to imagine that of him. "He was a good judge of character?"

"Nobody is *that* good! He was taking a risk."

"Don't you always take a risk whenever you hire someone?"

"Not for so sensitive a position. And not with someone so young. Do you realize how potentially disastrous your appointment was? Do you?"

"Not till now, Blake, but you're really bringin' it home.

How'd we get off on this? I thought we were going to look for a criminal."

Bauer tapped the ends of the folders on the table. "We are. But we can't study your background and activities and contacts without getting onto this subject, and it's a hot one for anyone in administration here."

"We were all that worrisome for everyone?"

"Oh, you bet."

"Were they all that jealous of our freedom?"

Bauer smirked. "You'd like to think that, wouldn't you? Maybe there was some of that. Maybe some of us would rather have been globe-trotting, carrying weapons, playing CIA. But mostly, as the number of you renegades dwindled and the dictates came down to quit spying on your own people, folks around here just thought the whole program ought to be thrown over. We thought we had you when you snuffed those guys in Cuba. Ho, man, Kettering! That just about did it. They could put up with you and yours when nobody but Rollins and a few others knew what you were doing, but when things got noisy, well . . . this agency was founded to intercept messages and decode them, and there you guys were, playing cloak-and-dagger games."

"Guilty. So now what? You want me to resign? I'm ready."

Bauer shook his head and looked back at his two assistants. They pretended to be bored with it all. He turned again to Jordan. "You know nobody's going to let you resign."

"*Let* me? How can they stop me?"

"You know too much, inside and out."

"I know too much *inside!* So, that's it. It isn't the federal secrets or the international intelligence. It's what I know about the NSA."

Bauer shrugged. "Maybe. I can offer you a three-step promotion and a significant raise, which both you and I know you don't need. You make almost as much as I do now, not that I have a problem with your bypassing me on salary. But, first, I have two tasks. And they're related. We feel an obligation to protect you from whoever is trying to kill you."

"I should think you would!"

"Well, don't go getting all uppity about that, Kettering! Not too many people in this agency get themselves in that kind of trouble."

Jordan stepped in front of Bauer and looked down on him in much the same way his own son had towered over him two days before. "So, I got *myself* in the trouble that killed my wife? Who do you think I was working for when I crossed whoever it was I crossed? You think I was on vacation? Moonlighting? Give me a break, Bauer! I may have been one of the only NSA men in the world— okay, the *only* one—doing that kind of work, but it was my assignment!"

Bauer looked as if he feared he was about to experience personally some of Jordan's legendary hand-to-hand combat skills. "What do you say we just calm down a little, huh, Kettering? Maybe I should have stated that a little more forcefully. In sincere appreciation for your putting your life on the line in the course of duty and in light of your tragic loss, we want to do everything in our power to apprehend the person or persons responsible. Okay? That's going to require careful scrutiny of your entire career. You know the case is otherwise strictly off-limits to you."

Jordan sat down. "I guessed that. But outside of Harley Rollins, whom you already have squirreled away in some two-bit desk job somewhere, you just finished implying I'm the only man in the NSA with the training and experience to handle the case."

"You're too close to it, those are my orders, and that's final. Don't fight me on this one. Now, are we ready for our second task here today and tomorrow, which, as I recall, was your original question? Here it is: I have to do the job, with or without Rollins's help, that he should have done when he hired you."

Jordan was clearly puzzled. "What didn't he do?"

"What I was driving at before, Jordan. He apparently had some seat-of-the-pants confidence in you as a young idealist, but he didn't document anything except your accepting and meeting a few challenges and answering a question or two about being gung ho—wherein you waxed eloquent about your father's war wounds. Your record after that is good, but we have to establish retroactively the solidity of your character."

Jordan sifted through the rhetoric until the full insult reached him. Then he wanted to dive across the table and inflict upon that soft, bureaucratic mug the pain deserved by people who would put him up to such a task. But the mind-trigger mechanism that had been so effectively impressed upon his brain by Harley Rollins shifted him quickly to a calm mode.

"Let's say I ignore the implications of that statement, Blake. Let's say I don't allow myself to absorb fully the slam at my record. Let's say I even agree there was some oversight in Harley's documentation. Doesn't my record speak for itself? Can't we say that even if he hired me on flimsy grounds, I proved myself in the ensuing years? Do you need a lie detector test? You wanna wire me up and ask me if I'm true blue?"

Bauer dabbed at his forehead with a handkerchief. "Jordan, I don't want to rile you, but I have to tell you this. I just hope you'll appreciate the fact that I'm telling you, because it was thought—and I hoped—that I would be more successful here if I didn't have to spell this all out."

"I can hardly wait."

"The fact is, we don't know enough about your activity

for several of the years you've been with us to know how credible you are."

"You think I could be subversive? A double agent of some kind?"

"I didn't say that! I'm telling you no, we can't just take a look at your record on paper and decide whether or not there will be any public embarrassment to this agency over what happened to your wife and what may happen to you as a result of that."

Jordan stared at Bauer. Then he looked down and scratched the back of his head. "Do you see the ridiculous side of this, if you carry it to its illogical conclusion? You could decide that I brought all this on myself by involving myself in some subversive activity or something on my own. Then what? You leave me to fend for myself? I'm confused, Blake. Do I get the promotion and the raise and the protection if I'm deemed okay, or if I'm *not* okay? And will you accept my resignation if I'm *not* okay, but not if I *am* okay?"

"You raise good points, Jordan."

At that, Jordan let his head fall back. He roared. "This is too much! And it feels so good to laugh!" Except that his laughter turned on him in a vulnerable instant, while his emotions were still raw, and became crying. Then he lurched forward to cover his mouth.

In the process he saw the eyes of Bauer and his assistants, and he knew why he had promised himself he would not break down during this session. But he couldn't help it. If only the emotion hadn't sneaked up on him, maybe he could have been ready. Maybe he could have reacted the opposite of the way he wanted to. Only isn't that what had happened?

He had wanted to laugh at the horrendous lack of logic. His mind, tuned to the paradox of the opposite frequency, read comedy and spit out tragedy. Now that he had failed and sat there sobbing, he wanted to scream at Bauer, to demand to know how he could impugn a perfect record.

He wanted to rage about his love for his country, his rock-solid belief in democracy and justice and peace and honesty. Yet he would not lower himself to speak while out of control. He fought for composure.

Bauer spoke haltingly. "Let's break, people. Mr. Rollins will be here this afternoon, and we'll take this up again then."

Nine

The ease with which NSA brass like Blake Bauer separated business and pleasure had always astounded Jordan. Bauer and his two young aides and Jordan were picked up in a motorized cart and deposited at a small, institutional, private dining room where they were served sandwiches in a manner all too formal for the fare.

For some reason, Bauer found it necessary to treat Jordan as a guest, an acquaintance he had invited to join his family for lunch. Jordan resisted the banter and refused to engage in small talk with the man who had so recently implied that he might be other than what he had been reputed all these years.

It wasn't enough that they had to make him endure a debriefing for the sake of finding his wife's assailant. No, now they would spring on him the fact that, for years, everyone who hadn't been engaged in his type of work had been jealous, even suspicious of him.

The only thing that warmed and encouraged Jordan during lunch was the knowledge that he would be seeing Harley Rollins before long. Bauer made a few half-hearted attempts at humor, trying to draw out Jordan. His efforts served only to disgust Jordan.

Bauer studied the empty plates before his aides. "Could you gentlemen excuse us for a few minutes? That is, if you're finished?" They left as if shot from their seats. "Jordan, there is another item, if you don't mind. Did you happen to bring your weapons with you?"

"No, I never do. You know that."

"I know that's standard, but this being a highly unusual visit, I thought maybe—."

"No, they're at home in the attic, in my locked trunk. Strictly regulation."

"Ah, good."

"Why?"

"Well, we'd sort of like to examine them for the purposes of this investigation."

"My weapons?"

"Yes, all of them."

"I didn't even take all of them with me on the last trip."

"Of course you didn't. You never carry them *all*, do you?"

"Only once. The Korean expedition. It was a chore getting them into the country."

"You have what, a couple of hundred pounds worth of munitions?"

"Oh, no. More. Probably double that."

Bauer shook his head, and it was clear to Jordan that he was more than surprised. His was a look of disgust, as if no one anywhere, and certainly not in the service of the National Security Agency needed any weapons, let alone a more than 400-pound arsenal.

"Some of those are personal weapons, Blake."

"Personal?"

"Yes. It's all in my files. I purchased sixteen Colt .45s a few years ago, soon after the Army announced it was switching to Berettas. They had over four hundred thousand Colts, not one newer than forty years old, some of them as old as seventy years."

"What in the world would you want with a .45, Jordan? What does one weigh? Two pounds?"

"Two and a half."

"And the recoil on that thing is enormous."

"That's what I like about it. That little nine-millimeter Beretta is like a BB gun."

Bauer raised his eyebrows, as if he knew more about

weapons than Jordan Kettering. "The Italians know how to make weapons. Our European allies have all gone to Berettas."

"Good reason for us to stay with the Colts. We've helped our allies a lot more than they've helped us, and one of the big reasons was our advanced weaponry. You wouldn't catch me laying out over six hundred bucks a piece for non-American-made toys like Berettas. But then I'm not in purchasing, except for myself. Got a couple of classics, and a dozen or so that are in perfect condition."

"Accurate?"

"That's never been one of the .45's traits, I know. Unless you get used to each weapon, learn its idiosyncrasies, and use it, rather than letting it use you."

Bauer looked as if he had taken that personally. Which was how Jordan had meant it. "You have a license to own those sixteen Colts?"

"What do you think?"

"I don't know. That's why I'm asking."

"I was a Boy Scout, remember? An honor student? Why, I've been in the selfless, patriotic service of my country for more than twenty years."

"Don't get sarcastic with me, Kettering."

"Me? Sarcastic? Just quit hoping you can get me on some local legal technicality. If you want to prove I'm the villain, that I brought this on myself, that the NSA has no responsibility in the matter, you'll have to do it based on my record, not on my gun-buying."

"Your gun-buying is part of your record. Anyway, who said I was trying to do what you just said I was trying to do?"

Jordan ignored the question. "Are you going to have to see my inventory?"

"Today or tomorrow, I'm afraid."

"Then you're going to have to let me go get my trunk."

"Can't do that. You're quarantined until tomorrow."

"You're not sending one of your flunkies into my home."

Bauer sighed and reached over to clap Jordan on the shoulder. Jordan hated that. "I don't have any flunkies, Jordie. I'm as proud of my young assistants as Harley Rollins was of you twenty years ago. They won't mess up anything in your castle, you can be sure of that."

Jordan stared straight into Bauer's eyes and shook his head. "You're not sending anyone into my house that I don't know. Forget it."

"Someone has already been assigned. We'd appreciate your permission, but it isn't required."

"What do you mean my permission isn't required? So now the NSA owns me *and* my house?"

"You know we can get in there in a minute, with or without your key. We feel this is crucial to our investigation. Remember that those weapons, all but the .45s, belong to the NSA."

"I have a few other pieces."

"Whatever for? Planning something?"

"Hardly. The only thing I'm planning is getting out of this organization."

Jordan thought he would jump all over that comment. But now it was Bauer's turn to do the ignoring. "Is there someone who would be acceptable to you, someone you would entrust with your keys?"

Jordan thought a moment. "This is that important? It has to be done before I go home tomorrow?" Bauer nodded. "Rollins, then."

"We can't afford the time. Rollins will be working with us today and tomorrow."

"Felix."

Bauer flinched. "Granger? You expect him to run an errand for you?"

"It's not for me, Blake. I'd leave those weapons right

where they are until I officially resign. Then I'd hand-deliver them."

"I don't know if Felix is even still in the country."

Jordan stood and strolled toward the door. "Wonderful. The man comes over here with me during the toughest time of my life and no one even lets me know when he's leaving to head back? Don't you think I might have wanted to thank him?"

"I guess I assumed you already had. I don't know. He may still be around. I'll check."

"You'd better, because no one else is allowed in my house—except Harley—unless you want a real noisy suit on your hands."

"Would you really do that?"

Jordan smiled patiently at Bauer. "Sounds horrible, doesn't it? Almost as horrible as breaking into the home of one of your own employees."

Bauer used a phone on the wall to learn that Felix Granger was scheduled to be driven to the airport within two hours. He told the driver to have Felix see him for an assignment first. As he walked Jordan back to the basement of S Building, he asked for his keys.

"Can't *I* give them to him?"

"We'll be busy with Harley. I'll let you see him when he gets back and before he leaves for the airport."

Harley Rollins wasn't the type of man one embraced, not even Jordan, though he hadn't seen his mentor for three years. There were a few more lines in the sculptured face, and Harley had let the crew cut grow out about a half an inch so he could bend over the result for a half-hearted attempt at something partable.

It was the same old Harley, though. Trim, fit, obviously running and working out. At fifty-five, he still looked as if he could take care of himself, regardless of the situation. He was guarded and suspicious around Blake Bauer, which reminded Jordan where he had learned to be that way.

The men shook hands, but were given no time to reminisce. Apparently that was calculated. Bauer pointed to a chair for Harley and began in his normal, formal tone. "You're here for three reasons, and I want to be very frank and very clear. First, we're searching for any clues in Mr. Kettering's career that might lead us to the identity of whoever might have paid to have him shot. Second, you're here to help us talk Mr. Kettering into at least putting off his decision to resign. And third, you are here to be assigned as the head of the field investigation to apprehend whoever is out to eliminate him."

Jordan looked first at Harley, then at Bauer. "Are you going to be *totally* frank and clear, Blake?"

"Meaning?"

"Are you going to tell Harley that you wonder about my competence, my loyalty, his job in selecting and recruiting me, and, best of all, that you really want me to delay my resigning until you determine whether I should be dismissed?"

Bauer hesitated and shouldn't have. Rollins was ready. "I can't wait to hear all this. Is that what it's come down to?"

For the next forty minutes, Jordan sat, almost amused, as Bauer took on Rollins in the same discussion/argument he had endured with Jordan that morning. Harley concluded in anger, "It's apparent I'm going to be a hostile witness, so now that we've both been very clear on everything, let's get on with it."

It was obvious that Blake Bauer was not used to having subordinates argue with him. Though he was ostensibly in charge, he was not in command of the situation, and he didn't like that. He quickly regained his stride, however, since Harley Rollins seemed to concede that the exercise was necessary.

Jordan longed for the chance to tell Harley of Stanley Stuart's terrible secret. Since Pearl Harbor, the United States had never been in as much danger. As far as Jordan knew, fewer Americans knew of this than knew of the Cuban missile crisis in its earliest stages, and he was the only one with the remotest ability to do anything about it.

But Jordan never got a minute alone with Harley. The study of his own file went long into the night. Dinner was brought in, quickly consumed, and cleared away. In spite of his inactivity and his good night's sleep, the exhaustion that had been dogging him for days was still with him.

Strange, he thought, that even hearing about himself, his hiring, his career, didn't keep him alert. He found his mind on the MiG-23s until Harley would mention something that jogged his memory. When his old boss mentioned the days in Washington during his college years, he was reminded of his firearms training. And that brought back to mind his own weapons arsenal at home. He interrupted the session.

"Hey! You said I could say good-bye to Felix!"

Bauer was ready for him. "I'm sorry about that, Kettering. They told me during dinner that he had made delivery and wasn't able to make connections with you. He sends you his best."

Jordan slammed his fists on the arms of his chair and glared at Bauer, who by now had shed his suit coat, unbuttoned his vest and his top shirt button, loosened his tie, and rolled up his sleeves. "How could you do that to me? It was a small request!"

Bauer didn't appear any more apologetic than he sounded. "Breakdown in communications. I tried. What can I say? You'll see him again."

Jordan shrugged and gestured with both hands to Harley. "An example of how I'm to be treated from here on out."

Bauer sighed. "Tell you what, Kettering. I'll authorize a nice long phone call to London for you. Just put it on your expense account."

Harley Rollins spoke softly but directly. "That isn't necessary, Blake. Give the man a break. He's been through an ordeal that you and I can be grateful we'll never have to endure."

Jordan recoiled. "Don't defend me, Harley! I can take care of myself. I don't want anybody feeling sorry for me."

Harley scowled at Jordan. "Be quiet!" And it was just like the old days when Harley was the boss. He could silence Jordan without humiliating him. He could tell him what to do and get instant obedience. He had earned the younger man's trust and devotion. Jordan knew Harley had his best interests at heart. "Now let's get back to the details of his file. Where were we?"

Bauer flipped through several more sheets. "Your training of Kettering in Washington."

Harley recited the details of how he put Jordan through his paces of diet, study, sleep, workouts, swimming, running, weight lifting, hand-to-hand combat, firearms training, and mind control. All that while Jordan worked in a date or two a week with Rosemary.

Bauer slid his chair back noisily, wood on concrete, and shot Rollins a double take. "Mind control? You mean like training him in case he gets caught and put in a concentration camp or something?"

"Not quite." Rollins briefly explained the basics of his "opposite triggers" thought processes.

Bauer was impressed. "Is that your creation, Rollins?"

"Sort of. I put it together from a lot of stuff I'd heard and read. By the time I taught Jordan, I'd been practicing it ten years. There's nothing mystical or weird or religious about the process, you know. No trances. No hypnotism. Just incredible concentration, attention to detail, and the training of your reflexes and reactions."

"How long did it take you to learn that, Kettering?"

"I'm still learning."

Rollins chuckled. "He's being falsely modest, Blake. Best I've ever seen, myself included. I remember the first time I tested him. Really tested him. You remember, Jordan?"

"How could I forget?"

Indeed, that test had been the most traumatic moment of his life up to that point. It was early in his days at International University. He was engaged to Rosemary, getting straight A's, and still trying to blend into the crowd in spite of his outstanding natural abilities. He ignored intramural sports, public speaking, and student government, though he would have shone in any one of those.

Most of his spare time was taken with studying and following Harley's regimen. Even his visits to or from Rosemary were carefully regulated, which neither of them appreciated until much later in their lives together.

One Saturday morning, Harley showed up with a rented vehicle equipped to take himself and Jordan up the ocean shore to a secluded spot. Thirty miles from civilization, they stripped down for a long, hard swim. Then they dried and dressed in military fatigues, carrying full battle gear, guns loaded with live ammunition.

"Follow me." Harley took off running in the sand with his big combat boots, carrying a heavy rifle, and wearing a helmet. After following him for two miles as fast as he could go, Jordan was about to drop. He was in the best shape of his life, yet this exercise called for all his energy.

If Harley had shown any sign of fatigue, any sign that he too was human, Jordan might have been able to go on. He knew he would incur Harley's wrath if he fell too far behind, so he kept pushing himself. But he knew he was in trouble when he quit sweating and felt his body temperature beginning to rise.

"Harley!" His voice was thick and weak. But apparently that had been what the older man had been waiting for. With Jordan's first word as an immediate cue, Harley stopped dead in his tracks, whirled, and fired his automatic rifle at Jordan.

Jordan froze, expecting the impact to knock him to the ground and for his system to relax gradually and let him feel the sharp pain. Then there would be blood, trauma, breathing difficulty. Yet he stood there, unscathed.

Harley circled him like a mad man, shooting again, then again. Each time, Jordan winced, almost shutting his eyes. Had Harley gone over the edge? Jordan's adrenalin told him his life was in danger.

His instincts told him to return the fire, but from six feet away? He'd have ripped the man's head off. Should he drop his rifle and go for a grenade? His pistol? How quickly could he shoot?

As if reading his mind, Harley tossed his empty rifle to the sand and drew his pistol. He fired several rounds past Jordan's head. The young man nearly passed out. Harley's wild look terrified him. Jordan counted the shots. When Harley was down to his last, he pulled back the hammer and held the barrel to his young student's temple.

Harley's voice was calm, almost a whisper, totally controlled. "If I was just playing with you, why would I hold a live weapon to your head with the mechanism cocked?"

Jordan's instincts were to leap into action, to karate chop the weapon hand away from his head and attack Harley. He feared his voice would betray his terror, but when he spoke he surprised both himself and Harley. "I don't know, sir."

Harley turned the weapon away from Jordan's head and fired the last round into the distance. It would be three days before Jordan's hearing would return in that ear. Yet he felt he had passed some sort of test, not breaking down and weeping, pleading for his life, running, or fighting. He remained calm, at least outwardly.

He failed, however, in the next few seconds. Harley slowly backed away from him, about ten feet, and coolly pulled a hand grenade from a pouch at his belt. He pulled the pin, released the lever, and lobbed the grenade toward Jordan.

The grenade landed squarely between Jordan's feet. Now he wanted to run, to jump, to dive for cover, to pick up the bomb, throw it back, kick it, anything. His entire body prepared for the explosion that would rip him to pieces and fling his body parts about the beach.

"Oh!" Harley shouted, running at him. "C-minus! And you were doing so well!" He deftly kicked the grenade through Jordan's legs at the last instant, lofting it forty or so feet toward the water. It exploded just before it hit, the force rocking Jordan and sending a water spout high into the air.

Harley grabbed Jordan's arm and pulled him to a low, sandy shelf where they sat down. Jordan's muscles ached. He was breathless and stiff. Harley let him catch his wind, then interrogated him.

"Did you know I wasn't going to kill you?"

"I didn't know for sure."

"What did you think?"

"At first I thought you wouldn't. And then I thought you would. And then I knew you would."

"You knew? When did you know? With the grenade?"

"No, with the last shot from the handgun."

"But I didn't. Then what did you think?"

"I didn't know."

"And the grenade?"

"Then I knew for sure."

"But you were wrong."

"Thankfully."

"When did you know you were wrong?"

"When you didn't dive for cover. I knew you weren't about to kill yourself to kill me."

"Did you think I was really mad at you?"

"At first, but I didn't know why. Then I knew you were testing me somehow."

"What was I testing?"

"I don't know."

"What did I mean by C-minus?"

"My grade, I guess, but I don't know."

"You had an A up till then, Jordie. You were beautiful, and you don't even know why, do you?" Jordan shook his head. "You don't know why you didn't run or fight, do you?" He shook his head again. "Your mind training is working. You were dead. I could have killed you if I'd wanted to. Easily. I had the drop on you. You didn't have a chance. Not for an instant. Not even when you thought you did."

"When did I think that?"

"When I held the pistol to your head, didn't you think that I should have killed you when I had the chance, because now, with the gun so near you, you had a fifty-fifty chance of subduing me? Didn't you think that?"

"I guess."

"But you failed when you let that grenade lay at your feet. We have to work on that. Your mind was so tuned into opposite triggers that instead of defending yourself—a good thing to avoid when you don't have a chance, but lethal when you do—you were going to stoically take it."

"What should I have done?"

"You knew you had between four and five seconds. It was kill or be killed unless I rescued you. You should have kicked that grenade right back at me."

"And what would you have done?"

"Depends on whether it came back straight or with

an arc. An arc would have wasted the remaining time and I would have had to dive for cover. If it had come back straight, I'd have kicked it, batted at it, or caught and thrown it."

He pulled another grenade from his pouch. "Seventeen ounces, five of which consist of component B. You don't need to know what that is, except that it turns serrated steel into fragments when it explodes."

Jordan was still shaken from the ordeal, wondering if Harley knew what he was doing. Harley sat there looking pleased with his student, though maybe a little shaken himself at how long Jordan had let the grenade lie at his feet and what a public relations mess the NSA would have had if word got out that he had killed his most promising disciple. Jordan reached for the new grenade and Harley dropped it into his palm. Jordan turned the weapon in his hand, idly studying it. He casually pulled the pin and sat staring at Harley, keeping the spring-loaded lever closed in his fist.

Harley smiled at him. "What're you going to do now, big boy?"

Jordan smiled back and tossed the grenade three feet in the air to Harley. The lever flew off just before Rollins caught the explosive, chuckled aloud, stood, and threw it about a hundred and fifty feet down the beach where it exploded. "Next time, Jordan, defend yourself. Everything else was perfect."

They walked slowly back to Harley's vehicle. "Just for the record, next time it won't be me. I put you through that test only once."

"Something's still bothering me, Harley. How was I supposed to feel when my mind was doing the opposite of what my body wanted to do?"

"Just the way you felt. As if you didn't have any choice. You want to feel cool and brave, the way you looked?" Jordan nodded. "Never happens.

If it does, you're certifiably crazy. Get out of the business then."

Blake Bauer heard the highlights of that first test. "You're both nuts." And he meant it.

Harley and Jordan looked at each other, bemused. Harley spoke. "You'd be the last person I'd want with me in a foxhole, Blake."

Bauer changed the subject. "So by the time Kettering was married and out of college, he was ready for this, uh, unusual sort of service within the NSA. Where was he assigned?"

"Everywhere." Rollins began a litany of clandestine operations at home and abroad, within and without the NSA. He was less than specific about the inside jobs, because he assumed Bauer was fully aware of such cases. It seemed, however, that the deputy was most interested in those. Rollins told only the basics, which Jordan appreciated.

But just as Harley got into the bulk of Jordan's work over the last two decades, Bauer held up a hand to stop him. He was digging through several transcripts. "Just a second here. Do you have supplementary files?"

"Supplementary files?"

"Is there an echo in here, Rollins? You heard me. There are some gaps in the records here. References to other material I can't seem to find."

"Like what?"

"Like conversations with Kettering that you recorded, but the transcripts of which are not included here."

"Some, well, much of that was classified information, sir."

"Nothing is classified to me in this investigation, Mr. Rollins. I want those supplementary files."

"I certainly wouldn't be able to tell you where to start looking. Anyway, I'm sure they're nothing to speak of."

"Then your memory better be awfully good, because you're going to have to recreate some of them for me."

128

"Such as?"

"Such as this." Bauer turned several pages slowly, recounting a conversation with Jordan that Harley Rollins had written of as "pertaining to clandestine activities in Indonesia during several months before Kettering's first semester at International University."

Jordan knew immediately the conversation Bauer was referring to. Their discussion had centered on his relationship with Cydya and would indeed have called into question Harley's judgment in selecting him for the NSA. He was shocked to know that material was in his file, and he said so.

Harley spoke softly. "Everything went into your file back then, Jordie."

"Everything?"

Harley nodded.

Bauer looked up, impatient. "But the transcript of the tape of that conversation is not here."

Jordan looked as puzzled as Harley pretended to be. "You taped that conversation?"

"Not easily." Jordan realized Harley was trying to signal him with his eyes. Through a series of hand signals that to anyone else in the room would have appeared to be nervousness or scratching, Jordan got the message: shut up.

Bauer was back on the offensive. "This record says you engaged in a sensitive conversation that is recorded in supplementary file JKb. What did it entail?"

"That was more than twenty years ago, Blake."

"Then where is the file?"

"Let me save you some time and trouble. If you can trust me and take my word for it, then get this: that transcript and every other supplemental document to these files are no longer in JKb. They were typed and maintained for years by Miss Gwendolyn Geoffrey."

"Your old secretary? The one with the highest clerical clearance level in the organization?"

"One and the same."

"And she's no longer with us, is she?"

"No, sir. Died about two years ago."

"And as for your knowing where this material is?"

"I couldn't say."

"Could be she shredded it years ago?"

"I haven't read it since it was typed, sir."

"Then you'd have a tough time recreating the file unless we found it."

"That's right. And you're not going to find it."

Ten

Three days later, Jordan sat at the kitchen table in his home, waiting impatiently for his first chance to speak privately to Harley Rollins and knowing full well that the house was still being staked out by NSA personnel. He had tidied up around the house, typed out his letter of resignation, and phoned the travel agency for his ticket to Muskegon, Michigan, to visit his Uncle Dexter Lee.

Jordan was ashamed that he was about to let his old boss and mentor see him unshaven, dressed in his grubbies, and without the tight tone that would have been obvious if he had been eating, sleeping, and running right. As was his custom, however, Harley wouldn't even reveal that he noticed.

The Friday night session with Blake Bauer had lasted until after midnight, and the Saturday session didn't end until just before dinner. Jordan had lost his cool on Saturday when a ballistics report showed that three of his weapons had been fired within the last several days.

Two of his own Colt .45s and one of the wooden pistols reportedly showed fresh powder burns. Jordan told Bauer that he hadn't fired a weapon anywhere, except on the practice range, in more than six months and that he had never fired the three weapons in question.

Harley had not defended Jordan's word or his honor in the dispute, and Jordan didn't want to say he was being framed by someone in ballistics. He had begun to wonder, however, if Bauer had purposely kept him from seeing Felix. He knew that if those guns had been fired, Felix would have noticed.

Jordan spoke angrily to Bauer, "If you can get me for unauthorized or unreported weapon fire, you can make me responsible for the attack on Rosemary and the others."

Blake had not argued the point. He ignored it and insisted that Jordan stay out of the investigation. Yet Jordan was determined to call London eventually. And he wanted to know why Harley would cover for him on some of the sensitive conversations they'd had in the past, yet seemed to take Bauer's side in the weapons dispute.

Typical of Jordan's ragged state of mind, he ignored the usual amenities when Harley finally arrived at the house. He ushered him in and pointed him to the sofa without even offering to take his coat.

"Harley, I've got so much to tell you. There's big trouble. My last night in Frank—." But Harley's desperate wave and piercing look stopped him in midsentence.

Rollins pulled a slip of paper from his pocket as he spoke. "Blake's a good man. I think we can help ourselves and the agency only if we cooperate fully." It was so unlike Harley to talk that way that Jordan was puzzled. Harley handed him the slip and he silently read: "Don't say much. House bugged."

Jordan needed a second to get in gear. "Yeah, I suppose you're right. It's difficult though. Hey, you wanna go for a ride or something, get a snack? I could use a break from here for a while."

"Sure, we can take my car."

As Harley pulled out of the driveway, Jordan unloaded. "Why do you think the house is bugged?"

"Just guessing. They had access to the house three days last week. Why risk anything?"

"Risk anything. I think I almost risked my life again if you're right. Harley, I think someone in the NSA is behind all this." He told Rollins the whole story of his meeting with Stanley Stuart in Frankfurt's old town.

Harley was so shaken by the news that he could hardly

drive. He kept checking his rear-view mirror, then pulled into the parking area of a forest preserve, several hundreds yards off the highway. "The only way out is the way we're going in, so there's no need for anyone following us to come in all the way, too. And you can bet we're being followed."

He parked and turned to face Jordan. "I have to ask you: is there any chance the old man's mind was playing tricks on him? I haven't seen Stu for years, Jordan. I mean, was he irrational enough to kill himself the next day?"

Jordan shook his head solemnly. "He showed me photographs, Harley."

"Genuine?"

"Looked real to me."

"So you don't think it was suicide. You think he was hit. Why? Because someone saw him with you?"

"What else can I think? If it weren't for dumb luck, we both would have been dead within a day of each other."

Harley stared out the windshield and clenched his fists on the steering wheel. Jordan had always been amazed at how quickly his mentor could summarize a situation and outline what needed to be done. "We can't go running to the Pentagon with news of Russian planes when we don't know where they are. And we don't know who to trust in the agency. Jordan, we'll need to work fast. I have to get to Frankfurt to see if Stu left the photos or any other documents around. If I can locate his contact person, maybe I can get a clue to who the inside man is. Top priority is to find something credible and specific to take to defense. I wish I could use you somehow."

"Harley, having Soviet planes inside our borders, whether or not they are nuclear equipped, makes me feel like I'm leaning over a gas tank with a cigarette in my lips."

"I know what you mean. I have to investigate this crazy thing with the brass on my tail, yet without their knowing what I'm really looking into. It won't be easy, and who knows how much time we have?"

Jordan shrugged. "I have no idea how long it would take to make those planes nuclear equipped. Who's to say they aren't already? What could the Soviets do with them, Harley?"

"Just about whatever they want, I guess. Doesn't sound like a bargaining chip in some negotiation, though, does it? If they merely told us about them to embarrass us, we'd find 'em and render 'em useless. No, we have to assume they're planning some kind of a first strike from within our country."

"Harley, I feel like the kid with his finger in the dike. We've got to locate those planes."

The older man nodded. "I'd like to expose whoever the creep in the agency is, but I suppose you can't do one without the other."

Jordan sat silently, breathing deeply, realizing that he and his former boss had never in their lives been involved in anything so volatile. Harley chuckled wryly. "Makes what I was gonna show you seem kinda insignificant right now."

"What have you got to show me?"

"How about file JKb?"

"You said you didn't know where that was?"

"I did not. I said I couldn't say and that my secretary was long since dead. The file is not in the file cabinet anymore because I have it. I've had it for years. I haven't read it, but I've had it."

"I don't understand you, Harley. You covered for me when Blake asked about all those conversations, yet you seemed to take his side on the gun business."

"What made you think I was taking his side?"

"You said some kind of wishy-washy thing about it being difficult to argue with a ballistics report."

"Well, it is! Do you think if they're trying to frame you, they're *not* going to shoot those weapons so the reports will be credible?"

"Yeah, but you acted like you didn't believe me either."

"Jordan, if there's one thing I've learned over the last twenty years, it's to believe you. I had to appear to side with Bauer a little if I was going to keep this assignment. You know no one else is qualified to handle it. No one else would care. And no one else would get any cooperation out of you."

"You'd better get it now because I'm leaving town Wednesday."

"Muskegon?"

"Where else?"

"You make your reservations under your own name?"

"Nope. K. Johnson."

"But from your home phone?"

Jordan nodded. "Which means the NSA will know I'm going to Muskegon. So what?"

Harley shrugged. "Might just be the best thing for us. You can hide out. I can start work in earnest on the case."

"You think the NSA will support you, Harley?"

"Are you kidding? They let me know that when I was put out to pasture three years ago. This assignment is a bone. If they can pin the whole problem on you in time, I'll be back to pencil-pushing in Florida."

"We can't let them do that."

"We can hardly stop them unless we find the money behind the assassin. And I hate to admit it, but Blake was on the right track. He was going about it the right way from the agency's point of view. To them, the key has to be something in your history, and unfortunately, it's more than likely hidden in the files that I separated from the main body years ago."

"Why did you separate them, Harley?"

"You wouldn't believe it."

"Try me."

"I started feeling guilty about them."

"You're right. I don't believe it."

"It's true. I left in everything I had recorded by hand with shorthand notes, memories of conversations, that kind of stuff. I took out everything I had recorded and transcribed without your permission."

"Was there a lot of stuff?"

"Several thousand pages."

Jordan could hardly believe what he was hearing. "Why *did* you record me?"

"Thought I needed to. You always had good insights and remembered lots of details I thought we needed."

"So why not ask if you could record me?"

"Never entered my mind. You might have said no, and then where would I have been?"

"And you think there's evidence there of who might have paid to have me killed?"

"I thought so until now. I know that material would have been the right place to look, and it's probably still worth your looking over. Some of the files are right here between the seats. The rest are in the trunk."

Jordan pulled the folders from between the seats. He noticed that the files were in order from most recent to most dated. "Listen, Harley, you're not going to keep me off this case, too, are you?"

"What do you mean? You're going to Michigan and that's probably the best place for you. I'd love to use you, but it would take all our energy just to hide you from our own people."

Jordan shook his head. "The official book is that I tell you whatever you need to know, and then I'm out of it. Pretty unrealistic, wouldn't you say?"

Harley seemed to study Jordan. "Maybe, but I guess I agree with that. You can't say you wouldn't be emotionally involved."

"That's the reason it's stupid to think I could stay away from this. Wouldn't you want to be in on it if it was your wife?"

"You forget, my wife left me. So if it was *my* wife, I'd probably be a *suspect*." Jordan didn't find that amusing just then and couldn't smile. Harley flushed. "Gee, forgive me, Jordie. That was a dumb thing to say."

Jordan had already turned to the file. Rollins unbuttoned his top coat and turned sideways in his seat behind the wheel. He peered over Jordan's shoulder. "You'll find that those things stopped about the same time I no longer had responsibility for you."

Jordan nodded. "About three years ago. I thought about quitting then. All of a sudden I went from working with the best field man in the business to working for a bunch of flabby bureaucrats."

Harley shook his head. "You think you had it bad. Look what I'm doing now compared to what I was doing then."

"Yeah. Until this week."

"I admit this gets my blood circulating, but I'm not totally uninvolved emotionally myself. Stu was a good friend of mine. I didn't totally respect him, I thought he took short cuts. But I liked the man. And I loved your wife. I mean, in the proper way, you know—."

"I know. You were special to her, too."

"I just want you to understand, Jordan, that for her sake, I want as much as you do to find out who's behind this."

Jordan nodded and turned his attention to the transcripts of long conversations he'd had with Harley over the years, debriefings on various cases that now stared back at him. Three quarters of the way through the stack, he reached the report on the Cuban assignment. He wasn't sure he wanted to read that one, but he was certainly glad Harley had pulled it from his permanent file. A couple of paragraphs caught his eye.

KETTERING: *Harley, it, uh, was my own fault. That thing you said, what you taught me . . . you know, about the hunches. About following the ones that protect you and not following the ones that make you take a risk.*

ROLLINS: *Right. Follow the hunches that make you cautious. Ignore those that make you take a risk.*

KETTERING: *Yeah. Well, I blew that. I mean, I didn't follow your advice that time.*

ROLLINS: *Sounds like you didn't. Your hunch was to wait, you should've waited. Then you would've had—*

KETTERING: *The advantage. And I could have jumped him instead of—*

ROLLINS: *Him jumping you.*

KETTERING: *Yeah.*

Harley interrupted Jordan's reverie. "I know which one you're most interested in."

"You do?"

"Course. And I've got it."

"You recorded that?"

"I already told you I did."

"And Gwen typed it?"

"Never told a soul."

"How do you know?"

"I knew Gwen, that's all."

"That was risky, Harley."

"So was what you did. Anyway, if I was going to live dangerously, I'd have left that file in your record. When do you think I riffled those files, before I came up here? I wouldn't have had access to 'em."

"When then?"

"When I saw the handwriting on the wall. When I knew my days as your supervisor were over. You think I didn't know it would come to this? This is just the culmination of years of political infighting and jealousy in the agency. They've been dying for a reason to lift the contraband on those files. Rosemary's death was the perfect opportunity. It was only a matter of time."

"So, where's the one you know I want to see?"

"In the trunk. You sure you want it? Do you need it? Or would you rather I destroy it?"

Jordan thought a moment. "I think I want to see it. Do I need it? No. I remember that conversation like it was yesterday. You were kind enough never to bring it up again."

"Maybe. But I kept an eye on you."

Jordan was shocked. "You're not serious."

"Of course I am. You think I wouldn't have known if you'd checked up on her once in a while? That would have been a natural thing."

"Maybe I figured you'd know and that's why I didn't. You check up on her, too?"

"Not a chance. I didn't want any part of that. None of my business." Jordan looked at him as if he were lying. Harley looked hurt. "Have I ever been anything but straight with you?" Jordan shook his head. "That's the story. You wanna see the file or not?"

"I do."

Harley got out and opened the trunk. Jordan found himself strangely nervous, as if he were about to be brought face to face with a past he had been trying to suppress for two decades. When he heard the trunk slam, he turned to watch Harley get back in the car. But Harley's hands were empty.

An NSA car slid to a stop behind their car. Jordan lurched around in his seat to see the agent on the driver's side talking to Harley. By the time Jordan leaped out and joined them, the agent was saying, "So get out of here. Anywhere. Back to headquarters, on a plane, whatever. But not in one of our cars."

The agent on the passenger side leaned over. "I can hot-wire that one, if you want to explain it to the owner."

Harley fired a glance at a late model, bright yellow sports car. "Perfect. Do it. I'll run him to the airport and then bring the car back here. Call ahead and get him a ticket under the name of, uh, K. Johnson. Route him wherever you want, just make sure he leaves soon and winds up in Muskegon."

"Muskegon?"

"You got it. Get some security to his kids. Tell 'em our story and that he will be in touch."

The roar of the sports car's engine brought a young couple running from the trees. "Hey! That's my car!"

The agents flashed their badges, then explained the need for the car and assured the owner he would be paid for his trouble. Harley turned toward Jordan. "Jump in."

"Not till someone tells me what's going on!"

"Sure! Right here in front of everyone. Get in the car!"

Jordan dropped into the front seat and slammed the door, angrily watching Harley finish barking instructions to the other agents. He got the keys from the owner and transferred the stuff from his own trunk to the backseat of the sports car. At last he joined Jordan.

Jordan expected Harley to bring him up to date immediately, but Harley didn't say anything as he streaked from the forest reserve and onto the highway. Jordan was mad. "I hope that whatever is going on, I still have time to run by my house. I haven't even shaved, and the clothes I'm wearing are all I have."

" 'Fraid not, Jordie. I've got bad news for you. Your house was obliterated about ten minutes ago. Rubble from one explosion. The windows were blown out of every house on the block and the houses on either side of your property are burning. Nobody hurt."

"Did the NSA do this?"

"No, that's not our style. You know that. We would have gotten the valuables and keepsakes out first."

"You're sure no one was hurt?"

"No one but you, pal. You were killed. Understand? You're dead, as of right now. That's the story that's going over the wires and to the papers and broadcast people. Can your kids be trusted with that secret?"

Jordan shrugged, unable to speak. How his kids would hate this. Now he was responsible not only for their mother's death, but for the destruction of the only home they had ever known, not to mention everything they owned other than what they had taken to college.

Harley was still talking. "That'll take some heat off you and give us time to figure out who's behind this, rather than spending all our time trying to protect you."

Jordan felt sarcastic. "Yeah, good job so far. How did anyone get past all that security?"

"You forget, we had men cruising the area. They saw us leave and knew where we were, but they don't have the place in view all the time. Whoever did this did it right. And with a huge charge. The place was vaporized. Just a black hole there now and what was left of the flooring is burning in the basement."

Jordan held his head in his hands. If he'd had any reservations about leaving the NSA, they were gone now. He never wanted another assignment, and he didn't care if the brass accepted his resignation or not. Of course, the letter he had typed that morning was in ashes now, too, but it wouldn't take long to draft another.

"Are you telling me that if you hadn't thought the place was bugged—by our own people, no less—and I hadn't wanted to get out of there, we'd both be history by now?"

Harley nodded. "Even some of our people, the back-ups on the stake out, think you bought it. They won't know differently until they're briefed at headquarters. They're really gonna keep a lid on this."

"And what am I supposed to do?"

"Go to your uncle's. Will he have you?" Jordan nodded. "You'll want to get some stuff. You still got your K. Johnson credit cards?" He nodded again. "Just hole up there until you hear from me. If we can't flush out the perpetrator, we may need to bring you back to life."

"For bait?"

"That's right."

"Not interested."

"What do you mean you're not interested? You want this guy or whoever or whatever to keep comin' after you and your family?"

"I just know I've had enough, Harley. I'm through."

"We'll talk later. I know how you must feel." Jordan doubted it. "Make sure you don't use your own cards; you'll leave a trail right to your uncle's place. And take any of these files you want."

"I don't want any of them."

"None?"

"Well, maybe that one we were talking about."

"It's a thick one."

"I've got nothing else to carry."

During a two-hour layover in Cleveland, Jordan got out to buy toiletries, a suitcase, and a couple of changes of clothes. He thought about running gear, but decided against it. He also wondered about calling his Uncle Dex, but he couldn't be sure his phone wasn't tapped until he got there to check it. He knew he was paranoid. How could anyone know about Uncle Dex?

Jordan couldn't bring himself to look at the file. He put it in the suitcase, but wouldn't risk checking it with the other baggage through to Muskegon. He carried the suitcase on board, and when it wouldn't fit beneath the seat, he put it in the overhead compartment. He fought sleep and watched warily anytime anyone came near it.

He needed to use the washroom before the plane landed in Detroit, but he couldn't leave the bag unattended and he knew he would attract too much attention if he took it with him. In Detroit, even though he wasn't changing planes—and was reminded of that by two flight attendants—he carried the suitcase with him through the terminal.

He finally arrived in Muskegon on a puddle jumper at nine in the evening and hailed a taxi. He asked to be let out a block and a half from his uncle's home. When he got to his uncle's street, he went through the alley and the gate to the back door of the rambling, two-story white frame. That huge, old house had hosted many a family gathering when he was a boy. But now most of the rooms were sealed off. His uncle lived by himself, occupying only a portion of the basement for his workshop, the living room and kitchen directly above that, and the bed and bath directly above that. There was a light on in the old man's bedroom.

Jordan set the suitcase down and tried to freshen himself up in his reflection in the back door. His two-toned hair, with his normal color starting to peek through at the roots of the brown dye, was greasy and matted. His eyes looked tired. He had gone two days without shaving, and his every-other-day five o'clock shadow was starting to show.

He rang the bell and glanced at the second floor window. His uncle peeked out from behind the shade. Then he saw the shade pulled aside completely and his uncle's head, nearly filling the window, as he tried to get a better look. Jordan waved apologetically, but Dexter Lee was already bounding down the stairs.

He burst out through the storm door wearing a plaid,

floor-length, flannel robe over his pajamas. His reading glasses were down on his nose, and his eyes were red and swollen. He was barefoot. Jordan was ready to explain his inability to phone ahead when the old man embraced him. "Oh, Jordan! Jordan! You survived. Come in, come in!"

His uncle carried his suitcase and led him up the back stairs to the kitchen. Lee's feathery white hair pointed several directions, and he couldn't quit talking. "I don't believe it. Don't believe it. Does anyone else know you're alive?"

"Not many."

"It was a setup then? Something your own people staged?"

Jordan shook his head. "Where did you hear about it?"

"On the news. The story was on all the stations. I had no reason not to believe it. I've been trying to call your kids all night. Jordan, I cried and cried. I couldn't imagine having to break it to your mother. I prayed it wasn't true. And now I can't believe you're here."

Though there was nothing he'd less rather do, Jordan took the time to tell his uncle the whole story. He had never kept anything from him, ever. Dexter was the only one, outside Harley Rollins, who knew everything. He knew more than Rosemary had known. He had even know about Cydya, though Jordan had never admitted his lingering curiosity about her.

It took all Jordan's remaining strength to express his fear about what his kids would think of him now. His uncle studied him, as was his custom. "You need a shower, maybe something hot to drink, and a good rest. Am I right?"

Jordan nodded and nearly wept. By the time he was out of the shower, his uncle had opened a heating duct to a spare bedroom and had arranged the bed and closet for Jordan. A cup of hot chocolate was ready. "Tell me, then, Jordan, are you basically in hiding?"

"Basically."

"Anything I can do for you? Get for you?"

"I'll give you a list in the morning. I'm going to need a few things to make myself look like an old friend of yours. Emphasis on the old. Gray hair, the whole bit. And don't worry if you hear me digging around in the basement in the morning. I'll just be checking your phone. Boy, I hate to put you through this, Dex. If you don't want to be involved, I'll understand."

Dexter Lee waved him off with both hands. "Don't even think that. I wouldn't have it any other way."

Still well before midnight, Jordan collapsed into bed and lay on his stomach. His right arm hung over the side and his hand rested atop the file he would read as soon as he felt up to it.

He awoke every few hours with weird dreams, wishing he had access to the miracle sleep aid he had been introduced to by Dr. Bradley at the NSA. He knew his uncle wouldn't disturb him if he wanted to sleep until noon. All he really wanted was enough sleep so he could think clearly, check his uncle's phone, get in touch with Ken and Judy, and get back into the hunt.

He knew that wouldn't please anybody at NSA, including Harley. In his rational moments, he realized that having the grieving husband look for his wife's slayer and his own pursuer made no sense. But Jordan didn't see that he had any choice.

Avenging Rosemary's death, protecting his children, and solving this case—the only one in his life that had ever really mattered—were the only reasons he would have for the rest of his life to look forward to waking up in the morning.

Eleven

Jordan slept well, surprising himself. He awoke early, long before dawn, and felt refreshed. He wandered to the bath and back down the hall to his room, tiptoeing so as not to bother his uncle and stretching as he went. When he awoke feeling like this, there was nothing he would rather do than head out for a brisk four-miler.

He sat on the edge of his saggy-springed bed, the same one he'd shared with a brother many times as a child. He lifted the JKb manila folder from the floor and laid it near his pillow. Lying on his stomach, his head supported by his left hand, elbow propped on the bed, he opened the file.

The transcription of his conversation with Harley Rollins seemed to begin in the middle. Harley had noted in his own handwriting: "Gwen, I wrote on the permanent file that when Kettering reacted to my checking out Rosemary by saying he might have to think about the job some more, he was kidding, that I checked her out carefully, found her solid, etc., etc. Let's hold the rest here for file JKb. Thanks."

ROLLINS: *Have I misjudged you, or do we call it quits right here?*

KETTERING: *Just call me Tuesday as early as you can. Is that too much to ask?*

ROLLINS: *(Unintelligible.) Listen, uh, while we're talking about women, I've got to ask you about Cydya LeMonde.*

KETTERING: *Who?*

ROLLINS: *Don't give me that, Jordan. Who do you think you're talking to?*

KETTERING: *What about her?*

ROLLINS: *You tell me.*

KETTERING: *Tell you what?*

ROLLINS: *Everything.*

KETTERING: *There's not much to tell. I met her in Indonesia.*

ROLLINS: *You worked with her.*

KETTERING: *You asking or telling?*

ROLLINS: *(Expletive.) I know you were supposed to replace her and instead you wound up working with her for months. Am I right?*

KETTERING: *Yeah.*

ROLLINS: *You like her?*

KETTERING: *What do you mean?*

ROLLINS: *Jordan, don't make this difficult for me, because that will only make it difficult for you.*

KETTERING: *What are you getting at? You already did my debriefing for Jakarta. You saw the thing, that diary you had me keep. Nobody else saw it.*

ROLLINS: *I'm asking you about Cydya LeMonde.*

KETTERING: *You mean, maybe she was CIA?*

ROLLINS: *You know better than that. Do I have to spell it out for you? Don't you think I know most of what happened, what you did there?*

KETTERING: *You mean me?*

ROLLINS: *Yes, you! We were watching you. I suppose you figured that.*

KETTERING: *I figured, but I had no idea who was there. Did you send somebody to infiltrate the corps or something?*

ROLLINS: *No! You were our only person on the inside, but there were visitors. They were with us. You didn't suspect anyone?*

KETTERING: *Huh-uh. Was that part of my test? I mean, should I have?*

ROLLINS: *No demerits this time for not noticing, but it's something to watch for next time. In this line of work, you'll find yourself suspecting everyone.*

KETTERING: *Sounds horrible.*

ROLLINS: *Sometimes it is. But don't try to get me off the subject. Tell me about her.*

KETTERING: *Who?*

ROLLINS: *(Expletive.)*

KETTERING: *Well, what do you know already? Or what do you not know and want to know?*

ROLLINS: *I want to know everything. She's a bit of a, uh, puzzle to us. You know where she's working now?*

KETTERING: *Yeah.*

ROLLINS: *She could be a friend in the future.*

KETTERING: *Not mine.*

ROLLINS: *Don't be silly. We work closely with those international agencies.*

KETTERING: *With Interpol?*

ROLLINS: *'Course. But listen, if there was anything there between you two, a relationship, you know, then I should know about it.*

KETTERING: *What did your people tell you, if they know so much?*

ROLLINS: *I didn't say they knew anything or told me anything, did I?*

KETTERING: *Then how did you even know her name?*

ROLLINS: *They told me. But all they said was that you spent more time with her than with anybody else there.*

KETTERING: *Oh, I don't know about that. I had to report to a woman and this other guy, too, and I—*

ROLLINS: *But you didn't, ah, go into the city with them whenever you got the chance and—*

KETTERING: *I didn't go with her either.*

ROLLINS: *You didn't?*

KETTERING: *Not every time I got the chance.*

ROLLINS: *Tell me how the relationship progressed.*

KETTERING: *Who said there was a relationship?*

ROLLINS: *(Expletive.) You're making me angry.*

KETTERING: *You're making me mad, too! Do I have to tell you every time I go to the bathroom? Don't I get a private life?*

ROLLINS: *'Fraid not. I don't need to know every detail, but I do have to know if there's anything, ah—*

KETTERING: *She was there that first night at the airport because of some policy or something that the person you're working with, the group leader, that woman, ah—*

ROLLINS: *Mickey.*

KETTERING: *See? You do know all this.*

ROLLINS: *LeMonde was a real looker, huh, Jordan?*

KETTERING: *A what?*

ROLLINS: *A looker, a good-looking girl, a doll. The kind of girl who made guys, you know, look.*

KETTERING: *Okay, I'll grant that.*

ROLLINS: *Did you find her distracting in trying to do your work?*

KETTERING: *(Pause.) Well, our job was to get the kids involved in games and stuff. Like badminton and—*

149

ROLLINS: *So you and Cydya worked closely together.*

KETTERING: *Not that closely, if you mean—*

ROLLINS: *Okay, but you worked together and you got to see this gorgeous girl running and jumping and playing sports with the kids.*

KETTERING: *It wasn't like I stood around watching her all the time. I had things to do, too, you know.*

ROLLINS: *What're you, a homosexual or something, Kettering?*

KETTERING: *What're you talking about?*

ROLLINS: *My people tell me this is a girl who would make any normal guy freeze in his tracks, and you're tellin' me you worked with her all day everyday, yet you weren't the least bit distracted?*

KETTERING: *I didn't say that. Okay, she was fun to work with. A good girl, you know. I mean, a really good girl. Straight. Smart. A good talker. Like, she said what she meant, you know?*

ROLLINS: *Uh-huh. And she wasn't making it with every guy there?*

KETTERING: *Who told you that?*

ROLLINS: *No one.*

KETTERING: *They were lying! She never was that way!*

ROLLINS: *I said no one told me that, okay? But some girls are like that, you know.*

KETTERING: *Not this one.*

ROLLINS: *You know that for sure?*

KETTERING: *You bet I do.*

ROLLINS: *So you had no relationship with her?*

KETTERING: *You mean—*

ROLLINS: *I mean, did you go with her or not, Jordan? Can't*

ROLLINS: *It went on longer than just a summer and it was more than just a romance, wasn't it, Jordan?*

KETTERING: *I don't know.*

ROLLINS: *C'mon!*

KETTERING: *What're you driving at, Harley?*

ROLLINS: *You're not writing to her?*

KETTERING: *Just once.*

ROLLINS: *Only once?*

KETTERING: *I'm sorry—twice. I told her we were through. But when she kept writing, I finally wrote and told her I wasn't going to open any more of her letters.*

ROLLINS: *Why not? What was so important about breaking up with her?*

KETTERING: *(Long pause.) There was no future for us.*

ROLLINS: *Looks like she thought there was.*

KETTERING: *She was too far away.*

ROLLINS: *Love isn't stopped by distance. Tell me, did she keep writing?*

KETTERING: *Yeah.*

ROLLINS: *How many letters?*

KETTERING: *Two.*

ROLLINS: *And you never opened them?*

KETTERING: *No.*

ROLLINS: *Jordan, let me give you some advice: Either get back in touch with the girl or forget her. Toss the letters and be done with it.*

KETTERING: *Someday I will. When I find someone else.*

ROLLINS: *You think this Rosemary is it?*

KETTERING: *That would be a little hasty, wouldn't it?*

153

ROLLINS: *That's your style.*

KETTERING: *It's not!*

ROLLINS: *You didn't waste any time with Cydya.*

KETTERING: *I just met Rosemary.*

ROLLINS: *And if you don't find someone else, are you going to look up Cydya again?*

KETTERING: *No.*

ROLLINS: *You're sure?*

KETTERING: *Absolutely.*

ROLLINS: *Jordan, I have to know: Was your relationship with Cydya appropriate?*

KETTERING: *You mean, did we—?*

ROLLINS: *Yeah.*

KETTERING: *We couldn't have if we'd wanted to.*

ROLLINS: *Why not?*

KETTERING: *For one thing, I had the fear of God in me. I told her all about my faith, church, God, everything.*

ROLLINS: *So she would have been disappointed in you if you'd tried anything inappropriate?*

KETTERING: *I guess so.*

ROLLINS: *Was she, um, experienced?*

KETTERING: *You mean with guys? I don't think so. She hadn't even dated that much.*

ROLLINS: *Maybe she didn't realize her own attractiveness.*

KETTERING: *You're right! We even talked about that. I couldn't believe it. All she had to do was look in the mirror.*

ROLLINS: *The eyes don't see what the mind doesn't believe. But tell me: What happened that night the two of you spent in Jakarta?*

KETTERING: *Huh?*

ROLLINS: *Jordan, I figure you were a virgin before you went to Indonesia. I know you had a few heavy necking sessions with a couple of different girls in high school, but not with any bad girls, and apparently you behaved yourself.*

KETTERING: *So what?*

ROLLINS: *So I haven't been able to check on Cydya and I didn't think it was worth contacting our French guys if you were able to tell me.*

KETTERING: *Tell you what?*

ROLLINS: *If Cydya was also a virgin when she got to Indonesia.*

KETTERING: *Why do you need to know that?*

ROLLINS: *Jordan, if your morals were compromised, if a loose girl made you do something you regret, it's significant to us, to me.*

KETTERING: *(No response.)*

ROLLINS: *The night before she was supposed to fly back to the states and then on to France, you went to Jakarta with her.*

KETTERING: *We had the day off. We went shopping. Harley, she was a virgin, I swear it.*

ROLLINS: *That's good to hear. But you didn't go back to corps headquarters that night.*

KETTERING: *No. We missed the bus. I called Mickey and she checked with her supervisor. We swore we'd stay in separate rooms.*

ROLLINS: *Did you stay in them?*

KETTERING: *Of course.*

ROLLINS: *So you weren't in her room?*

KETTERING: *No.*

ROLLINS: *Not at all?*

KETTERING: *Well, yes. I kissed her good night. But we didn't sleep together, if that's what you mean.*

ROLLINS: *Bet you wanted to.*

KETTERING: *(No response.)*

ROLLINS: *Bet you were really excited to be alone with her, miles away from anyone who knew you and more than ten thousand miles from home.*

KETTERING: *(No response.)*

ROLLINS: *Jordan, you can tell me you didn't sleep together, I have no way of knowing. But I do know you were in her room for several hours, until about two or three. Are you telling me you didn't sleep with her because you didn't fall asleep, or are you saying you weren't intimate with her?*

KETTERING: *(No response.)*

ROLLINS: *I know it must have been difficult for you. But I also know something must have happened that night. Because the next morning, when you got the news that your father had died and that you had to get back to the states, you left without telling her. Didn't even leave her a note. You just hurried back to the headquarters and arranged for the next military plane out. Why?*

KETTERING: *It was over. That's all.*

ROLLINS: *No, it wasn't, was it? Maybe it is now, or maybe it will be when you can forget her, but I think you slept with her that night, Jordan.*

KETTERING: *I told you—*

ROLLINS: *All right! Neither of you fell asleep. But it happened, didn't it, Jordan? And then you felt terrible about it. Maybe she didn't, but you did. And when the news about your father came, you couldn't separate what you'd done from what had happened to him. Maybe you even felt you had been judged.*

And Cydya's letters told you she didn't feel that way, that what the two of you'd done was not so terrible.

KETTERING: *(No response.)*

ROLLINS: *Jordan, let me tell you something: I believe that you were in love with this girl and that she was in love with you. I also believe that she was a girl of character, because everything else bears that out. If she'd had a bad reputation and could drag you down with her, I would lose all interest in you for the NSA. But I believe your failure was honest. Don't be so hard on yourself. It was a passionate mistake.*

KETTERING: *It was still wrong. But it's over now.*

ROLLINS: *I'm no psychologist, Jordan. And I'd be the last person to argue with anybody over his religion, but if nothing else ever comes of this conversation, I've got to get you to separate your mistake—if that's what you want to call it—from your father's death. Can you do that?*

KETTERING: *Not easy.*

ROLLINS: *Will you think about it?*

KETTERING: *I guess.*

Yet twenty years later, the issues raised in that conversation were still a problem for Jordan. He no longer felt remorse for the lack of willpower, for going against his convictions, for taking advantage of the girl he loved. But the memory was so closely associated with his father's death, and he felt guilty because he felt more remorse about his relationship than about the loss of his father. And never having told his wife about such a deep, intense love, one he had never been able to shake, a curiosity he had never been able to satisfy, made him feel almost unfaithful. He knew it was invalid. He knew it was childish. But still, he had never closed the wound by talking it over with his wife. Something told him that the confession probably would have been easy and that Rosemary would have been her typically—and wonderfully—understanding self. But now it was too late.

The transcript went on and on about training regimen, diet, and all the rest, but the words were swimming. Jordan buried his head in the pillow and sobbed.

Twelve

The smell of eggs and sausage made Jordan ravenous. He knew his uncle would come checking on him soon. He buried the file in his suitcase and padded to the shower. As he toweled off a few minutes later, he discovered his bed had been made, a clear signal that breakfast was ready. He threw on his new change of clothes, a casual outfit with cuffed trousers and a pullover shirt.

He was grateful his uncle was not one for small talk in the morning. Without a word to Jordan, the old man straddled his chair, sat heavily, and prayed aloud. Jordan had always enjoyed hearing his uncle pray. He was personal, informal, and somehow specific. He never just rattled off the blessings of life, but rather thanked God for "loving us in spite of ourselves, for never changing or even casting a shadow of turning." He even admitted that "we don't understand what's happening and confess that, in our finite wisdom, we wouldn't have allowed what You have allowed. But we love You and we trust You."

Jordan wished he himself could pray that way again. He agreed silently that yes, he did love God and he did trust Him, but how long had it been since he had really prayed? Things were so different now, so removed from his childhood when everything was black and white and made sense. He wasn't doubting, wasn't challenging. As a boy, he had had an experience with God. A transaction had taken place that nothing could take away. He had prayed to receive Christ under the guidance of his mother. But he felt he had drifted so dreadfully far. What did his faith mean now, today, with his wife in the ground, his country in peril, and his heart full of vengeance and anger? Perhaps, he thought, it was God who had brought him back to this place, this person, at this moment.

Rosemary and Uncle Dexter were the only people anywhere outside the NSA who knew the name of the agency for which Jordan worked. And not even Rosemary knew precisely what he did, except that he used disguises. She had never known about Cydya either. Dex Lee had.

It had been Jordan's uncle who pointed out to him the irony of his "continuing, schoolboy-like guilt and curiosity over a long-lost love, in contrast with a sort of utilitarian angst over having to kill two men in Cuba."

Jordan had thought about that one a long time, trying to reconcile his feelings with his faith, his morals, his upbringing, his training. Over the years, he had quit talking to his uncle about Cydya, hoping Dexter would suppose he had forgotten her. Well-placed questions from the old man exposed him, however. Their visits were less frequent than they once had been, but were always poignant. Whenever Jordan got an R & R message from Harley, he would consider himself assigned to Muskegon and spend a day or two there before flying home to Rosemary.

Therapeutic. Being with Dexter always was. Strange, he thought, to read that old transcript in this very house. And then to weep, shower, dress, and eat breakfast in front of his lifelong confidant without letting on. His uncle sighed. "How long can you stay with me? Nothing to rush off for, is there?"

Jordan shrugged. "Never know. Depends on what Harley finds. See, Dex, I don't know if anyone connected with the London thing followed me to the States. I mean, the fact that I'm without a house should tell you something, but so far, none of our people have seen anything or anybody who could be linked with the attack."

Lee pressed a thick palm over his mouth, then pulled it away. "And even if someone did follow you from London—assuming whoever had the shooting done also had the house bombed—I s'pose there's little chance he followed you here."

"You'd think not, unless he was fortunate enough to see me leave with Harley, talk with the other agents, and switch cars. Then I guess I'd be fairly easy to track. But I doubt it."

"Did you check the phones?"

Jordan shook his head, trying not to give away his own surprise at the lapse. He had said he would, but then he started reading that file. . . .

While his uncle washed the dishes, Jordan crawled around in the basement with a flashlight. It was clear no one had messed with the phone lines in that house for years. He fished around in his uncle's tools till he found a small voltage tester. He used a tiny alligator clip to dig through the extension phone wire and then picked up the receiver.

He listened for the telltale click that would have exposed an old-fashioned bugging device hooked to the line from outside the house. Nothing. He dialed for local information and asked for the number of time and temperature. Was it just his imagination, or was there a fluctuation of voltage when the call was placed?

He watched the meter carefully as he dialed the time and temperature number again. There had been a minute change when he picked up the receiver, of course, and when the dialed phone began ringing. But when the call was answered, there was a noticeable diminution of wattage. He slammed his fist against the wall.

He grabbed a pliers, two screwdrivers, and a hammer and headed up the stairs and out the back door. He sensed his uncle watching from the window as he followed the phone lines to a pole in the alley. Then he followed the poles until the third one, which had a series of drab green boxes at its base.

Quickly surveying the area, Jordan determined he was alone and out of the line of sight of any nosy neighbor's window. It was impossible to tell which of the green boxes contained the wiring from his uncle's house, unless his hunch was right. Only one of the boxes appeared to have been tampered with. Paint covered the screws and bolts on the other two.

Jordan quickly opened the box with the pliers and screwdriver. There, attached to several thin wires, was a platinum-colored strip that looked no bigger than a child's toy watch band. Only one intelligence organization in the world was even aware of such a device. It served as a self-contained transmitter that put the tapped conversations on a special frequency, which could then be monitored by cellular technology from miles away.

Jordan left the bug in place and secured the box again. He ran back to the house. His uncle sat at the kitchen table, reading the paper. "Everything all right, Jordan?"

" 'Fraid not." His uncle put down the paper and stared at him. Jordan shook his head. "The only outfit bugging this place is the NSA. I've had it."

"What are you talking about?"

"Your phone is being tapped from the area signal box by *NSA* equipment!"

"When would they have had time to do that?"

"Somebody knew I was coming, so they just assigned local people!"

"Could it have been authorized by your own superiors for your own good?"

"No way! If I don't see Harley soon, there's no guarantee where I'll go or what I'll do. I just hope he's not already out of the country."

Jordan walked past his uncle and through the dining room to the living room where he flopped onto the couch, his hands behind his head. Dexter Lee joined him a few minutes later, sitting in an easy chair with his legs propped up on an ottoman. He mirrored Jordan's pose, hands behind head, and stared at his nephew.

Jordan was nervous, agitated. He hated being immobile. He knew he should place calls to his kids, but what if he'd been wrong about the tap? Why had he been so sure it was from the NSA? Not even the CIA was on to that type of bug, yet who knew? It could be stolen. He should have removed the device, he knew. But it wouldn't be smart to go tinkering again. "Do me a favor, would you, Dex?"

"Anything."

"Call my kids from a pay phone. Give 'em my love. Tell 'em I'm all right and that I'll be getting back with them as soon as I can."

"You sure you want *me* to do that?"

"I can't go out, Dex. Not until I'm ready to make a run for it. I don't want anyone to know where I'm going, not even the NSA."

"Not even Rollins?"

"Rollins I trust. But he thinks I'm safe and sound for awhile. He's doing what he's supposed to be doing, and I'm getting bugged by my own people. And if I'm not, whoever it is can trace my calls."

"So rip out the bug."

"I could, but if it *isn't* ours, then someone knows I'm here anyway. That puts *you* in danger. You know what happened to the last place I was living."

His uncle showed no fear. "Is that a real possibility?"

Jordan shrugged. "This whole thing's getting crazy. Who knows? All I know is, I have to get out and do something."

While Jordan fumed, his uncle sat calmly. "I've never seen you this way."

Jordan was almost irritated, something he'd never felt toward Dexter Lee. "Well, I've never lost my wife and home before. Or been pursued in this country. Do you realize that? Nobody in the international community, until now, even knew where I lived. That was the beauty of working with the NSA."

"You're usually so calm and rational, much more than I would be in the same situations. You seem a little paranoid now, not that you don't have a right to be."

The phone rang. Jordan bolted upright. "Go ahead and answer it, Dex. If it's personal for you, I'll back off immediately." Jordan stooped to put his ear next to Dex's, and his uncle spoke.

"Hello?"

"Mr. Lee? This is Western Union calling. We have a telegram for you."

"Thank you, ma'am."

"May I read it to you?"

"Certainly."

"We'll mail you your own copy and you should receive it tomorrow."

"Is it long? Should I get a pencil?"

"The message isn't long, sir, but you might want to jot it down."

"I'm ready."

"It reads:

HAVE YOUR MONKEY TRAVEL FIVE CENTURIES ON THE HOOSIER EGG AND HE'LL BE RIGHT WHERE THE HOG WANTS HIM, PRECISION TUNED. WORTH HIS WHILE. TWO HUNDRED AND FORTY POUNDS OF YOURS, MINE, AND YOU-KNOW-WHO'S. YOUR COCCINELLIDAE.

"Could you spell that last word for me, honey?"

"Certainly."

"And this was sent from where?"

"The origination point is in code, sir, and I'm not aware of it myself. The message came through our New York facility."

When Dexter Lee hung up, Jordan was a different man. "I *love* Harley! I *love* him!"

"Gee, Jordan, what's it all about? You understand this?"

"All I know is, it's from Harley. He's never sent me one I've figured out in less than four hours. Can I have a pencil and some paper and a place to work?"

"Sure, but—."

"And would you want to run some errands for me?"

"Sure, Jordan, I—."

"I hate to put you out, Uncle Dex—."

"Nonsense. You know I'd do anything to help. What do you need?"

"Call the kids, and call a friend in London for me?"

Lee nodded.

"Here's his number. His name is Felix Granger, and be sure to talk only to him. Just tell him I know he knows most everything that's going on and that I appreciate him more than I can say. Someday I'll try to make it all up to him. He rode back with me on the plane."

"You told me about him."

"I did?"

"Many times."

"Well, if you don't mind—."

"I'll look forward to talking to him."

Jordan also made a list of items he needed from the store. Various kinds of makeup, some dumb bells, running shoes and sweats, and hair dye. By the time his uncle returned with a late lunch in midafternoon, Jordan had cracked the telegram. He enjoyed sharing it with Lee.

"The first thing you have to decide with a piece like this is whether the sender is playing word games, using the first letter of each word to spell out the message, or jumbling the word order, or whatever. That's not usually Harley's style, but he's good at it."

"Is that what this is?"

"No, this one is more deductive. Let me walk you through it. The telegram is to you, right?" His uncle nodded. "And so who would he be referring to—assuming the sender is Harley, and who else would it be—by sending you a wire in code?"

Dexter shrugged.

"C'mon, Dex. He'd have to be talking about me, right?"

"So you're my monkey?"

"Exactly, if we can make that idea make sense."

"And can we?"

"Well, if I'm your monkey, what are you?"

"What am I? Hm. I'm your uncle."

"Right! You're a monkey's uncle! All of a sudden, it makes sense, doesn't it? See how easy it is?"

"No."

"Let's keep going."

"I'm lost."

"Stay with me. What does he want you to have me do?"

"Travel five centuries on the Hoosier egg."

"Good!"

"Good nothin'! I'm readin' it verbatim!"

"Don't take it at face value. The word *travel* is the tip-off that *centuries* doesn't mean years, get it?"

"No."

"You don't really travel in time. You travel in distance. So traveling five centuries would, or could, mean 500 miles."

"Yeah?"

"Yeah. Does that make anything else make sense?"

"Well, Hoosiers are from Indiana, right?"

"Good, Dex! Ever hear of anything in Indiana connected with traveling 500 miles?"

"The Indy 500!"

"Right!"

"He wants you to go to Indianapolis?"

"I don't think so. Look how he words it. What's the Hoosier egg?"

"How should I know?"

"What shape is an egg?"

"Oval."

"So?"

"The egg is the track?"

"I think so."

"Then he *does* want you to go to Indy."

"Maybe, but I don't think so. Look at it this way: If you did get to Indy and you did travel 500 miles, from start to finish, where would you be?"

"In the winner's circle?"

"Not unless you won. All the guys who make the whole 500 miles wind up somewhere. Where?"

"Right back where they started from."

"Exactly!"

"Exactly what, Jordan? I'm glad to be just an old lumberjack turned furniture man!"

Jordan laughed. "He may want someone who intercepts this message to think I'm going to Indianapolis to meet him at the track, but to me it means, stay right where you are. Move and run and travel 500 miles if you want, but—just like at Indy—you'll end up right where you started. So I stay here."

Dexter Lee looked dubious. "So how do you know it's from Rollins?"

"That was the easiest part."

"I was afraid of that."

"No, it's easy, look. He says that's where the hog wants me. Almost too simple. What kind of hog would you be likely to find around a race track?" Lee was still puzzled. Jordan gave him another hint. "Think: motorcycles."

"Harley Davidson!"

"Right! Because *hog* is slang for a big Harley Davidson. A *hog* is a Harley and Harley Rollins is the hog. And the next phrases, 'precision tuned' and 'worth his while,' mean just what they say. They fit the parlance he's using, but he wants me in shape for a good assignment. Which can only mean he's got a place for me on the case he's working on."

"How can that be? I thought you weren't allowed on that one."

"What else could he mean?"

"I'm sure I don't know."

"That's my guess, Dex. And I think he wants to see me in ten days. Don't know if I can wait that long."

"Where in the world do you get ten days out of that crazy message?"

" 'Two hundred and forty' relates to the missing word implied by 'yours, mine, and you-know-who's'—which is?"

" 'Ours'?"

"Right, but take it phonetically. Hours. Two hundred forty hours is ten days."

"Why not pounds?"

"Because things are never the way they seem."

"Could you be totally off on this, Jordan? Could you have got on the wrong track—pardon the pun—and missed the whole point?"

"Possible. Doubt it. One of my specialties."

"You seem almost high on this."

"Beats sitting around. Never thought I'd say that again."

"Staying with the NSA?"

"No way. But I'll go anywhere, do anything for Harley Rollins."

"The hog."

"Right."

"And what's the strange sign off?"

"Didn't know myself until I looked it up. Glad you're well read and have lots of reference books. The term was obviously biological, so I started there. It means ladybug, Dex. He's 'Your Coccinellidae' or 'our bug.' That tells me that *he* had the phone tapped, so I can quit worrying about it."

"I think you made all this up."

"Could have been wishful thinking. But Harley and I used to communicate like this all the time. Actually, it's quite amateurish. We were decoded many times."

"You won't be this time."

"I hope not, Dex."

Thirteen

Frequently during the next week, Jordan had second thoughts about his ability to decipher Harley's coded telegram. But, he wondered, what was the alternative? He had to go with his instincts, trust his own judgment.

During the next week, Jordan worked out hard every day, mostly indoors. He ran in place and did multiple series of push-ups, chin-ups, and isometrics. He alternated periods of exercise, when he tried to keep his pulse at around 140 for twenty minutes, with ten-minute breaks, when he sat perspiring in his new hooded sweats.

Dexter Lee busied himself with errands and projects around the house for much of each day, always sure to be home when Jordan was out running. Jordan told him precisely when he planned to return. "If I'm forty seconds late, come looking for me." But he never was. If anything, he was early, to set his uncle's mind at ease.

From dinner until bedtime, the two talked. Night after night they chatted, going over old ground, dredging up memories. Dex Lee even raised some subjects Jordan had long forgotten, and every night he smoothly worked the conversation to the areas he thought were most necessary for Jordan to deal with.

Jordan felt his uncle urging him to talk about Rosemary, about his grief, about his guilt, even about his short-circuited spiritual life since her death.

"I know you wished I'd have reacted more consistently with what I believe, Dex, but I've got to tell you, I don't know what to believe anymore."

The old man was curled up on the end of the couch near the fireplace. He stared at Jordan before speaking.

"Jordan, did I say how I thought you should react?" Jordan shook his head. "I couldn't hope to prescribe how a person should react to a trauma like yours. I lost your aunt in what was supposed to be the most natural, humane, easiest way to lose a person. She fell ill, she got worse, her condition was aggravated by age, and the doctor prepared me. She didn't suffer long, and we were both ready for it.

"Still, I cried for weeks. Knowing the end was coming didn't cushion the shock, at least as far as I could tell. I had nothing to compare the experience to, but I recall that punched-in-the-gut feeling of shock, if not surprise, when she was suddenly wrenched from me. I can't imagine how it must have been for you."

With several evenings of therapeutic sessions already behind him, Jordan was feeling as comfortable as ever with his uncle.

"But surely you wished I'd evidenced at least some of that 'peace that passes understanding.' "

Dexter sat up and planted both feet on the floor, resting his elbows on his knees. The fire illuminated only the right side of his face, and a beard would have made him look like a just-arrived Santa.

"Oh, but you have, Jordie. Don't kid yourself. Did you fire your weapon when you knew your wife was dead? Did you kill yourself? Did you go crazy?"

"That wasn't as much peace as it was Harley Rollins's mind training."

"Come now. Even Harley says you were the best mind trainee he ever saw. Even better than himself."

"He's being modest."

"But never falsely so. No, Jordan, you were the best because you have that bedrock peace. Peace doesn't mean giddiness or even happiness. It's deeper. It's more solid. It's the sense that God is sovereign."

Jordan didn't feel entirely convinced, but as the hours of talk mounted, he found himself quicker on the emotional trigger. He wept when they spoke of Rosemary, which became more frequently. He grew open and spoke his mind, as his uncle advised him to do over and over. When he felt mad, angry, ignored, cheated, he said so. When he thought the whole situation was God's fault, he said that, too. When he disagreed with Dexter, he said so. He was feeling healthier.

He was still careful to check the area around the house every night. He was confident that the only person who knew he was there was Harley. And he grew eager to see him. On Sunday he ventured out with his uncle to go to church. It was a strange, awkward experience, because the people in the tiny congregation were friendly and curious, and he wasn't in the mood, nor had he ever been disposed, to say much about himself. But especially now.

Late Sunday night, after another meaningful talk with Dexter, Jordan found himself anxious, pensive. It was still a few days before he expected Harley, yet he was energized. He paced his room, conscious that his body was lean and hard, his mind sharper than it had been since the Germany assignment. Indeed, the conversations with his uncle had covered more than Jordan and his troubles. Dexter Lee was well-read and a thoughtful historian. He loved to gas about politics and economics.

Jordan turned off his reading light and lay listening to a light rain. He heard splashing footsteps in the street. A jogger at this time of night? Jordan sat up and peered out. He worried about the figure of the man who bounced along past the house.

Could the jogger have studied the house as he ran? He faced straight ahead as he went under the light directly in front of Jordan's window, but he could have checked out the house on his way. Jordan chastised himself for being paranoid, but didn't the man take longer to get past than he should have?

The runner appeared young and stocky, an orange-clad, plodding type whose thighs looked like they could handle more speed. Jordan strained to look far down the street. The jogger was still heading that way. Jordan wondered whether he would be able to tell if the man doubled back.

His heart raced and he nearly laughed aloud. Had he taken such a long break from the action that he was oversensitized? Was he too excited about Harley's promise of an assignment? He began to breathe deeply to counteract his pulse, and just as he felt his body relaxing, he saw the jogger reappear on the near side of the street, heading his way.

There was no question now. The man slowed and carefully cased the house as he went by. Jordan felt adrenalin flood his system and his mind shift into its opposite trigger mode. He crept downstairs in the darkness. His uncle kept no weapons in the house, and Jordan was unarmed. He'd been in the same position before, not knowing if his opponent had a weapon. It called for the coolest head, the best strategy. If indeed the jogger was more than a jogger, Jordan would have to surprise him.

He stayed out of the rays of light that broke in between shades and drapes, trying to follow the image of the jogger down the street. The man should have run under the light at the corner by now, but he had not appeared. Was he on his way back, or had he cut between houses to head back through the alley toward the Lee home? Either way, Jordan knew he'd feel safer outside.

He grabbed his sweats from a pile near the front door and pulled on his shoes. There was no time to find any sort of weapon now. While his uncle snored from the second floor bedroom, Jordan slipped out the front door and knelt in the damp earth behind the bushes. It was cold. The jogger was no longer on the street.

Jordan crept around the house to the back where the outside light was on. He stood still to listen, but his pounding heart and his shallow breath made that difficult. He willed his system to relax, and as his body began to respond, he heard footsteps in the alley. He squinted in the mist and was startled when the orange figure emerged from the bushes and strode up the back walk. The man pulled a small slip of paper from his sweat shirt and read it in the back light.

He pocketed the paper, studied the house, looked up and down the other back yards, sighed, and sat on a bench at the side of the steps, his back to Jordan. He was breathing heavily as if he either had run a long way or was not used to running at all. His physique suggested the former.

Jordan stepped lightly in the grass and surveyed the man to see if he was armed. Then he approached to within a few feet of the jogger, and when he knew he would be heard if he tiptoed another step, he leapt at the man, throwing his left forearm around and under his chin, pressing hard but not lethally on his Adam's apple. With his right hand, he pressed forward on the back of the head.

Jordan was shocked at the hardness of the man, wondering if he had been wise in attacking. Rocklike fists reached up and back in an attempt to pull Jordan over, but he had prepared himself for that. All his weight was on his heels and he lifted them from the ground, making himself a dead weight, a choking, suffocating albatross.

He knew both wind pipe and voice box had been incapacitated and that the man would have to relax or move with Jordan's pressure to be able to breathe. Jordan lowered his mouth and spoke near the man's ear, which was still hidden by the hood. "Talk to me."

A straining, gurgling sound came from the jogger's throat, but when Jordan loosened his grip slightly, he felt the man tense for action. He reapplied the pressure, feeling soft tissue constrict around the larynx. The message had been transmitted, and Jordan loosened his grip again.

The voice was husky. "Harley Rollins."

Jordan flinched. This wasn't Harley Rollins. This man was much thicker, much more muscular. "What about him?"

"Sent me. He's here. Wants to see you."

Jordan slid his hand away from the man's throat and felt the man's pocket for a weapon. Nothing. Then he felt the man tense again, and he would have gone for his throat once more, if the man had not raised his hands in surrender. Jordan stepped back and wheeled around in front of him in a karate stance. "I'm not expecting Harley for three days."

The man shrugged, swallowing. "I don't know nothin' about that. I've got a van around the corner and I can take you to him. He's at the beach."

"The beach? Lake Michigan?"

The man nodded and extended his hand. "Call me Roscoe."

"You could be anybody, Roscoe. How do I know you're with Harley?"

Roscoe loosened the string at his neck and pulled his hood down. His face was wide with pale blue eyes and close-cropped blond hair. He looked to be in his late twenties, close to six feet tall and weighing at least two hundred pounds. "Ask me somethin'."

"You got a last name?"

"Roscoe."

"Okay. You got a first name?"

"Nope."

"Uh-huh. What's my wife's name?"

"Rosemary, sir. Maiden name Holub."

"Am I happily married?"

"You were, sir. I'm sorry."

"Lots of people know that."

"I'm answerin' *your* questions, sir."

"You military?"

"Was."

"Now?"

"I work for Harley, same as you used to."

"Can't be."

Roscoe shrugged.

"Did I surprise you, Roscoe?"

"No, sir. Harley said to make myself a little obvious and you'd come to me. You were a little earlier than I expected, but Harley's seldom wrong."

Jordan studied him. "Harley give you any passwords?"

"J.K.B., sir, whatever that means."

"You don't know what it means?"

"No, sir."

"Harley didn't tell you?"

"Roscoe shook his head again.

"And what did Harley say to try if I said a lot of people knew about J.K.B.?"

"He said you might say that Bauer's people knew about that and that you might think I was workin' for them, sir."

"And you're going to prove that isn't the case?"

"Yes, sir. He said they wouldn't know about C. L. from France."

Jordan fought for composure. "And you do?"

"No, sir. He just said that would convince you."

Jordan nodded. "It did. Meet you at the corner."

He poked his head in the front door to be sure his uncle was still asleep and left a note on the mat inside the door. Ten minutes and a silent drive later, he found himself sitting under a bluff, his back to the wind, with Harley. Roscoe stayed in the van.

"What'd you find in London?"

"Nothing to speak of yet."

Jordan had stretched the truth the same way himself. He eyed Harley. His old boss had to be onto something. "I wasn't expecting you just now."

"What do you mean 'just now'?"

"I expected you in three days."

Harley studied him in the faint light from cottages on the shore. "Why?"

"Your message said 240 'ours,' which I took to mean hours. That would have been ten days."

"What are you talking about?"

Jordan was embarrassed. "Okay, apparently I misunderstood part of it. At least I didn't head off to the Indy track."

"What are you telling me?"

Jordan felt cold all over, and it wasn't because of the rain and wind. "I got your telegram, the one telling me to stay put for ten days and to stay in shape and you'd make it worth my while. You signed it, in essence, 'My bug,' which told me you were the one who put the NSA tap on the phone."

Harley said nothing at first. He just looked out across the lake and rubbed a hand over his mouth. Finally he spoke. "What else did it say?"

"You didn't send it?"

"What else did it say, Jordan? You'd better be sure about the timing or we're going to have to get your uncle out of there."

Jordan recited the telegram as carefully as his memory allowed. "You've got to admit, it even sounds like you."

Harley nodded, rising and heading toward the van. "Your uncle have a garage?"

"Uh-huh."

"And you're sure the bug is ours?"

"Pretty sure."

"Let's check it out."

Roscoe waited in the van at the end of the alley while Harley took some tools and followed Jordan to the phone box. He removed the tap and put it in his pocket, swearing under his breath. "Can we put the van in the garage without waking your uncle?"

"Think so."

"And is there somewhere we can talk, now, without bothering him?"

Jordan led Roscoe to the garage, then both of them to the kitchen. He showed Harley the telegram. His former boss squinted and shook his head. "If I didn't know better, I'd have thought you wrote it."

Jordan nearly laughed. "Me? I thought it had you written all over it."

"It does. And that scares me. I do have an assignment for you, Jordan. But I wouldn't have thought to encourage you to stay in shape. I would have assumed you would do that."

Jordan felt guilty, but he didn't correct Harley. "Who else knew you had an assignment for me?"

"Not many. Of course, we're always under surveillance. You're sure there's no bug in here, other than the one that was on the phone?"

Jordan nodded.

Harley looked at Roscoe, then at Jordan. "Looks like we've got three days then."

"For what?"

Harley shrugged. "Before company arrives."

Roscoe spoke for the first time since he'd talked with Jordan in the backyard. "You want us out of the country before that, don't you, sir?"

Harley nodded. "I haven't mentioned that to Kettering yet."

"Sorry."

"It's all right. I will. But now we have to figure out what we want to do about whoever is coming here in three days. Do we leave him an empty house? Or, if he's looking for some action, do we not disappoint him?"

Jordan shook his head. "If it's the same one who had my wife and Stu killed and my house blown up, I'd just as soon stay and fight."

"Yeah, and risk your uncle's life, not to mention your own. And put both of our careers on the line."

"When has that ever bothered you?"

"I'm getting old, Jordan."

"You'll never get that old."

"All I need is to let the brass know that I let you back onto the case and that we knew about this threat three days before it came. Uh-uh, no, forget it."

"I don't understand."

"I'd rather case the place, stake it out, get your uncle out of here, and see if we can surprise someone. Meanwhile, I've got work for you and Roscoe."

"Related to my case?"

"Course. And if we don't succeed, it'll cost me my job."

Jordan studied the alert, tense figure of Roscoe. "Harley, who sent me the telegram?"

The older man looked tired. "I hate to admit I don't know."

"Is there any doubt in your mind that Stanley Stuart was right? Isn't this clearly an inside job by someone very strategically placed in the agency?"

"Fraid so. Hate to think it."

"I do too, Harley, but it's someone who knows my comings and goings, who knows I'm here and has access to NSA bugging devices, who knows your style of messages and even knew you had plans for me."

"That could have been a coincidence. A ruse."

"Could have been. But how likely?"

"Not very."

"So, what'd you turn up, Harley?"

"I've been a busy boy. I spent a day in London with Felix. He had just gotten back from the States. Appreciated your call, or your uncle's call anyway."

"He's a good friend and a good man."

"You betcha. Then I went straight to Frankfurt. Jordan, I hit the jackpot. I was there three days and scored, that's all I can tell you."

"What do you mean, that's all you can tell me? You're gonna tell me everything. How'd you score?"

"I got a peek at Stu's personal effects, things found in the room with him when he died. Jordan, I hate to tell you, but it was indeed a suicide."

"I don't believe it, Harley. It doesn't sound like him."

"Look at this." Harley spread a photocopied sheet before Jordan. It read: "The news from the northwest is true, and it's my fault."

Jordan covered his mouth with his hand. "London?"

Harley nodded. "That's all it can be. He heard about the shooting in the airport and assumed you had been killed. When his contact person confirmed it, he figured it was his fault for dragging you into the situation."

Jordan stood and faced the wall. He could hardly speak above a whisper. "I have to know for sure, Harley. How can we know?"

"We know, partner. I'm sorry. Among the miscellaneous items in his apartment that were stuffed in a manila envelope were some bills he'd paid and receipts from the post office. The man cleared up his affairs before he shot himself, Jordan. Bills were paid, the place tidied up, even his work at the office was up to date. He had to go back to the office in the evening to do that."

Jordan shook his head. "That sounds more like the Stu I knew."

"Me, too. But Jordan, I believe the man saved your

life and tried to preserve the security of the United States before he died. One of the post office receipts was for an overnight package flown to the States. He listed the contents as 'Miscellaneous returned catalog items' and addressed the package to HER LTD. at my personal post office box in Florida. You and Stu are the only two people in the NSA who know that address. I use my home address for everything else. That box is just for my private family or business or confidential stuff."

"So, what'd he send? The photos?"

Harley nodded, suppressing a smile. "Like I said, I've been busy. I slipped the receipt out of the envelope so no one else would be aware of it and so Washington wouldn't come nosing around. Then I called my post office and told them to hold that package for me. Picked it up yesterday. I was lucky enough to locate Roscoe last night and find him hungry for work."

"I still can't get over your stealing evidence from an NSA suicide scene."

"Hey, Jordie, they put me on this case. I'm in charge of stuff like that."

"They didn't assign you to Stu's case."

"Well, I had to trace your whereabouts up to the time of the attack in London, and that trail led to Stu, okay? So, you wanna see the package or not?"

Jordan sat back down.

Harley pulled the envelope from his bag as he spoke. "I'm going to want to pay a visit to Western Union tomorrow and find out where that telegram came from. We're safe tonight. Anywhere we can sleep?"

"The living room."

"And scare your uncle when he stumbles over us? Why don't *you* sleep there and we'll sleep in your room."

"Deal. Now show me the stuff."

Roscoe sighed. "I've seen all this. I'd just as soon turn in. Where do you want me to sleep at?"

Jordan led him upstairs and shook his hand in silent apology for having had to apply the choke hold. When he returned to Harley, the veteran was just opening his eyes. "One hundred twenty seconds."

"What's that?"

"You were gone 120 seconds. I prescribed myself an intense, two-minute nap. The subconscious never—."

"I know, never misses. Keeps perfect time and all that."

Jordan recognized the three photographs on the table. Harley said he didn't see anything in them that could be a clue as to precisely where the hangar was. "Foliage sure looks like southern U.S. though, doesn't it?"

Jordan nodded. "Any message from Stu?"

"I was saving the best till last." He slid a sheet across the table. In neat, hand-printed, block letters, Stanley Stuart had written:

DESPONDENT OVER YOUR LOSS. THEY'RE MOVING THE CINCINNATI CLUB TO ALABAMA AND PREPARATIONS FOR SAM'S RITES WILL BE HELD AT THE MALDONADO FUNERAL CHAPEL NEAR 78TH AND 1ST, THE 20TH OF THIS MONTH. THE ENTIRE FAMILY WILL BE THERE. IF OUR MUTUAL FRIEND DID NOT GET TO YOU BEFORE HIS DEMISE, THIS WILL BE MEANINGLESS TO YOU AND ALL IS LOST. FOR MY CONTRIBUTION TO THAT CATASTROPHE, I PRAY FOR ABSOLUTION. SEE ATTACHED.

Attached was a carbon copy of Stu's hand-scrawled note to a Michala Diego at an apartment in downtown Frankfurt:

THE LONDON ACTIVITY CONVINCES ME I'M IN OVER MY HEAD. I WANT OUT. COUNT

FLORIDA CONTACT IN, THE ONE I TOLD YOU
ABOUT. HE'LL SEE YOU THE 20TH.

Jordan looked to Harley. "I'm lost."

"Don't feel bad. This one took me six hours and
several trans-Atlantic cables to Interpol. If this Diego
trusted Stu, we're making progress. If the suicide spooks
him or he finds out that the Florida contact—that's me—
goes back a long way with you, he'll smell a rat and we'll
come up empty."

"But what was Stu saying in his note? And who's
Diego?"

"Okay, my loss that he's despondent over is you. He
thinks you were wiped out in the London attack. The
Cincinnati club would be the Reds, right? The Russians.
That's a clue to the location of the MiG-23s in the photographs. Sam's rites took me a while, but he's referring
to the death of Uncle Sam if we don't do something about
the Reds in Alabama. The next part took the longest. I
went to the library and looked up funeral homes in the
telephone books of a hundred cities and didn't find anything remotely close to Maldonado's or anything at an
address like that. I discovered what he was talking about
by accident.

"I was frustrated, so I took a walk through the library.
In one room, I found a globe and gave it a spin. When
it stopped, I noticed the latitude and longitude lines.
Guess what's near 78th and 1st?"

Jordan spoke in a monotone. "Maldonado, Ecuador."

"You've been there, have you?"

"Not right there, but I had two assignments in Ecuador, one in the late sixties and one in the early seventies
that took me south of Quito into that sweep of four fairly
big cities—Ambato, Riobamba, Guaranda, and, um, that
northernmost one."

"Latacunga."

"Yeah. I hated it. Hot, muggy, buggy, smelly. Reminded me of Indonesia."

"Not all your memories of Indonesia are that bad are they?"

Jordan nodded absently. "Uh-huh."

"But you got north, near Maldonado?"

"Somewhat. Seems we flew in or out of Ibarra. Probably out because I remember being happy on the plane."

"That would have been in '72, right?"

"Probably. Is that when the government was overthrown and they went away from the 1967 constitution and back to the 1945 one?"

Harley nodded. "Good memory."

"A curse as well as a blessing, if you know what I mean." Harley didn't respond.

"Horrible climate."

"Yeah, especially this time of the year. It's around a 100 degrees all the time and humid."

"So, what's happening there on the twentieth?"

Harley scratched his head. "Best I can figure, it's a strategic meeting about the MiGs and what comes next. If the entire family is there, I expect people from Mexico, Cuba, and South America. Maybe even from the Soviet Union."

"But where in Maldonado are these people supposed to meet? And what do we do if we find them? Do you know how hard it is to get weapons into South America?"

"That's your job. As to where they're going to meet, that's mine. I'll spend the next few days in Frankfurt, tracking down this Diego character. I've already got a lead on him from Interpol. If everything works out right, I'll win him over and come to Maldonado with him. You and Roscoe can bring weapons in from the other direction and we'll rendezvous somewhere."

"What's Interpol got on this Diego character? Why'd you start there?"

"I didn't start there. I ended there. I tried him with everybody. FBI, CIA, NSA. They've all got something on him, but of course Michala Diego is just one of his many aliases. Interpol provided the most information. He's from the Galápagos Islands."

"What's he doing so far from home? The islands are what, five or six hundred miles into the Pacific from Ecuador, and he's in Germany?"

Harley nodded. "No one really knows. Just like Lister, he's a hired man."

"Just like Roscoe."

Harley jumped. "Don't ever put criminals in Roscoe's category, Jordan. At least he's always on the right side."

"Just checking."

"Sure, and what did your comment imply about me and my choice of people to team up with you?"

"Sorry. I didn't mean it. Tell me more about Diego."

"Well, the only time he was even spotted on the Ecuador mainland was about four years ago when Interpol was on his tail for narcotics traffic as far north as Texas and as far south as Chile."

"He's a dope smuggler? Did he take advantage of the radar gap Stu told me about?"

"Likely. Maybe that's how he got connected with others who wanted to do the same, only on a much grander scale. He was into weapons, too."

"Big ones? Like MiGs?"

"Not before this. Just firearms and small munitions. I think this is his first time in the big leagues. I mean, he's a bad boy, but he's never played for these stakes before. No doubt he's the junior man in this operation, just a mouthpiece and message carrier. Most likely, he told Stu he was going to have you killed because he talked to you without his permission. When the London attack was broadcast, Stu told him I was a better bet anyway and then blamed himself for your death."

Jordan stretched and shut his eyes. "Harley, I want this guy. I know how important the whole thing is, but I want him for myself."

"Let's not get carried away just yet, Jordan. We still don't know Diego's contact in the agency, and until we know that, all we can do is try to get next to the guy and see what he's up to. That won't be easy because he's not going to immediately trust the new recommendation from a guy who tried to go behind his back and then killed himself when the thing blew up in his face."

"How you gonna get around that?"

Harley shook his head. "I have no idea yet. I'll just have to turn on the charm, I guess. Convince him I've been stiffed by the NSA and the United States for so many years that now I want to do something for myself. I could sure use the money." He winked at Jordan.

"And you want Roscoe and me to get to Ecuador from the other direction?"

"I've made almost all the contacts already. The rest will be made by the time you get there and need them."

"So when do we leave? I have to do something before I go crazy."

"Not till you know what you're up against."

"So tell me."

"First off, you have to know that this is a totally clandestine operation."

"They always are."

"You didn't hear me. I said, totally clandestine."

"What does that mean?"

"That means no one knows about it right now. No one but Felix and me, you and Roscoe."

"I need to know all about Roscoe, you know. If I'm going to be spending several days with him and maybe depending on him for my next breath."

Harley told Jordan he'd met Roscoe—"last name's the same as the first, though he denies it"—when Roscoe was a Marine recruit. "Different kind of a kid. Mercenary, and all physical. Doesn't have the double dose you've got with the body and the brain, but he's not stupid. Quiet. Built like a fireplug. Could beat you in a sprint and a mile. Probably not any longer distance than that."

"I can break five minutes in the mile, Harley."

Harley smiled. "Not bad for a middle-aged man. Would you believe 4:36 for this kid every time he goes out?"

"What else does he do?"

"Name it. Self-defense, kill skills, hand-to-hand combat, especially strength tests."

"Like?"

"Push-ups, chin-ups, weights, that kind of thing."

"*You're* still ahead of me in that area, Harley. Does he beat you?"

"By a third, all the way around."

"Firearms?"

"Nothing heady. He can use 'em, but he doesn't know what makes 'em tick the way you do."

"So, what's he doing here? You're not telling me he's tomorrow's version of Jordan Kettering."

"Nope. No contact with NSA at all. Strictly freelance. He didn't like military pay, so he hires himself out. He'll do anything legal for a flat fee. Only none of the fees I've ever paid him have been flat."

"Harley, you in shape?"

"Wanna arm wrestle?"

Jordan laughed. "For you to suggest that, when you've never beaten me, tells me you're either in shape or dreaming, as always."

Fourteen

The next morning, Harley visited the local Western Union office and Roscoe found himself at breakfast answering Dexter Lee's curious questions, some of them ones Jordan had wanted to ask the night before. The husky man finished his meal and dragged a napkin across his mouth, his pale eyes darting everywhere except at Dexter, who had posed the question.

"What made you leave the military?"

"You mean besides the fact that Harley's a legend?"

"That's right."

"Bucks."

Dexter was smiling. "I don't mean to offend, but you're apparently a multitalented man. Yet you're motivated only by money?"

Roscoe shrugged and leaned forward, resting his weight on his elbows. "'Course. Aren't *you*? Looks like you've done all right for yourself."

The old man's smile remained, but the twinkle left the eyes. "I'm not motivated by great amounts of money. No."

"Well, then what motivates you?"

"It might sound a little pious to you, Mr. Roscoe."

Roscoe shot a glance at Jordan. "Yeah, Harley told me Jordan was a bit of a Holy Roller. I guess it runs in the family."

Jordan was offended. "Neither my uncle nor I could be considered Holy Rollers. Did Harley really say that?"

"Maybe not in so many words, but he made it clear you were religious."

Jordan rolled his eyes and threw his hands up in disgust. His uncle intervened. "Let me speak to this, Jordan. You're not in any condition—."

"Dex! I'm not in any condition to do what?" But he realized immediately that his uncle was right. The fact that he had snapped at Dexter in front of a stranger only proved the point.

The older man began slowly. "Our faith is not in religion. It's a way of life, yes, but we believe in a Person, not in a creed."

Roscoe shook his head. "Yeah, I've heard that Person business before. But the Person is God, right?"

"Well, Jesus."

"Okay, Jesus then, but if you don't think believing in *that* person makes you religious, you're just kiddin' yourselves."

Dexter Lee cocked his head. "Perhaps we have a semantical problem. Call it faith, religion, Christianity, the Person of Christ, whatever. The fact is, He is my life, and that's a better investment than any I could ever have made in the stockmarket."

Roscoe looked around the room. "I still think a few shekels have passed through your fingers in your time."

"I feel fortunate, sure. But I've had more than this place represents. I've invested a lot of my resources in the Lord's work, too."

"You can say that and tell me you're not religious? C'mon! I'm happy to say I've never been taken in by a preacher with his hand out."

"Neither have I."

Roscoe was clearly irritated. "I can see where this is goin'. You're going to wind up workin' on me. Let me tell you somethin'. I was raised in Indiana on a dirt farm. Picked vegetables from the time I got up in the morning till it was time to go to school. My daddy figured that if his kids picked until eleven minutes before school started, we could wash up, jump on the back of the truck, and be drove to school—he'd get more bushels out of us than if we took the school bus that came by twenty minutes earlier."

"Seems to have made quite a man of you."

"I wouldn't say that's what did it. I did it. I had to pick when I got home, too, ya know."

"No play time?"

"Not much, but I didn't mind that. There wasn't much to play with. I played in my head." He looked away, almost as if he'd wished he hadn't said that. Jordan got the feeling that Roscoe rarely talked about himself at all. But Dexter Lee could get anyone to talk.

Roscoe pursed his lips, as if he was about to reveal something he had never let out before. "When I was fifteen, workin' barefoot in the cabbage patch, dust makin' me gag, Willie Floyd come drivin' past real fast, honkin' and wavin' from his red and black convertible. That sucker was just sixteen years old, and he had a brand-new car. A Merc. A beauty."

Lee nodded, silent.

"When he come back by, I knew he wanted me to come runnin' and see it and all. He skidded up to the fence and I could see him from maybe fifty feet away, only I pretended I didn't. He honked and hollered and waved, and I just kept pickin'. He never dared to pull that thing onto our property. Might get it dirty."

"Where did you know him from?"

"School. We didn't really know him, 'cept who he was. A rich kid. Spoiled. Loved to show off."

Dexter smiled. "Surely you didn't want to be like him."

Roscoe shrugged. "Nope. But I figured if I could ever get a car like that, that would be enough. People would know I had to have *some* money, and they might guess I was free, too. I wouldn't have to be a rotten guy like Willy."

"And did you get it?"

"Soon's I got out of the service. Big monthly payments. Lived in a cheap apartment. I hated livin' there, but I loved drivin' that car."

"Still got it?"

"Yup. Don't drive it much no more. Too busy. Got a nice place now. Lots of stuff. Want more."

"So you do what?"

"I do whatever anybody wants me to that's legal and that they'll pay for."

"And who hires you?"

"I've been workin' for the military and for Harley about three years."

Jordan nearly jumped. "Really? He never told me about you."

"He told me enough about you, man. Made me look forward to workin' with you, but I never thought I'd get the chance. He'd always say, 'Gotta get you on a case with Jordan K.'"

Jordan raised his eyebrows. "This case has to mean more than money to you. Can you get worked up about Soviet planes in Alabama?"

Roscoe shrugged. "No question. I'll do the right thing, if that's what you mean. I know the good guys from the bad guys, but for me it's a business. If I get dead, I don't get the bread. Follow?"

Dexter Lee broke in, gently. "And if you get dead, as you say, before you deal with God's claim on your life, then where are you?"

"I don't think about that. I believe in me, and I've taken care of myself all right up till now."

"But sometime during this mission, you might want to discuss this more with my nephew."

Jordan wasn't sure what he thought about that. He supposed that he cared about Roscoe's eternal soul as much as Uncle Dexter did, but he didn't feel he was up to that kind of responsibility just then. He didn't have to worry about it, though. Roscoe wanted no spiritual guidance. He gestured and pointed at each of them as he spoke. "Tell you what. That'll be my business, Okay? If I want to talk about it, I'll raise the subject. But if I don't, I'll thank you to stay off my case. Deal?"

Jordan nodded, but his uncle offered a warning: "Just don't wait to raise the subject until it's too late."

Roscoe waved him off. Yet his expression revealed admiration for the old man's persistence.

Jordan changed the subject back. "If your philosophy is that this is just a business deal, and it doesn't do anything to your gut that we may be on the verge of a world war, maybe you're not right for this assignment."

"Don't worry about me. I work for whoever's payin' me. But don't expect me to get into it the way you do."

Jordan didn't like Roscoe's attitude, but he trusted Harley completely to have handpicked the right person. He wanted to argue, but he knew it was pointless.

"If I decide to do this, I'll count on you."

Roscoe leaned back in his chair and tugged at his belt. "You've already decided, and you know it." Jordan decided Roscoe wasn't as slow as he sounded. The young man smiled at him and stood. "I'm takin' a walk."

With Roscoe gone, Dexter leaned forward. "Look after that young man, Jordie. This is a dangerous mission. Before it's over, he may find he needs something more to believe in than just himself."

"Dex, I don't know."

"Jordan, you have a responsibility. Within reason, don't worry about offending him. You may just be courteous enough to let him go to hell."

Jordan still didn't feel comfortable with the thought of pushing his faith on an unwilling listener, but he wasn't up to arguing with his uncle about it. Besides, Dex's point was hard to refute. "Hey, can I still get an ear around here myself? I need a little more therapy."

"Sure. Shoot."

Jordan reminisced about the days soon after he had begun training with Harley, developing his mind and body for government service. He had tested well under pressure. Harley would argue with him, berate him about his Pollyanna beliefs about America and patriotism and his faith. He would argue about capitalism, world hunger, peace, social issues.

Harley would play the devil's advocate, arguing against the system, against the United States, against a traditional system of justice. Down deep Jordan knew Harley didn't believe the position he was taking or he wouldn't have been such a loyal NSA staffer, but still he pressed Jordan to articulate his ideals.

"And I had them. I had ideals when I went in. I didn't get them from Harley." It was coming to him almost as a revelation now. "I've always feared that he brainwashed me, made me a super patriot. I wondered what would have happened if I had been recruited by the wrong guy, the wrong branch? Would I have turned out the opposite? But Harley couldn't shake me. He used to tell me how no one else had ever been able to stand up under his barrage of criticism and accusations.

"The ultimate test, after that hand grenade incident, was when he came to me acting very cold and somber and sad. He drove me to a country road where we just walked for miles. Then he told me he was leaving the NSA, had lost his zeal. I laughed at him, told him I didn't believe him, told him it was too late to fool me with this kind of a test. But he finally convinced me. By the end of that hike, I was pleading with him, arguing with him. Nearly crying. For the last half hour before we got back to the car, he quit talking. Wouldn't say anything. I asked him over and over if he would reconsider, what was he thinking, would he sleep on it? He had already told me who my new superior would be and that there were no guarantees about what my assignment might be.

"I begged him all the way back to my apartment to consider his worth to the United States, to the NSA, to the world. I got the impression that if he had tried to talk, he might have choked up. When he wouldn't answer me, I just left the car and trudged up to my apartment. I didn't sleep."

Dexter Lee leaned forward. "Obviously, he didn't carry out his threat."

Jordan laughed. "The next morning he showed up early, woke me, dragged me out of bed and down to the beach for our usual workout. It was weeks before he'd admit that he'd just been testing me again. I thought it was unfair, almost as unfair as the grenade. I was mad at him and I let him know it. I told him I wouldn't have done that to someone. He said it was the first time he had been totally convinced I was genuine. He used to say, 'None of us can tell what makes us or anyone else genuine in his passions, but once we become convinced, there's no wavering.'"

Jordan sat in silence, wondering why he or Harley hadn't told Blake Bauer that story. It might have exonerated him in the deputy's eyes. But, for Jordan, the anecdote was too personal, too revealing. It was Harley's story to tell, and he had chosen not to. Bauer could believe what he wanted. Not only had Jordan's loyalty and commitment been tested thoroughly before he was put on any sensitive assignments, but he had also proved himself countless times during the next two decades.

When Harley returned to Dexter Lee's home, he pulled Jordan off to the side. "Some things I can tell you; some things I can't. You'll have to trust me as usual." Jordan nodded. "I'm working on a few leads from the scene of the shooting, and some interesting ones from Felix and Huck Williamsby, but this telegram still has me baffled.

You know how tight Western Union can be. They gave me zip. I called the code at the top into our ciphering guys in Washington, but all they could tell me was that the message came from Europe and that, while the text itself was originated in English, the code was originally in Spanish."

"Spanish?"

"I don't know what to make of that either, Jordan. But I'll be working on it. Regardless, it's no joke. I'm going to get your uncle out of here by tomorrow and stake out the place myself. Maybe with some help."

"Not mine though, right?"

"Course not. This Ecuador thing won't wait."

"But what about all the—."

"Arrangements? What do you think? You remember what it was like working for me, don't you?"

"Yeah, but—."

"Yeah but nothing. The first thing I did was get your weapons from headquarters. I told them I needed to examine them myself, all but the ones that had been fired. They wouldn't let me touch those. And we're going to have to talk about those someday."

"Let's talk about them now, Harley, so you'll be clear. I wasn't lying about that. I never fired those weapons."

"Frankly, I was kinda hoping you had and that there was some creative reason for it. Would have made my job much easier. Anyway, I've stored the extra weapons, the wood pistols, and so forth, and I've shipped a half dozen .45s toward Ecuador. They'll be waiting for you when you get into the country."

"We're going in conventionally?"

"No. Not enough time for phony I.D.'s, shots, passports, visas. You'll fly from Muskegon to Chicago, from Chicago to Mexico City, then take a puddle jumper to Panama and two boats to San Lorenzo. Roscoe has all the contact people. You know one of 'em. Paul Paveli."

"Really? Good! Good man. First or second leg?"

"Second. He'll take you right into the harbor on his fishing boat. You'll still be about seventy-five miles from your destination, but you're on your own after that."

"How will I keep in touch with you?"

"You won't. I'll find you."

"You're pretty confident."

"Shouldn't I be? I've got the best in the business and three others who know how to follow orders."

"And the weapons?"

"Roscoe has that contact, too."

"And the other two men?"

"They're Cubans."

"Ouch."

"Should be good for you."

"They have a vested interest?"

" 'Fraid not. They're just like Roscoe."

"They know about me?"

"About your eliminating two of their countrymen? No, and if they did, they couldn't care less. They wouldn't be any more sympathetic to their government's agents than to ours. I've worked with these boys before. They know the jungle and they know the languages. They'll prove valuable. You'll meet them there and they may have the best idea where Diego and his people are meeting. They'll also have bikes."

"Motorcycles?"

Harley nodded. "Course they'll only get you so far. Then you're talking canoe and foot. Here are your tickets."

Jordan studied them. "Tonight? I need a few things."

"Such as?"

"Such as time to discuss strategy with you. Alternate plans. And gear."

"You still the same size you were three years ago?"

Jordan nodded.

"Check the van. It's in the driveway."

The crisp morning air and sunshine felt good. Jordan climbed in the back and dug through several bags from an army surplus store. He couldn't have chosen better himself. Some of the stuff was obviously for Roscoe, but they both would be fully outfitted with clothing designed for heat and humidity, camouflage, and comfort. Even the sleeping bags and tents were super-lightweight. Jordan's juices were flowing again.

He spent the afternoon and early evening on the phone with his son and daughter and in intense planning sessions with Roscoe and Harley. By that night, he felt better about Roscoe. The young man was full of bluster and make-believe earthiness, but he could plan brilliant strategy, distinguishing between the wise and the foolish. And Jordan had no doubt he was fearless.

At the airport, Harley asked Roscoe to get everything checked and loaded. Harley stood outside with Jordan and put a hand on each of his shoulders. "I want to tell you something, something important. But I will tell you only if you promise me you will not act upon it."

So Harley *had* discovered something already. Was the inside man someone they knew? Jordan's mind raced. But Harley pressed him again. "Swear to me. You won't do anything until I get there."

Jordan nodded, wondering if he could keep his promise, not fully knowing what he might do if he heard the name of someone who had tried to kill him, who had murdered his wife, who had caused the suicide of an old friend, blown up his house, bugged his uncle's phone, and might even be on his way to Muskegon now.

"Jordan, Felix tells me that about six months ago, he began getting inquiries about you from Interpol."

"Interpol? You mean, as a criminal or a suspect in some case?"

"No."

And Jordan knew. The inquiries were not official

Interpol business, but from someone there. "Cydya?" The name sounded strange in the night air. Harley tightened his grip and nodded. "But why?"

"I don't know, Jordan. The first inquiry came as a formal request on official letterhead. Felix told no one in Washington and ignored it."

"Why would she write to Felix?"

"Maybe she didn't want to get too close to where you were. I don't know. She even visited him, finally dropping the official business charade. Admitted it was personal."

"She couldn't be involved—not after making herself known to him."

"I'm not saying she was involved, Jordan."

Jordan tried to make it all make sense. "Why didn't Felix tell me?"

"He never put the pieces together until I was over there investigating."

Jordan was incredulous. "You told him about her."

"No. I told him the types of things I was looking for in your tenure with the agency. Then he recalled the inquiries."

"Did he give her any information?"

"He stalled her. Hasn't heard from her for a while." Harley studied him. "You all right, Jordan? Can you sit on this?"

Jordan felt a compulsion to change his flight, to fly to France, to find Cydya, to ask what she wanted. What he really wanted, he knew, was to eliminate her from any suspicion in his mind. "Do I have a choice?"

Fifteen

By the time Jordan and Roscoe boarded a Spanish frigate bound for Malpelo Island, about 150 miles due west of Buenaventura, Colombia, they had endured delays in both Mexico City and Panama.

Roscoe had told Jordan that they were to speak to no one but the captain and to say only, "Malpelo." Their fare was to be $250 each and they were to provide their own food. They didn't know whether the captain was a friend of Harley's, a mercenary, a criminal, or neutral. It had been Jordan's experience that his clandestine aides could be anything from Harley's old service buddies— men like Paul Paveli—to mysterious, closed-mouthed types like this one.

The stony captain, haggard and blood-shot as if under the influence, looked at Jordan. His voice was gravelly and weak.

"Roscoe?" Jordan nodded toward his young companion. The captain spoke again, in a thick Spanish accent. "Five hundred American dollars each." He extended his hand.

Roscoe dug deep in his clothes for a roll of bills and peeled off $500 in twenties. "Not each. Total." The captain didn't argue. He just pocketed the cash and pointed down into the hold, then held up three fingers. After he turned his back on them, Jordan and Roscoe neither saw nor heard from him again during the entire trip. They lugged their stuff into the hold, but could find no light in the narrow hallway.

Roscoe lit a match and found a battered door with a

"3" hand-painted near the handle. Inside, a single bulb hung from the ceiling on a long cord that swayed with the pitch of the ship. There were nine crew members, Jordan and Roscoe were the only passengers, and all but the captain shared a toilet that was not convenient to cabin number 3. Such as it was.

Distrusting the integrity of ancient wire mesh, Jordan opted for the top-most of two short, narrow bunks. He had pictured Roscoe falling on him in the middle of the night and decided it would be less cataclysmic if he fell on Roscoe. There was a small round table in the room, but no chairs. With their gear, the two men had barely enough room to get from the bunks to the door. With the door shut and the light off, the cabin was tomb black even at noon.

Roscoe hadn't spoken since he paid the captain. He sat on the edge of the bottom bunk. Jordan leaned back against a trunk and studied him. "Prone to claustrophobia or seasickness?"

Roscoe shook his head. In the dim light he looked weary. That didn't surprise Jordan. There was nothing he hated so passionately as a long, cramped, inconvenient, delayed trip. Without a word, Roscoe lay back on the tiny bed with his hands behind his head. One shoulder pressed against the wall; the other protruded over the side of the bunk by half a foot.

Jordan had never had a problem with either claustrophobia or seasickness, but he knew this box would provide the true test. Fortunately, the weather was uneventful and the sea calm. The captain didn't appear to be in any hurry, and occasionally Jordan had to ascend to the bridge to assure himself the craft was moving at all. His only clue was the deafening clack of the engine room not twenty feet from his bunk.

Thankfully, he was able to sleep. The two occupied themselves talking and working out in the corridor. It was clear the crew had been instructed not to speak or even look at them. They were avoided as if they had been contagious. He and Roscoe subsisted on sausages, cheese, fruit, crackers, bread, and bottled water.

Jordan was amazed at the body strength of his companion. After relieving himself in the morning, Roscoe would return to the cubicle, wrap his hands around an overhead pipe, and do ten slow-motion pull-ups, forcing himself to spend fifteen seconds on the way up and ten on the way down, resting no more than three seconds between each one.

Jordan had seen the exercise done before, but never ten repetitions. He found himself glancing at his watch and timing the man. The entire exercise took more than four minutes, and during the second five pull-ups, Roscoe's massive arms shook with effort. Jordan was shocked when his companion tried the ninth maneuver; he had seen the sweat stream down his body during the excruciating eighth rep. But when Roscoe began the tenth, Jordan worried.

What if he tried another? Should Jordan stop him? Roscoe had been so unusually quiet since they boarded the ship, Jordan wondered if he was becoming despondent or depressed. He gave no indication of motion sickness or weakness.

The tenth pull-up took everything Roscoe had. His biceps, triceps, deltoids, and trapezius contracted into grotesque knots. His eyes were shut, his cheeks full of air, his face nearly purple. Though his whole body quivered, he kept his ankles pressed together and his legs straight.

When he reached the zenith of the tenth pull, he exhaled slowly but still forced himself to lower his weight gradually. When he dropped to the floor, he staggered toward his bunk as if light-headed.

Jordan was stunned. "I don't believe I just saw that."

Roscoe had formed his lips into a circle and puffed to catch his breath, his massive chest heaving. He spoke between gasps. "Won a hundred . . . bucks. From Harley. Said I could . . . do fifteen. He said he'd . . . give me . . . fifty for every . . . one over ten. Ha!"

"You did twelve? I can hardly believe it."

"Ask . . . Harley. Truth is . . . I did fourteen . . . once. Alone. Not even . . . anybody to . . . show off to!"

Jordan whipped through his two-hour routine of speed and high-repetition strength exercises, but after watching Roscoe for two days, he thought of renaming his workouts. Next to Roscoe's, Jordan's were more like limbering up. Roscoe did his push-ups the same way he did his pull-ups. On toes and fingertips, with his back perfectly straight, he forced himself up and down in slow motion.

Late into the night the new partners talked, mostly of Harley. Jordan found it remarkable that Roscoe had endured many of the same training regimens he had, yet there had been a definite difference. Apparently, Harley had almost exclusively emphasized physical discipline with Roscoe. But Jordan's training, more than fifteen years before Harley met Roscoe, had been a blend of the mental, the physical, and even the academic. Roscoe, Jordan decided, had been conditioned as a tool.

"Did Harley ever wax eloquent with you after you returned from an assignment, Roscoe?"

The big man had been breathing heavily and deep, and Jordan wouldn't have been surprised if he didn't respond. But he wasn't asleep. "Nah. You?"

"Oh, yeah. For some reason, he always got the impression I was a little down or depressed after a job was over. Then he would pep-talk me, hard-sell me. Once I was out of International and into the agency full time, he quit testing me by bad-mouthing the agency and the country and the policies. His real self came out, and he was what I had suspected all along. He could go on for hours about how our form of government, how democracy itself, was the only sensible, humane political system on the face of the earth.

"He would remind me of injustices all over the globe, the real stories behind all the wars and the petty egos that affected the lives—and deaths—of millions. By the time he was finished with me, I was ready to head back out and do anything for him and for the country. What he didn't know was that I didn't need the pep talks. They were helpful, of course, but I wasn't down or depressed. I was just tired. The work was exhausting. I was ready for a break." Jordan fell silent for a few minutes when Roscoe began snoring. Then he finished anyway: "There were times I faked a dour look just to elicit one of those speeches."

It didn't make any difference if Jordan's eyes were open or shut in that room in the middle of the night. He found himself playing mind games to fall asleep. "Hey, Roscoe. Ten bucks says I can blow you away in arm wrestling."

"Hm?"

Jordan flinched. "Nothing. Sorry. Go back to sleep." He buried his head in the musty pillow and laughed.

The ship's first and only stop after it chugged out of Panama was Malpelo Island. Roscoe seemed loggy to Jordan, yet he carried ashore more than his share.

The younger man set a trunk on its side and sat atop it. He spoke softly, sounding weary despite all the rest he'd gotten. "Harley said you'd know Paveli's boat by sight."

Jordan snorted. "That's easy. Paveli will have the rattiest looking tub in the drink." He scanned the horizon. "Two more hours of daylight. He'll be along." For some reason, though he knew it was much too early to fear detection, Jordan felt too visible, too vulnerable. It bothered him to sit in the sand in the daylight, as if on stage.

Roscoe appeared to be daydreaming. Jordan lifted half the gear and trudged off close to the pier where they might more easily blend into the crowd. He had an uneasy feeling about Roscoe, who was slow on the uptake but eventually followed at a distance. Jordan wished he'd had more experience traveling with him; maybe Roscoe always lost his spark when he journeyed.

Or maybe there really wasn't a spark to the man anyway. Yet Jordan felt he had seen some animation in him in Muskegon. He wasn't humorous or wry, but he seemed to have an opinion, something to add to the strategy. He usually responded when spoken to. "You feeling all right, Roscoe?"

The big blond shrugged. "Not ready for a jog up the beach, if that's what you mean. But I could take you on in arm wrestling."

Jordan squinted at him. He saw no hint of a smile, but it was clear Roscoe wasn't being mean. Jordan wondered if Roscoe had heard him the night before, or if his comment had planted a subconscious trigger. "Arm wrestling? Not unless I can use two hands."

Roscoe appeared to laugh, but no sound came out. During the next hour, neither man spoke, and as daylight faded, Roscoe sat in the sand, his back to the trunk. Fifteen minutes later, he had stretched out, feet crossed at the ankles, hands clasped over his chest. His cap was pulled down over his eyes, and he was soon snoring.

When the sun was gone and the temperature dropped a few degrees, Roscoe turned on his side and drew his feet up behind him. Jordan draped a khaki fatigue over the wide shoulders and worried that his right-hand man was not well.

Jordan strolled along the beach, keeping an eye on

his companion and their gear. He heard Paul Paveli's forty-foot sloop before he saw its lights on the horizon. He imagined he could hear Paul singing, but that was impossible.

Jordan waited until Paul had docked and taken on fuel and supplies. He knew the tiny, wiry Italian could see him. Neither waved, and Jordan felt his wisest course was to head back to Roscoe and let Paul come to him. He thought about waking the young man, but Roscoe was sleeping so soundly that he decided against it.

Finally, Paul approached. His black beard and stringy hair were grayer than Jordan remembered, but he had the same pointed nose, big ears, and telltale, sea-weathered forehead and cheekbones. His black eyes were nearly invisible in the low light.

They embraced, the seaman giving Jordan a viselike bear hug around the waist. "Bad, bad news about your wife, Jordan. I was shocked. You doin' all right?" Jordan nodded and thanked him. "And this must be Rip Van Roscoe?" Paul bent to help carry things to the boat.

Jordan fell in a step behind. "I'm worried about him. Young, energetic, an ox, but out of sorts the last few days."

Paul turned to look back. "Just looks tired to me. You'll both sleep well on my rig. Not fancy, but comfortable. You got the cash, Jordan? This is gonna be a risky one, ya know."

"Roscoe has it. Need it now?"

The Italian shook his head. "One more trip with your junk and then it'll take both of us to load sleepin' beauty."

Jordan laughed. "I'll wake him." He looked around the boat. Although the sloop was a fraction of the size of the frigate, there was living, walking, breathing, eating, and sleeping space.

Paul moved close to Jordan and stood with his hands on his hips. "He's the only thing left on the beach. I'll leave him to you. Listen, we're gonna be a little heavy with the extra fuel I needed to store to get us all the way to the harbor at San Lorenzo. But I'm gonna stoke 'er up and do some hard pushin' tonight. See how much we can get accomplished. Once she's up to speed, you can hold 'er a while and I'll make you boys a hot meal. Beans and corn meal. I'll even see if I can scrounge up some canned meat chunks. Good stuff. U.S. government surplus."

To Jordan it sounded like heaven. He went ashore and knelt near Roscoe, wondering if he had looked that zeroed-out when he had taken the sodium pentothal. He put a hand on Roscoe's shoulder.

"Time to get aboard, big guy." Roscoe didn't stir. Jordan patted him gently. "Let's go, Roscoe." Still no reaction. Jordan shook him and spoke loudly in his ear. "Get up, Roscoe. We've got to move!"

"Huh?"

"Come on. Let's get up." The man staggered to his feet and walked stiff-legged toward the sloop. On board Jordan guided him to a built-in cot where Roscoe collapsed and immediately slept again.

Paul leaned close to look at him. "A young one, ain't he? I'll bet he never woke up. Won't remember the walk to the boat. Should I fix him anything to eat?"

"Maybe you'd better. Otherwise *you* can deal with him if he wakes up hungry while we're eating."

But Roscoe didn't wake up for dinner. At midnight, when Paul and Jordan had finished bringing each other up to date since their last visit, Roscoe had not changed position. Jordan threw a wool blanket over him.

"Paul, he's shivering."

"It's cooling down, Jordie, but not that much. Give 'im another blanket. I got plenty."

Jordan spread another blanket on him and heard his teeth chattering. "Chills. Wonder if he's got a fever."

"If he does, it'll wake him up and we can fill him full of aspirin, huh?"

"I hope so."

"You're not worrying about malaria, are you, Jordan?"

"That crossed my mind. You know, if he's got it, he'll be no good to me. He could be out of commission for weeks. And what would I do with him?"

Paveli shook his head. "If it's malaria, and we can't treat it with chloroquine or primaquine, you're gonna wind up leaving him in Tumaco or Valdez. There isn't much you or I could do for him."

"You've got medication?"

"Just those two. If it's your basic treatable type, we might be in luck. Can't guarantee how fresh the stuff is. Never opened."

"Should be good then. Worth a try later, but let's not assume the worst. I'll sleep near him and try to get some medication down him at the first sign he's awake."

Paveli let Jordan pilot the craft while he dug in his supplies for the malaria medicine. "What's he supposed to be doing for you, anyway? I mean, without tellin' me any specifics."

"I really can't say, Pauly. I'm sorry. The most I can tell you is that he could wind up as my body guard or fellow soldier. Clear enough?"

Paul nodded. "I wasn't trying to pry. He a good man?"

Jordan shrugged. "Haven't seen him in action yet, but I'll say this: I'd rather be on his side than not. Strictly mercenary, you know?"

"Just like me."

"I don't believe that for a second, Pauly. You care."

"I care for friends, not ideas."

"Sure. You care for Harley because of his ideas. Right?"

Paveli cocked his head and nodded in resignation. "So, what do I know? I guess I'd work for Harley for nothing. And I wouldn't work for the other side for any price, if you know what I mean."

"I know."

Paul smiled wide. "But, hey, a deal is a deal and I'm not doin' this job free."

Jordan laughed and clapped him on the shoulder. "Well, Roscoe's got the money. If you want to wake a sick giant, he's all yours."

Paul waved him off and they switched places. Jordan approached Roscoe. The mercenary's body was shaking and heaving. Jordan put the chilly back of his hand against the big man's forehead, "I don't like this."

Paul hollered over. "What's the story?"

"Bad news. High fever. We've got a sick man on our hands."

"Need some help?"

"Maybe."

Paul cut the engine and let the boat drift. Jordan stepped aside as he approached. "He's hot, but shivering. Pretty ironic, Pauly. Looks like my greatest strength is going to be my biggest weakness."

"Don't give up too soon, kid. Let's get 'im sat up and you can pour somethin' down him. Wanna start with aspirin?"

"How much should I give him?"

Paveli shrugged. "A handful, I s'pose."

"No, I'd rather go straight to the strong stuff."

Paveli nodded slowly. "He's your responsibility, Jordan. I don't know doses for that stuff either. Pretty potent, though. I oughta know."

"You've suffered?"

"You betcha."

"What do you use?"

"Prima, but that's only after I was tested and experimented on and everything."

"But you must've got your malaria down here some-where, huh?"

"Maybe. Or could have been in Europe, who knows? If you wanna try primaquine because I use it, that's up to you. Maybe neither of them will work, so one's just as good or bad as the other."

"Encouraging."

Paveli shrugged again. "Your business has always been riskier than mine, Jordan."

"Help me sit him up."

Jordan studied the tiny bottle in the scant light and pried the cap off. He didn't know if the medicine should smell strong or weak, but he assumed it was fresh when he heard air rush in as he opened the bottle. He replaced the cap, buried the bottle in his palm, and wrestled Roscoe to an upright position.

Roscoe groaned and struggled weakly. Jordan slapped his face a few times. "Let's get some medicine down you, big guy. How 'bout it?"

Roscoe stirred and squinted at Jordan. "When's your friend gettin' here?"

"He's here! We're on his boat!"

"He'd better hurry. Tired of lyin' on this beach. Hot, Jordan. Hot."

"Take a drink."

"Whatcha got?"

"Something cold. Refreshing."

Roscoe held out a hand. Jordan ignored it.

"Here, I'll give you a drink. Open up."

Like a child, Roscoe opened his mouth and tilted his head back. Jordan assumed he would gag if the medicine tasted anything like it smelled, so he decided to pour in as much as he could, hoping Roscoe would swallow enough to make a difference.

He put the bottle to Roscoe's lips and upended it. A

huge swallow was followed by a gurgle and a roar. Then the big man swore. "What was that?"

"Good for ya. Medicine. You need it. You're sick."

"I'm tired!"

"Sure you are. Let's get you back down."

"Hot, Jordan! Gotta take my coat off. Hot!"

Jordan looked at Paul. There would be little arguing with Roscoe. Paul shook his head. "He's your patient."

Jordan helped him get the coat off. Then Roscoe wanted his shirt off. Soon he lay there bare chested, barefoot, wearing only khaki camouflage pants. He was sweating and breathing heavily. "It's so hot, Jordan. So hot."

Paveli went off to start the engine. Jordan knelt next to Roscoe and tried to calm him. "You're sick, Roscoe. High fever. That's why you're hot. It may be malaria. I gave you some medicine. The fever should come down now. Try to relax."

"Hot. Too hot."

"I know, partner, but you've got to lie still and you should be covered."

"No covers!"

"All right. But at least lie still, okay?"

Roscoe put his hands behind his back and stopped fidgeting. Jordan found it hard to believe he wasn't freezing in the chilly ocean breeze with the boat at full power. Roscoe took a labored breath and seemed to hiss, as if the effort made him hotter.

When the big man's breathing evened out, Jordan wondered if he was asleep. Roscoe still squirmed as if he were uncomfortable and hot. Jordan touched his forehead. Still warm. Maybe not as hot as before. Or was that wishful thinking?

Eventually Roscoe involuntarily curled up, and his hands were tucked under his chin. Jordan leaned close to monitor the steady breathing, then piled blankets on the man. He met no resistance. He fished through Roscoe's shirt and jacket pockets until he found a roll of large American bills.

Jordan paid Paul and settled into his own cot. He was more than a continent away from home, with mystery behind and ahead of him, and still his dreams raced immediately to Rosemary.

But he awoke with Cydya on his mind. Something gnawed at him. That same something bothered him for hours in the sun, while he helped Paul guide the boat through the ocean, played nursemaid to Roscoe, and planned strategy for his mission.

Roscoe seemed to be coming around, gaining strength. Only then did Jordan realize how panicky he had been. He hadn't allowed his fears to invade his conscious mind until Roscoe seemed out of danger, and now he wondered what he would have done without help in a strange and unforgiving climate with an agenda of unknowns before him.

Sixteen

Just before midnight Monday, Paul Paveli shut down the engine on his fishing vessel and raised a tattered sail. The balmy tropical air made Jordan feel good, and he was encouraged by Roscoe's recovery.

Roscoe had been more active that day and had even engaged in conversation. He was reluctant to say much in front of Paveli, but when he had the chance, he recounted to Jordan more of their instructions from Harley Rollins.

Paveli maneuvered the craft between rocky bluffs north of the harbor town of San Lorenzo. Jordan and Roscoe kept their eyes on the shore, but neither detected a signal from their contacts. Jordan looked at Roscoe. "Still feeling weak?"

The younger man nodded. "I'll carry my share, though."

"No, you won't. Let me do the lugging tonight. Save your strength for the trip into the interior."

"There's nothing to riding a cycle. I'll be all right."

Paveli kept his sloop as close to the rocks as he dared. "Want me to hang around until you've made contact?"

Roscoe shook his head. "Nah. You're probably scarin' 'em off as it is."

Paul shrugged. "Probably." He shook Roscoe's hand and clapped him on the back. "Stay well."

Jordan embraced Paul. "Be careful."

"I will. Greet Harley for me when you get back."

"*If* we get back."

More than half an hour later, after Jordan and Roscoe

had slogged ashore in the foot-deep water with Jordan carrying most of the gear, they heard Paul start the engine and knew he was dropping the sail. Jordan was amazed at the seaman's ability to elude detection. He'd gotten them into Ecuador easily; now all they had to do was make contact with the Cubans.

Roscoe sat with his head in his hands. "Dull headache. Hungry."

"Me, too. What do we do if they don't show?"

"They'll show. We've still got some sausage, but it's probably gone bad by now. Maybe that's what made me sick."

Jordan hoped that was true. He didn't need a sick man on his hands. Except for some morphine, there was no more medicine, and he didn't relish carrying the behemoth through the jungle, even on a motorcycle. Especially on a motorcycle. "You realize we're pretty vulnerable out here, Roscoe? Unarmed, I mean."

"The only people besides us who would be out here would be people who already know we're here. If they want to take us out, they'll take us out, armed or not."

Jordan shrugged and nodded at the logic. He started to speak, but froze when he heard what sounded like fingers snapping in a staccato rhythm. *Dot dot, dot dash, dot dash dot, dot dash dot dot, dot, dash dot dash dash.* Silence.

Roscoe turned toward Jordan. "Hope they repeat it. I missed a lot."

"I got most of it. I-A-R-L-E-Y."

"Really? You'd think even a couple of Cubans could spell Harley."

"Assuming I missed the first part of the first letter, it could have been four dots."

"An H."

"Yeah." Jordan pursed his lips and whistled back R-O-L-L-I-N-S in short and long bursts of code.

He and Roscoe struggled to their feet, left their gear,

and scrambled in the sand toward the sound. Silhouetted against the sky was the short, stocky figure of a lone man standing beside a motorcycle he had apparently pushed for miles. As Jordan drew closer, he was amazed to see the immense load the bike carried. Stacks of boxes and cans towered high over the Cuban's head.

Roscoe extended his hand. "Harley."

The Cuban ignored his hand at first, secured the cycle by resting the kickstand on a rock, then responded in a thick Spanish accent: "Rollins."

"I'm Roscoe. This is Kettering."

The Cuban did not respond. He collapsed and slumped to the ground. Jordan helped Roscoe lay him on his back. "You're alone?"

"*Sí*. Bad news for you. Message from States. Uncle safe. Mentor dead. Machala Diego staying in Germany. I no go with you. My partner no come. You get no guide."

The message sent Jordan reeling. He wanted to scream, to beat his fists against the rocky ground. Could it be true? Could Harley have sacrificed himself for Dexter Lee? Or was the message a sham? Just phony intelligence? There was no way to tell. And his mind wouldn't let him dwell on it.

"Where's the other cycle?"

"In box." The Cuban nodded toward the pile. "Instructions and tools inside. Easy. Both bikes hold extra gas. Long range."

Jordan could see from the unusual construction of the assembled cycle that several areas had been expanded to hold fuel. "And the weapons?"

The Cuban nodded toward the pile again. "American .45s. Five."

"Should be six."

"Five."

"You received them?"

"My partner."

"He stole one of our guns. Why would he do that?"

"No need. He got plenty of guns."

Jordan kicked at the ground. The Cuban sat up, breathing more easily. "I leave now."

"Why?"

"You're on your own, man."

He ran off across the sand. Roscoe looked to Jordan. "You want me to run him down?"

"No. He's spooked. So's his partner, I guess. I'm surprised they're afraid of Diego, though. Thought they knew what they were getting into."

Roscoe surveyed the pile of gear. "Must be a thousand pounds. Wonder how far he walked this sucker."

"Long enough so we couldn't hear him. Can't believe he didn't hang around for the money."

"Where'd you put my dough after you paid Paul?"

"Same pocket of your jacket."

"Seriously?"

" 'Course. Maybe the other pocket."

"Both empty."

"C'mon, Roscoe."

"Really."

Jordan was furious. "Nine bills, all hundreds, right?"

"Right. You think he pickpocketed me when we laid him down?"

Jordan toyed with the idea of dumping the supplies off the bike and heading after the Cuban. But the noise would have drawn more attention than the money was worth. "Got any more?"

"Four hundred in my shoe and about a thousand in the trunk. I know he didn't get in there."

"How do you know?"

Without a word, Roscoe headed back down toward their gear, moving more quickly than he had for days. When he heard him swear, Jordan knew his hunch had been correct. "What'd they get?"

215

"Just the money . . . no, the morphine, too!" Roscoe swore again. So, the Cuban's partner *had* been there, doubling back behind them while they were helping the other.

Jordan helped Roscoe lug their stuff toward the cycle. "Not like Harley to put us together with a couple of losers."

When all their stuff was together, Jordan sank down onto the sand. He suddenly felt alone, tired, hopeless. He didn't know what to believe. In his gut, he felt Harley was gone. He didn't know why. He'd also been sure Harley wrote the first telegram, and he'd been dead wrong. But now. This. Why was there a ring of truth to the message that had come to him from a cowardly mercenary who had ripped him off?

"Better find the .45s first."

Roscoe was already searching. "Guns here, but no ammo."

"Got to be there somewhere."

"I don't know, Jordan. The rest of the stuff is just canned food, fuel, and cycle parts."

"You mechanical?"

"Yeah, but I can't read Spanish instructions."

"You're kidding."

"Nope."

"I can."

"Whew."

"But I'm not mechanical."

"Wonderful. It'll take a team effort, Jordan."

"Let's get out of the open and find a place to sleep."

By the time they had carted everything into the underbrush and set up a small tent, Roscoe was faint and feverish again. But he wouldn't admit it. Jordan warned him: "Man, I'm tellin' you, we're out of medicine, so don't do this to yourself. Don't do this to me. I need you."

"I won't let you down, Jordan. You know that."

Jordan stretched out his sleeping bag. "I know nothing. All I know is that you're strong and agile and not as dense as you'd like me to believe. For all I know, you could steal the guns and the cycle and I'd be in this thing alone."

Roscoe studied him for a moment. "Yeah, well, maybe that'll keep you on your toes. You'll sleep lighter. More alert."

Jordan chuckled, but he ached at the thought of losing Harley. Though they hadn't been close for three years, no one in his life had ever meant as much to him. Not Dexter Lee. Not Rosemary—not really. Not even Cydya.

He wanted to bury his head and sob, but he knew his physical and mental training had been complete when he could almost feel his mind shift gears. He was into the opposite trigger mode and his mind raced with the schedule for the next morning. He wanted to sleep deep and sound and then rise at dawn to assemble the other bike.

Roscoe lay on his back and sighed. "Think our Cuban friends'll be back for more?"

Jordan turned on his side. "Not unless they think I'm totally unprepared." From deep inside his bedroll he produced two full clips of .45-caliber ammunition. "It may be all we have, but it'll be more than enough."

Roscoe traded him a weapon for one of the clips and they loaded the guns. "For tonight, maybe. But is this all there is for Diego, too?"

"Hey, we're only after him and a few companions, right? We're not aiming for the hostages."

Jordan slept soundly, but he awoke well before dawn and his first thought was to mourn for Harley. Much as he tried to tell himself it was just a lie told by the Cuban to throw him off, he couldn't shake his dread.

If Harley had been killed, who was behind it? Who knew Harley and his itinerary well enough to pull off such an assassination? He didn't allow himself to consider Cydya's involvement. It couldn't be. It mustn't be. If indeed his wife and his oldest friend were now gone, then he would need the elusive dream that Cydya embodied more than ever.

Roscoe's steady breathing was encouraging. Jordan was tempted to feel his forehead for signs of fever, but didn't want to risk waking him. He thought of trying to doze another half hour, but something caught his eye from far down along the waterfront. A light. Dancing. Moving, as if coming up the beach.

It was a flashlight, he was sure. And no one looking for him—at least anyone who really thought he was nearby—would use a bright beam and give himself away. He imagined he could make out a small figure following his and Roscoe's tracks to where they had first stowed their gear.

He slowly raised himself to his elbows and knees and buried the handle of the .45 deep in his palm. The figure paused at the site, then moved up to where they'd met the Cuban. The flashlight shone around and followed their clear trail in the sand toward the underbrush.

Should he wake Roscoe and risk the half-asleep noises he might emit? Jordan knew he didn't want to be caught on his hands and knees in a small tent when fate sought him out. He slipped out of the tent and circled around to kneel behind foliage where the tracker would have to come if he followed the trail to the tent.

He released the safety on the gun and gingerly cocked it. The figure passed within inches of him. He was about to leap out and press the barrel against the back of the man's head when he recognized him. "Pauly?"

"Ah!" The little man jumped and fell to his knees. "Oh! Jordan! Oh!"

"Pauly, what're you doing here?"

"Jordan, am I glad I found you! I thought you'd be on the trail by now."

"Shh!" He led the Italian out of the underbrush away from the tent.

"Whoever's tryin' to get a hold of you thought it was worth breakin' radio silence, Jordie. At first I almost didn't notice they were sending, but through all the static and everything, I finally made out the message. They even used your names."

"You're not serious."

"Roscoe and Kettering. Repeated several times. Anybody who wanted that message must have heard it. I think it was sent from a U.S. military ship somewhere down here."

"They give any indication of where we are?"

"No, they tried to make it sound like an international call. I wrote it down. It's in code." He swore. "I never thought I'd find you. Hope this is important enough for me to be riskin' my boat." He handed Jordan the slip.

Paveli looked out to his boat. "If they get my boat, I'm with you."

"What do you mean?"

"If I spot anybody nosin' around my boat, I can't go back. I'm in restricted waters. Forget it. I'd be joinin' your expedition."

"Not unless you've got a cycle, you're not."

Paveli held the flashlight so Jordan could read. The old man's handwriting was atrocious, but the message was clear—at least to Jordan.

"DELAY VACATION. TRAVEL AGENT CLOSED FOR GOOD. NEW INFO ON TOUR HOST IN CLOSEST CAPITAL. IGNORE CIGAR SMOKERS. THEY GOT A BETTER DEAL UP THE ROAD. SIGNED, ADVISER."

"You sure you got everything, Paul?"

"They repeated it several times, Jordan. That's the message. Mean anything to you?"

" 'Fraid so. Listen, you got any medicine left?"

"For Roscoe? No. Not any more of the stuff you gave him."

"Morphine?"

"Yeah, I got some."

"Aspirin?"

"Yeah."

"I also need that money we gave you. You know we'll wire it back to you as soon as we can."

"I know. But Jordan, if you want anything off the boat, we've got to get it now. As soon as the sun is up, I'm nothin' but a target. You want anything, you come and get it now."

Jordan followed Paul down to the water, debating what to tell him. The horizon was pink when he filled his pockets with cash and medicine. "I'm leaving Roscoe to recuperate for awhile. What's the closest capital from here?"

Paveli pulled a roll of maps from a drawer. "Looks like Ibarra and Tulcan are about the same."

Jordan looked over his shoulder. "Yeah, but if I go south, Esmeraldas is closer than both, right?"

Paul nodded. "And the message came over the water, so they must've figured they'd catch you before you got started inland. If the message got to you in the jungle, you'd have to figure Tulcan."

"I'll try Esmeraldas."

"Anything else in that message you can tell a curious ol' captain?"

Jordan nodded and swallowed. "Pauly, I'm afraid Harley is dead. Our contact told me he got a message that said my mentor was dead, and Harley was the one who arranged this trip. He's the travel agent."

Paveli looked stunned. "What does the rest of it mean?"

"Nothing I can talk about, except we've already been hoodwinked by the cigar smokers. Our Cuban contacts. Apparently they've been paid more by the other side. Anyway, Paul, I'm pretty sure about Harley, and I thought you'd want to know."

Jordan doubted Paul Paveli had wept in decades, let alone in front of anyone. Now the old seaman cursed the rising sun and turned his back on Jordan to get his boat ready to move. There was no more talk, no good-byes, just a stiff, formal wave as he pushed off. Harley had been their only link, and Jordan had the feeling they would never see each other again.

In Esmeraldas he would try the International Telephone and Telegraph office for anything addressed to any of his aliases. He would leave Roscoe behind to assemble the other cycle, to use the medicine as necessary, and to get himself in shape for whatever might be left of their original mission.

While Roscoe dozed, Jordan packed necessities and his only change of civilized clothes. Then he fired up the cycle. It brayed harsh and annoyingly, but evidenced enough jumpy power to help him elude any curious authorities.

Roscoe stirred, rolled onto one side and opened his eyes, squinting at Jordan. Jordan told him the news. Roscoe sat up in his sleeping bag, Indian style, like a toddler. He was quiet, shaking his head. Finally he managed to speak. "So, who do you think you're supposed to see in Esmeraldas?"

"Don't know. One of our guys stationed down here, maybe. Might even be CIA, but I doubt it. Wish it was somebody from Washington." Jordan told himself he wouldn't even mind seeing Blake Bauer right then if he could get some definitive word on Harley.

He had been careful to leave enough food and water

for Roscoe, and was about to walk the cycle back up over the rolling sand hills when an explosion from the water rocked the beachhead. He left the motorcycle, grabbed his .45 and hollered to Roscoe.

"Stay with the stuff!"

He scrambled down the rocky shore, tumbling twice, scraping elbows and knees, and reached the water in time to recognize small fragments of Paveli's boat floating in the distance. He realized someone had to have planted a charge in that boat while Paul had been talking with him on the beach.

He scanned the horizon and thought he saw bubbles a hundred yards from the sight of the explosion. *If that's a diver, he'll never reach shore alive,* Jordan vowed. He sprinted up the beach. A head appeared from the water, and the diver pulled off his mask, looking back to see the results of his handiwork.

Paul couldn't have survived, Jordan knew. But why bomb the boat? Did someone think Jordan had been with him? They had to know better.

No way his .45 would be effective from that distance, so Jordan slipped behind a rock to wait for the diver to swim closer. When the diver was nearly within range, Jordan dropped to a crouch, both hands on the weapon. He edged out onto the shore and drew a bead. The diver was still a miniscule target, but incentive and adrenalin were on Jordan's side. Ten feet closer and he knew he could kill the man.

But the diver stopped in the water and bobbed. Jordan heard a motor boat fire up, though he couldn't see it. The diver would wait for the boat and wouldn't get any closer! Jordan had to close the gap himself. He charged into the shallow water and fired, screaming for his partner.

"Roscoe, the boat! The boat!"

Jordan's shot splashed within two feet of the diver

and sent him underwater again. The only possibility now was to sink the boat. It sped wildly into view from behind a bluff, and Jordan fired again. It was no bigger than a row boat. The occupants dove into the hull for cover as the bullet splashed in front of them. Jordan only hoped his shot had not skipped too high off the water. He wanted to put a hole in the craft under the water line. *Where's Roscoe?*

As he aimed again, he heard shots ring out from up near the tent. But Roscoe knew better than that! He couldn't come close from up there! As Jordan listened in horror, a total of nine shots were fired, all with the same, deliberate two seconds between them.

By now the boat had picked up the diver and sped out beyond his range before heading up the coast. Jordan had seven bullets left, and—he feared—no allies. He stayed close to the rocks as he crept up the shore until he was directly beneath the tent site. The way up from there was treacherous and steep, but he had to stay out of sight. That couldn't have been Roscoe firing from the tent.

When Jordan was within sight of the tent, he pressed against a rock and waited, calming his heart and listening for any sound. He heard nothing. He crept to the back of the tent. A light breeze made the flap smack against the side. He wanted to call out for Roscoe, but he had no idea what or whom he might encounter inside.

He crawled along the side, his weapon out in front of him. Satisfied that no one was around, he peered into the tent. The young mercenary was lying on his back, feet and legs spread wide, eyes and mouth open. His weapon lay on his sternum, just beneath his heart, through which nine .45-caliber slugs had passed. Someone had surprised Roscoe, then wasted him with his own weapon.

Jordan trembled, near collapse. He backed out of the tent and stood. "I'm here, you cowards! Try me! Come on!" He wiped his eyes and waved his gun. "There'd better be more than seven of you! Come on! Come on!"

The response was silence and the maddening billowing of the tent flap. Jordan fell to his knees and knew he was alone. More alone than he had ever been in his life. Within seconds he shuddered at his crazed reaction. He could have easily been cut down by snipers. Either they didn't want him or they were gone.

Why had he reacted so impulsively, so unlike himself? It was the carnage. Roscoe was just another in a line of five, *five*, that led back to his wife. While there were still maddening puzzles, one thing was clear. This was more than espionage, more than politics. This could be the start or the end of a world war that would live up to its name.

Jordan had been willing to take on all the Cubans or Russians or Mexicans or South Americans who had killed Paul and Roscoe because it seemed to him that nearly everyone he had cared about was gone. But as he forced his pulse and nervous system to calm down, he realized there was still Uncle Dex, Judy, Ken, and Felix.

But, most important, there were those Soviet planes in the United States. For the future of the country, he vowed never to react irrationally again, no matter who else was slaughtered in an attempt to get at him. He would tune his mind to a sharpness that would make Harley proud, and he would fulfill this mission, even if it was his last.

Seventeen

The twentieth of the month was two days away, and the beach had not proven safe for anyone, but Jordan took the time to bury Roscoe anyway. As he shoveled the last blade of sand over the hole, he thought grimly of his uncle's warnings. To Roscoe, he had said not to wait until it was too late to raise the subject of God. To Jordan, he had said not to wait for Roscoe to raise it. And now Jordan couldn't even bring himself to say anything or pray over the grave.

He carefully made note of the area so he would be able to have someone exhume the body for return to the States, if that ever became necessary. He hid the still-crated cycle and other equipment he couldn't carry and pushed the assembled motorcycle a half mile up the sandy beach to a back road, wondering how the turncoat Cuban had managed such a load. As soon as he hit asphalt, he jumped aboard and slowly got used to the feel of the machine.

Within minutes he had the cycle up to seventy miles an hour, and when no other vehicles were in sight, he opened the throttle all the way. He felt exposed without a helmet and wondered if the Cubans had made off with those as well. The wind felt good in his hair, but the day was heating up.

By midmorning he grew nervous about the stares he was attracting from people in pickup trucks and buses. With only a compass, Jordan kept to the back roads as he tried to stay on course to Esmeraldas, capital of the province of the same name.

He crossed two rivers via bridges before the longest part of the trip, knowing that he would likely have to ferry across the Rio Esmeraldas to get to the coastal capital. The back roads were tortuous and slow, but he felt safer on them. When he came within sight of the big river just before noon, his shirt was soaked and he guessed the temperature at more than ninety.

He rode off the road along the bank until he thought his kidneys would burst. He kept looking for narrow, shallow crossings and was even prepared to wade across with the bike on his shoulders, if necessary.

Eventually he realized he was going to have to head north to Tachina and take the ferry directly across to the capital. At midday, the crossing was busy. Jordan knew he looked conspicuously un-South American, but he refused to return any stares.

As the ferry filled, he doubted whether he'd be able to squeeze on. He didn't want to wait for the next one. The man at the gate held up both hands to signify that the ferry was full, spurring an outburst from the half dozen or so hopefuls in front of Jordan. They jabbered and shouted at the man while Jordan calmly held up an American $100 bill so only the gatekeeper could see it. When any of the others turned, Jordan hid the money in his palm.

The gatekeeper's eyes grew wide and he bellowed in broken English. "Yankee emergency! Medical!" The crowd opened for Jordan. He smiled at the gateman and pressed the bill into his hand. By midafternoon, Jordan was a spectacle in the capital city. He didn't intend to disturb anyone's siesta, but he couldn't wait to get to the telegraph office. When he located it, he was angry at himself. The office was, of course, closed until late afternoon.

He found a spot on a side street to park the bike and to sit in its shadow until the town slowly came back to life. Still ignoring stares from the curious, he made his way back to the telegraph office and entered a swinging screen door that slapped shut with a twangy spring.

Jordan pretended to be more interested in the messages on the walls than in talking to the woman behind the desk. He didn't know which name to use in asking for a message, so he just browsed until he could steal a glance behind her where large envelopes bore the names of recipients. There were just five, and only one appeared to be printed in other than Spanish.

When she reached for the phone, he leaned forward and peered at the name: *Blanc, P. Gaston.* Jordan was rocked to see the name he had used the night his wife was killed. He realized that whoever was using it was intimately acquainted with that episode. He also realized he had no identification. Even here, he knew, the receptionist would require something of him. His mind raced.

Would he be able to get a phony I.D. on the black market? How long would it take and what was the risk? The woman hung up and smiled at him, speaking pleasantly. In his best French accent, he tried to speak very poor, rudimentary Spanish, telling her he didn't understand her language.

He sputtered in French, pointing to his message. She asked for identification and pantomimed reaching in her back pocket. Jordan pleaded with her in French and flashed another big American bill. He was near tears by the time she smiled at him, took the bill, gave him a few pesos in return, and handed him the message. He hurried outside, tearing at the envelope.

WELCOME. YOU ARE BOOKED AT THE ESMERALDAS GRANDE. DINNER AT NINE IN THE LOUNGE. SIGNED, ADVISER.

Jordan wheeled his cycle onto a major street and stopped in front of a taxi, drawing an angry honk and shouts from the passengers. He leaned in the driver's window and shouted. "Esmeraldas Grande?"

The driver cursed him in Spanish, but pointed north and held up two fingers, then pointed to the right and held up one. Jordan found the place quickly. It was magnificent. Had he been in a normal state of mind, the breathtaking marble lobby would have made him feel like a pilgrim at the portals of heaven. Under present circumstances, however, the reception area had an antiseptic, funereal feel. Jordan was sticky and miserable and desperately in need of a shave and shower.

Nothing was more representative of the contrasts in the busy capital than the palatial Grande Hotel. Within its shadow lay squalor, yet inside its revolving doors was an air-conditioned world of opulence. Apart from the grim task at hand, such comfort would have been just what Jordan's weary body and mind needed.

He approached the desk. "Blanc."

The clerk asked in three languages which he preferred—Spanish, French, or English. To remain in character, he chose French. He couldn't relax until he had changed one of his hundreds, tipped the bellman, checked his room, and double-locked his door. When he was certain he was finally alone and safe, he shaved and showered, letting the questions roll around in his head.

Something was working on him, but it wasn't coming together. He dug deep into his pack and laid out slip-on shoes, socks, knit pants, a cotton pullover shirt, and a light sportscoat. They were a mass of wrinkles. He hung them over the shower rod, turned on the hot water, and closed the door to let the steam smooth them out.

He lay on the bed in his underwear, his .45 in his hand. There were three hours before he was expected at dinner, and he needed the time to rest and think. Was his "adviser" CIA, NSA, or military? Could he be someone in Ecuadoran intelligence? Whoever it was had used his French alias, so he must have had contact with Rollins, Granger, or Williamsby. Of course, there were those in the NSA who knew of the Blanc alias from the past, but they wouldn't have known where to find him if Harley was really dead, unless Felix had briefed them. Whoever it was had to know what had happened to Harley.

In his anxiety, he needed every ounce of mind training he'd ever learned to allow himself to sleep. But he accomplished it as a tribute to Harley. As he dropped off, Jordan tried to focus on one set of questions, hoping his subconscious mind could make the answers fit together somehow as he slept. He wondered why the NSA thought he had fired weapons he hadn't fired? How did someone get past NSA security to level his house? How was he tracked to Muskegon? How had they gotten to Harley? And why had Cydya been talking to Felix?

When Jordan awoke, one thing was clear: He needed to know who his "adviser" was before he dined with him at nine. He also needed to be armed. He checked his watch. It was only seven, but he was anxious. He paced the room, sifting the details, trying to force them to make sense. He dressed, then wished he hadn't because he felt too warm. He left his room and went to the lounge to scout out casually which table would give him the best view of the rest of the place, particularly the entrance. He reserved the table for eight-thirty, pressing more money into yet another palm.

By eight o'clock he was back in his room, not sure whether he was going to be briefed by someone who would add to his knowledge of his prey, or whether he was about to become the prey himself. Half an hour later, he left for the lounge again with the .45 in his waistband at the back. Calming himself was more of a chore than he expected. If there was anything he hated, it was the unknown. Finding out, knowing in advance, setting up his own scenarios had been his specialty for twenty years.

And now, inside a few weeks, his wife had been slaughtered, an old friend driven to suicide, his home demolished, his oldest, dearest friend killed, a valued contact man and sailor eliminated, and Harley's hand-picked compatriot for him assassinated while Jordan was within earshot.

He felt more dread with every step. Was he foolish to subject himself to this surprise? The table was placed well, and he would have some protection, being armed and in public and—he hoped—already seated and able to get a good look at his adviser as he approached. Yet Jordan still felt vulnerable, the one feeling that could gnaw at him until he was ready to change plans at the last minute, stand up his host, and wait in his room until trouble came knocking.

Maybe he should stake out his own room and see who came asking for Gaston Blanc. There was no sense sitting there with his back to the wall and his gun out if he was hopelessly outnumbered. Or if his adviser was a friend.

Jordan decided that within the next twenty seconds he would make his decision and either go through with his original plan and wait in the restaurant, or retreat and regroup for a more controllable situation. But he was distracted as he passed a bank of pay telephones. Felix! Felix was on the phone with his back to him!

Tall, black-haired, and double-knit clad, the image was so comforting that Jordan felt weak-kneed. What a relief! Felix would know what happened to Harley. He would know everything. And he would care. Things couldn't be better!

He approached the big man from behind and gently put a hand on his shoulder. Felix told his party to hold on a second and turned to see who had greeted him. But it wasn't Felix! Jordan was stunned. "Sorry, sir. Mistook you for someone. Sorry."

The man on the phone smiled and went back to his

conversation. Jordan was embarrassed, but worse, he was confused. He had wanted so badly for the man to be Felix that he now found it hard to believe he'd been wrong. In the lounge, the head waiter smiled at him.

"Your eight-thirty table is ready, Señor Blanc."

The table in the back was set for two, and Jordan took the seat that faced the entrance. He told the waiter his guest would not arrive for half an hour and that he would not care for anything until then.

Jordan's mind was such a jumble that he pressed his fingers to his temples and shut his eyes. Mistaking that man on the phone for Felix had made something fall into place. He was sure his adviser was Felix. It had to be Felix! Felix knew him well. He knew Harley well. He would have known Jordan was meeting his wife in London after his meeting with Stanley Stuart in Frankfurt. Lister blew the assignment, missing the fact that Jordan and his wife would not be on the same plane, but the hit directive had to have come from Felix.

Felix had to be the high-level NSA man that Stu had warned him about—though Stu never suspected! Felix had removed all suspicion from himself by accompanying Jordan back to the States. He had access to the house, to the weapons, to Harley's confidences in England while Jordan was in Muskegon. He could have planted the bomb, fired Jordan's weapons, and then had the NSA-style bug planted outside Dexter Lee's home to keep track of Jordan. He could have sent the telegram in an attempt to keep Jordan at his uncle's home until it was bombed or ambushed.

He must have killed Harley trying to get at Jordan. And once Harley was out of the picture, Felix tried to jump back in as Jordan's protector by sending the cable Paul Paveli received. But that had to just be an attempt to keep Jordan from his assignment. If Harley was dead, who else would know where to reach Jordan?

231

Jordan couldn't imagine a motive besides greed or lust for power. Felix was one of his oldest and most-favored acquaintances in the agency. True, he had been passed over as a mentor for one of the new recruits when Harley had Jordan and Stu was assigned a protégé. And before Felix was named BRUSA director six years before, he had been an expert on radar as the U.S.'s last line of defense. He was the perfect inside man for the Soviets.

The question was how much Harley had told Felix about what he learned in Frankfurt. Felix must know why Jordan was in Ecuador, and he must also know that Jordan didn't know where in Maldonado Diego and the others would meet regarding the MiG-23s.

Adrenalin pumped through Jordan's body. All Felix had to do was make sure he didn't find out where the meeting was or learn any more about the location or nuclear capabilities of the MiGs. There was no one else alive who could slow the process. How long had Felix been involved with the Soviets? His whole life? It was hard to imagine. Yet even if he was a recent traitor, with some greedy or vengeful motive, it was clear he was well connected. He had already proved able to dispatch terrorist hitmen, bombers, and guerrillas.

And all the while, he was still in the good graces of the NSA director and Deputy Bauer, not to mention Harley and Jordan and virtually every other influential person in the NSA. Felix's connection with Cydya and Interpol jarred Jordan. He didn't know what to believe. Had she really come to Felix, or had he gone to her? Could Felix have known about Jordan and Cydya? Surely Harley had never mentioned it before. He'd kept the information from everybody. And if Cydya was in fact involved in Felix's scheme, why would he have told Harley about her?

Jordan suddenly felt vulnerable again. Felix was

involved, no doubt, but would he send a hired gun? If Felix himself came, would he eliminate Jordan at the first opportunity or would he still pretend to be an ally? It was ten to nine when Jordan casually but quickly stood and strode toward the head waiter. "I'll be back shortly. Would you direct my party to my table? They'll ask for me."

He trotted up one flight of carpeted stairs to a mezzanine portico that overlooked the lounge. There he could loiter inconspicuously with a good view of his table, while anyone sitting there would have to crane awkwardly to notice him.

Jordan kept an eye on the head waiter for any sign of Felix or anyone who looked as if he might have been sent by him. Moments later, a beautiful woman appeared in the lounge. From Jordan's perch, she looked to be in her late thirties, long, lithe, and tanned in a cream-colored chiffon dress. She chatted briefly with the head waiter, then followed him to Jordan's table.

Oh, no, he's not giving away my table! Now Jordan would just have to wait until Felix, or whomever, asked for Gaston Blanc, and the waiter realized he had made a mistake. *I should have ordered something to drink and left the glass there.*

Jordan scanned the room again, but his attention was drawn back to the woman at his table. She sneaked a peek at herself in a mirror from her tiny handbag, and he noticed her hands shaking as she put the bag next to her on the seat and crossed her legs. As she turned to survey the room, Jordan saw her face. Those huge, green eyes. He was staggered. It was Cydya.

He nearly panicked as a half dozen thoughts invaded his mind. He couldn't turn his eyes from her, marveling at how the years had done nothing but enhance her beauty. Jordan felt that if he dared even to blink, she would disappear. No doubt the head waiter had told her that, indeed, Señor Blanc had been there and would be back soon.

So, it was true. She was involved. What was her motive? His legs felt rubbery as he headed back to the stairs. He glanced behind him and moved his weapon from the back of his trousers to the hip pocket of his coat. How ironic to fear that the lost love of his life might soon cut him down in public with, perhaps, a fancy derringer from her handbag.

He could have retreated to his room or checked the lounge for accomplices. But he was so curious, so drawn to her, unable to turn away. He nodded to the head waiter as he strode the length of the lounge and approached her from behind.

The long neck, the majestic carriage, the velvety hair. He would touch her shoulder and greet her by name as he had done to the man at the pay phone. Only, this time, he would not be mistaken. He wondered if his voice would fail him. Somewhere at the periphery of his consciousness, he was aware of his mind trying to shift into the opposite trigger mode, pushing him to be calm. It was no use; he'd have to fake that.

His hand brushed her shoulder as he came around the table and sat across from her. What he said then was more of a quiet pronouncement than a question, because there was no question in his mind.

"Cydya."

She didn't flinch, didn't jump, didn't move. It was as if she had seen him coming. His nervousness, his pain, his anxiety must have been obvious. She looked at him pleasantly, but without a smile. It was as if she knew everything, as if she knew what he was going through and understood.

He was looking into the green eyes of the twenty-year-old he dreamed of. The expression, the direct look, the knowing gaze had not changed. She leaned forward and delicately put her elbows on the table, cupping her face in her hands. And when she spoke his name, he was transported to Indonesia. Why had he only ever seen her thousands of miles from home?

"Jordan Kettering."

There was a slightly more mature timber to the voice, but he would have recognized it anywhere, even over the phone. He had questions, but neither the breath nor the nerve to ask them. He was ashamed to realize that he had instinctively slipped his right hand into his jacket pocket as he sat down and now sat there with his fingers wrapped around a .45. He could no more shoot this woman than he could shoot a member of his own family. If she had a part in any of the deaths that surrounded him or was involved in a plot to attack her own homeland from within, he'd just as soon she dropped him on the spot. He knew that feeling would pass, but at the moment he was only impressed that something, someone, had been able to override his mind training, at least for a while.

He sensed that his face had flushed as he stared at her. She was radiant. But what was she doing here? He didn't have to ask. Jordan noticed a waiter approaching and finally spoke again to Cydya, "Are you hungry?"

She smiled and shook her head. He pressed a bill into the waiter's hand and whispered. "We'd like to be left alone for a couple of hours."

"*Sí. Bueno.*"

Cydya was still smiling. "We meet in the strangest places." How like her younger self she was! So glib, so warm.

He nearly laughed. "Cydya, forgive me, but I wasn't expecting you."

"Really? Whom were you expecting? Harley?"

Was she being sarcastic? She had to know Harley was dead if Felix had sent her. "Not funny. I was expecting Granger. Is he here?"

Her smile faded. She quickly reached out and covered the back of his hand with her palm.

"Jordan, Felix Granger thinks you're dead. He thinks Harley's dead, too."

"Harley's alive?"

"Oh, Jordan, yes. I'm sorry. We thought you'd see through that message. In case Felix's people intercepted the message to the boat, we wanted them to think you were being informed of Harley's death. That couldn't be better for us right now, but I'm so sorry you were misled. I know how close you are to Harley."

"That's all right if Harley's alive. But if you're telling the truth, then that message also told them that Roscoe and I were still alive, if not exactly where we were. I'm so confused now, you'll have to straighten me out."

"I will, Jordan. I'll tell you everything. I've been involved in this only since the night you left Muskegon with that mercenary Harley hired. Roscoe?"

"Right."

"Is he with you, Jordan?"

Jordan still hadn't heard enough to know whether to tell her he had buried Roscoe that very morning. "No, I left him back where Paveli dropped us."

"And, of course, Mr. Paveli got our message to you because here you are."

Jordan nodded, not smiling. He wondered if she was aware of Paveli's tragedy. "You'd better start from the beginning, Cydya."

"Right. Well, one morning last week, I got a call at Interpol from Mr. Rollins. He said it was 3:00 A.M. in Muskegon, but he'd been thinking about me and he wanted to come and talk to me right away, if that was all right."

"You didn't even know him, did you?"

"Well, yes. I had met him in Indonesia, but at the time I thought he was CIA."

Jordan shook his head, amazed. "That dog! What was his scheme there?"

"He just said he was checking on other branches of the U.S. government and whether they were trying to infiltrate the Peace Corps. He wanted to know if I had any knowledge of anyone doing that. I told him I didn't and he asked that I not mention our meeting to anyone."

"You didn't even tell me. I didn't know he was in Indonesia when I was, the second time at least."

"I know. I learned that later. But I decided not to tell you because I knew my work with Interpol was likely to involve a lot of confidences and I wanted to see if I could handle it. The incident didn't seem significant at the time. I certainly didn't suspect you were with the NSA. I wouldn't have known what that was back then anyway.

"Shortly after I arrived in France and began at Interpol, Mr. Rollins visited me again and admitted he was with the NSA and that he and some associates had actually been evaluating your performance. In a way, I was proud of you that you had said nothing about your real mission in Indonesia, but my pride may not have shown through. I'm afraid I wasn't very good at covering my feelings about our, you know, our broken—."

"Relationship."

"Well, that's what I thought it was, Jordan, but when I learned you were actually an NSA trainee, I wondered if we'd had a real relationship. Mr. Rollins said I didn't have to answer any of his personal questions, but he did want to know if I thought we would eventually marry. I felt almost as if I were betraying you, Jordan, but since you had made it clear in your letter, I told him no, there was not going to be a future for us."

Jordan was reeling from the revelation that Harley had met and talked with Cydya twice in person and who knew how many times by phone or correspondence over the years. He wanted to assure her that their relationship had been real and not affected by his NSA involvement, but that would have to wait.

"Cydya, can I ask you something?"

"Anything."

"Did Harley ask you about the night we spent in Jakarta?"

Cydya looked away for the first time since he had sat down with her. When she looked back, her eyes were moist.

"No, he didn't. Did he ask you about it?"

Jordan nodded. "I just wondered if he had heard about it from you first."

She shook her head. "So, you're saying he knew about it before he came to see me?"

"Yes." Jordan entwined his fingers and rested his chin on them. "Did you keep in touch with him then—after that, I mean?"

"No. I never heard from him again until last week. I did keep tabs on you, though. I suppose you figured that. You know, at Interpol we have files on almost everyone, from international criminals to everybody in intelligence in the world."

Jordan was embarrassed. "So, what have I been up to?"

"You've been everything I knew you would be, except I confess I wondered if you'd have staying power when things got tight." Jordan winced, and she continued. "You're a globe-trotting specialist in political and criminal undercover work, the best disguise man in the business. In fact, you're somewhat in disguise now, hiding blond hair that hasn't grayed yet. A good husband and father of two, Judith and Kenneth, bright and talented children." She hesitated, as if remembering. "Oh, Jordan, I was so sorry to hear about your wife. I didn't know until Mr. Rollins told me late that evening he called. He flew to France that very day."

"Thank you."

"I'm sure she was a wonderful woman." Cydya's eyes filled with tears again. She opened her small bag and searched for a tissue. Not finding one, she closed the bag and stood. "I'm sorry. I'll be right back."

As she hurried away, Jordan impulsively ran his hand over the bag she had left on the table. Nothing hard or heavy. Still, he was curious enough to open it and feel through the contents. Nothing but the usual. He felt guilty and paranoid for having his weapon in his jacket pocket. He quickly replaced it in his waistband at the back.

Was he being set up? He told himself not to be careless. For all he knew, she could have dreamed up this whole story by piecing together information from Felix. Had she left the bag on purpose to put his mind at ease, all the while planning to come back with a weapon? There had been nothing in her manner that indicated she felt she deserved vengeance. An answer to her letters, an apology for running from her perhaps, but not revenge.

What were the odds that she was the same, straightforward woman she had been when he met her? That would be too good to be true. One thing that stunned him about her story of Harley's first visit with her in Indonesia was that she had kept it from him back then. To his knowledge, she had never kept anything else from him.

In the event that she was telling him the truth, which he so badly wanted to believe, what would be the harm in showing off a bit of his memory from more than twenty years ago? He signaled the waiter. "Is your lobster good?"

"Oh, sí! Fresh from the Pacific everyday!"

While she was gone, Jordan ordered her favorite meal, everything from the lobster tail to the salad dressing. The waiter disappeared just before she returned. As she sat down, she whispered, "You know, Jordan, I am getting a little hungry now."

"Me too, but let's wait a bit longer. There's so much more I need to hear."

Eighteen

Jordan could not, would not be played the fool by someone simply because he had bailed out of an adolescent romance. In his heart he knew it had been more than that, but he didn't know what she thought. Could she have held a grudge all these years? He had trusted Felix Granger almost like a member of his family. Yet now it was clear that Felix, whom Jordan had once watched torturing a fly to pass the time, was slowly pulling off Jordan's wings and would crush him between his thumb and forefinger at the first opportunity.

Could Cydya be Felix's pawn? Had he somehow learned of her despite Harley's efforts to suppress the files? What else had Harley done or said that Jordan never knew about? Rosemary was dead, Stanley Stuart was dead, Roscoe was most certainly dead, and Harley could be dead for all Jordan knew. This was no time to let his emotions take over. He took the offensive.

"Felix told Harley that you wrote to his office, officially requesting information on me for Interpol, and that you later visited him on your own and admitted your interest was personal. Is that true?"

"No." Her gaze was steady and there was no dilation of the pupils. "As I told Mr. Rollins, I was at BRUSA in London on Interpol business and asked an agent if he was aware of an American-based operative named Jordan Kettering. He said of course, but that he had never met you. He said his boss was an old friend of yours and then he introduced me to Mr. Granger. Frankly, I was impressed with him, the down-home charm, the wit, the personal interest."

"What did you tell him about us?"

"Precious little. I told him I had met you when we were both in the Peace Corps and that we had dated. He offered to remember me to you and I asked him if he would please not do that. He agreed and didn't ask me why not."

"What *was* your reason, Cydya?"

She looked up and took a deep breath. "Jordan, it was clear to me that if you wanted any reminder of me, you knew where I was. Not only did you apparently not read my letters, but neither did I hear one word from you over the next twenty-plus years. Of course, once I knew you were married, I didn't expect to. I knew your principles. I shared them." Her voice had grown shaky and she was unable to continue.

"Felix never contacted you again, nor you him?" She shook her head. "Then why did he imply to Harley that you were much more involved in trying to find me, even to the point where you could have had something to do with the attempts on my life?"

Cydya looked directly at Jordan. "Listen to what you're saying. I haven't even finished my story about Mr. Rollins contacting me last week, yet you're letting a Felix Granger color your view of me. It's been a long time, Jordan, but you should know me better than that. Is Felix Granger a credible judge of character?"

Jordan reached across the table and gently took her hand. "No, you're right. I'm sorry. Please finish."

Cydya tilted her head back and lightly shook out her hair. "When I told Mr. Rollins about my one, brief encounter with Felix Granger, I got the impression he believed me. He asked me about my life since he'd seen me last, but he quickly got to the point. He wanted to know if I had been aware of the attempt on your life and of the death of your wife. I was shocked, but in a way, the magnitude of the problem wasn't surprising. For him to call me from the States in the middle of the night and then come immediately to France—well, I knew it had to be something big. I had no idea how big, though."

Cydya said Harley gave her a complete rundown on everything that had happened to Jordan from the time he met with Stanley Stuart until he left for Ecuador. Jordan was dubious and said so. Cydya looked hurt. "So now what, Jordan? Am I supposed to plead with you to believe me?"

"I'm sorry. It just doesn't sound like Harley to tell everything. He's the most tight-lipped man in the business."

"Maybe *he* sensed he could trust me, even if you don't."

It was a shot. "Don't think it's easy for me to sit here unable to pretend that I fully believe you, Cydya. The sad fact is that there is nothing I would rather do. But I've seen people die right and left, and the stakes have never been higher."

Cydya just stared at him, as if to ask what else she could say or do that would put his mind at ease. When she spoke again, her voice was quavery. "Mr. Rollins said that he couldn't sleep the night you left. He rolled the thing over and over in his mind and came to the conclusion that Felix Granger was the only common denominator in the whole mess. He was the only one who knew everything and everyone and had access to you and your house and your weapons."

"As usual, Harley beat me to the solution by a week."

Cydya ignored his remark as if she hadn't heard it or didn't understand it. "He said he was certain that the next step was for someone to try to kill you before you left for South America, and that while Granger knew of the plans, he probably assumed you would be going a few days later than you actually did."

For the first time, Jordan was encouraged. *That* sounded

like Harley. "So he hustled back to Muskegon to get my uncle out of the house and make it look like both he and I had been there when, what? The place blew?"

She nodded. Jordan smiled, but his mind told him to not jump to conclusions. This could still all be the work of a very crafty Southern mind. *Southern!* Felix was from Mississippi, but his family owned acreage throughout the South! If the Soviet MiGs landed on property Felix owned, there wouldn't be anyone within a hundred miles who would notice or care. No one would come snooping, no one would report unusual activity. If Jordan could be certain about Alabama, then land owned by a Granger would be a good place for U.S. Air Force reconnaissance pilots to start looking.

Jordan's reverie was interrupted by the delivery of their meals. Cydya glowed. "Jordan."

When everything was in place and the servers had left, Jordan felt the need to push just once more. "Cydya, I have to be very frank with you. I want to believe you, but everything you've told me up to now is known by many people within the NSA. True, there are a few nuances that sound like vintage Harley. But isn't there something you can tell me, something that will assure me that you're working with Harley and not someone who just knows him well?" She shook her head and her face contorted to fight back tears. "Cydya, I don't want to offend you, you must understand. Forgive me, but care, worry, wariness—they're occupational hazards. They've allowed me to reach middle age in a short-term business. Listen, I've never begged someone to convince me before. At least be complimented by that."

She began picking at her salad. "Do you remember what you used to do when we shared a meal together?"

She had ignored his plea and he was rattled. "No, Cydya. What did I do?"

"You prayed. You prayed before every meal, whether or not we were alone. It didn't bother you. I was impressed with that. You were a good, devout boy. Are you still?"

He shrugged. "I still believe, if that's what you mean. The devout part is tenuous just now."

A smile played at the corners of her mouth. "Would the fearless international operative have the guts to take the hand of an old flame and ask the blessing right here on the equator in the middle of nowhere, just for old time's sake?"

It was a challenge, hard to compare with the previous challenges of the day, but for some reason no less difficult. Awkwardly he reached for her hand and bowed his head. He was embarrassed. He had not prayed aloud for so long that the only prayer that came to him was a rote phrase that had become meaningless through repetition as a child.

"Lord, for what we are about to receive, may we be truly thankful."

As he opened his eyes and lifted his head, he wondered if he would find himself staring down the barrel of a gun. But all he saw were Cydya's tears and he had to bite the inside of his cheek to prevent his own. He could see that his small gesture had stripped away the years for Cydya. When his hand was atop hers and their eyes were closed and he was whispering that simple line, somehow they had been transported back more than twenty years, across thousands of miles to the land of eternal humidity.

For that instant, he was no longer a middle-aged widower whose world was crashing in on him. He was not a father of two college students, not a professional agent whose old friend was trying to kill him for God knew what reason. He was not a man whose yellow hair was peeking out at the roots of brown-dyed strands.

He was a devout nineteen-year-old who had won her

heart, who had fallen for her so hard, so fast, so completely. And she had come to love him so deeply that they knew nothing would ever come between them.

She had not been a believer as he had been, but when they slept together that last night in Jakarta before he was suddenly called home to his father's funeral, it violated every standard she had ever set for herself. As awkward and fumbling and passionate as they had been, she considered that night a mistake, a failure, wrong, just as much as he did.

He knew she never expected it to come between them. She had assumed that when he got back to Jakarta, he would write to her in France and they would pick up where they left off, except that they would resolve never to sleep together again until after they were married. That was what they both wanted, what they both believed to be right.

But he had written only twice, once to tell her it was over, and once to tell her he would not open any more letters from her. And that's when she had to know she was on her own, her dreams shattered. He knew it had to hurt her to realize that her love and commitment were deeper than his. But there was no arguing it. There was only getting over it. And from the expression on her face when Jordan looked up from praying, he knew she never had.

Cydya pressed a tissue under her eyes and nose. She seemed to force herself to start eating. And she changed the subject.

"Mr. Rollins told me to tell you about the receipt he stole from the evidence in Mr. Stuart's apartment."

Jordan stared at her. Now they were getting somewhere. Or were they? Could Felix have known that? Could JOSAF have recorded that receipt before Harley got there and then reported it missing after he left?

"What was it for, Cydya?"

"For sending a package to Harley at his private post

office box in the States. Jordan, this is delicious and you were sweet to remember."

She was smiling, but he wasn't. His head ached from the possibilities. Had her last comment been intended to keep him off balance? He chastised himself. *You're so paranoid, your own mother couldn't convince you she was trustworthy.*

He knew that if JOSAF had recorded the seemingly insignificant receipt, the address would have been on it.

"What was in the package?"

Cydya's mouth was full. She swallowed and dabbed at her lips before she answered, "Photos of the Soviet planes and a message to Mr. Rollins about the Maldonado meeting."

Jordan held his breath. "Anything else?"

She repeated the question, "Anything else?"

His heart sank. Anyone could guess that Stu would have sent the photos and a message. But who would know what else he sent? Only Harley. And Cydya, if he told her.

She cleared her throat. "A copy of his note to Michala Diego, opting out and recommending Mr. Rollins."

Just as Jordan began to smile and relax, another doubt hit him: *Harley might have told Felix all that before he began to suspect him. JOSAF or the local authorities could have discovered the carbon paper in the apartment.* Jordan was still troubled and couldn't hide it.

Cydya's shoulders sagged. She held up empty hands before Jordan and pleaded with him, "What are you afraid of? What do you want? What do you need? Jordan, face it. You don't have a choice. You have to trust me. If I'm lying, then Harley is dead and Felix knows where you are. But if I'm here because Mr. Rollins sent me, because he was pretending to be dead while actually doubling back to follow Diego to Maldonado, then you have to stick with me."

Jordan had a bite of steak in his cheek. "That's his

plan? Stay out of Felix's sight and follow Diego?" She nodded. "Very risky. Very difficult."

She cocked her head. "He said you'd say that."

That sounds like him, too. He decided to try another tack before answering her question about what he was afraid of. "Cydya, what would you say if I told you that I saw Paul Paveli blown to bits this morning and that I buried Roscoe."

She shoved her meal aside. "Don't play games with me. Don't test me. I'm too tired."

"It's true."

She covered her mouth with her hand. "Oh, Jordan. No. That means Felix knows you're in South America."

Jordan was stony. "You see why I would be wary of anybody associated with this case? I'm sorry, but I have to think Harley wouldn't know who he could trust, and so he wouldn't trust anyone but me."

That hurt her. She wept. "And you trust only him, is that it?"

He threw up his hands and whispered, "Cydya, do you blame me? Do you see what's happening all around me? I want to hear something rock solid that will convince me everything you have told me so far is true and has come straight from Harley—or I'll have an answer to your question."

"Which one?"

"The one about what I'm afraid of."

"I understand what you're afraid of, Jordan, if you saw two men die today. But do you see the position Mr. Rollins is in? What if Felix finds out he escaped the bombing of your uncle's house and *then* something happens to Mr. Rollins? He needed to tell the whole story to someone he could trust, but his options were limited. He trusted his intuition and took a chance on me. I think his confidence was well placed. Do *I* make you fear for your life?"

He stared at her long and hard before answering, "Until I hear something that Felix couldn't have gotten through NSA channels, yes, I fear for my life. I see your tears and I watched your reaction to the news that Paul and Roscoe were dead. If I was talking to the twenty-year-old Cydya LeMonde I knew in Indonesia, I wouldn't think you could fake that. But it's not just my own hide I'm worried about now. If Harley *is* dead and I fail in this mission, then nobody else anywhere can do anything about those MiGs in Alabama, and you know what that means."

Cydya picked up her linen napkin and dabbed her face. "Are you finished eating, Jordan? Could we go for a walk?"

He waved to the waiter. "Check, *por favor.*" Jordan paid in cash and followed Cydya out. She had not tried to meet his last request. Was it because she couldn't? Had she given up? Was he being unreasonable? He didn't think so, not with the security of the United States at stake.

His imagination played games with him, making him wonder if she wasn't taking him somewhere to be eliminated. While her back was to him, he moved his weapon again, this time to his right trouser pocket for easiest access. If he was wrong, which he prayed he was, he would feel like a fool and would owe her a huge apology. Yet he couldn't let down his guard for a minute.

He found himself not wanting to offend her by suggesting that they stay on the main boulevard and avoid the dimly lit side streets, yet he didn't want to die for his manners. Instead, he suggested their route. "On the way to the hotel, I saw a pier with a concrete bench surrounding a miniature lighthouse. Would you like to sit out there?"

She nodded and he touched her elbow as they started toward the ocean. He sensed a stiffness in her gait and told himself it was due to his continuing to reject her after all these years. How he wanted to believe her!

"Would you like my coat around your shoulders?"

She shook her head. It was true the night was warm, even muggy, but she hadn't spoken since she suggested the walk and he was trying to elicit any response. Was her silence an ominous harbinger? He told himself to quit worrying.

Nearly ten minutes later, they reached the sand. She held onto his arm for balance as she removed her shoes, and he was hit with a wave of anxiety he couldn't shake. He searched his mind for the reason. As she held out her hand to return the favor and he slipped off his shoes, he remembered: that same polite gesture had been offered his wife just before she was killed. A man showing courtesy had innocently confirmed to a mistaken terrorist that he had found his target.

They worked their way across the sand a hundred yards to the pier, which jutted another fifty yards into the ocean. The farther they got from the road, the darker it became. With their shoes in one hand and the other hand outstretched for balance, they bumped into each other a couple of times. He thought he heard her giggle, the way she had years ago.

Finally they reached the pier and stepped up out of the sand. They steadied each other while they put on their shoes again, then headed out toward the little lighthouse at the end. The pier was just ten feet wide, yet Jordan didn't feel comfortable with any physical contact except to touch her arm occasionally when she appeared to get too near the edge.

As they came within the radius of the lighthouse, which was solely for pedestrians, Jordan couldn't help but notice that Cydya had virtually not changed in twenty years. He recalled how naturally and easily they had once walked with their arms around each others' waists. Only the years and the circumstances kept him from instinctively reaching for her now.

When they reached the circular bench surrounding the light, Jordan passed Cydya and sat facing the ocean, his back to the beach. She sat a couple of feet away and they both listened to the lazy slap of the waves against the pier. "It is beautiful out here, Jordan. Leave it to you to see this place in the daytime and picture how it would be at night."

He didn't respond. He had always found ocean sounds and smells therapeutic. Cydya's light perfume was other than therapeutic. Jordan turned to look at her as she gazed out onto the water. For years he had not been able to think of her name or picture her face without being reminded of the terrible news about his father.

There had been so much guilt—still was—regarding his relationship with his father. They had never been close, and he had often felt oppressed under the man. It wasn't that his father had died young, just unexpectedly. And for a teenager who had just broken one of the commandments, the news came at the worst possible time.

Jordan had outgrown his fear that his father's death was a direct result of his own sin. Even though Rosemary never knew of Cydya, it was she who had introduced him to a view of God based in love and understanding and forgiveness. His faith had matured over the years, and while he still believed in a righteous, holy, just God, he quit believing that God killed his father to punish him for his sin. Rather, he came to believe that God gave his Son to forgive him for his sin.

When Jordan finally spoke, his voice sounded eerie over the water. "This walk was your idea. Did you have an agenda?"

She turned toward him, and her face, lit from above, looked just as she had looked twenty years before. "Yes.

I want to tell you something, and I want to show you something."

She pulled the handbag from under her arm and removed a wallet. "Jordan, I never married." He nodded. He'd wondered. "I was mad at you, but I never fell out of love with you. I didn't talk about you specifically. There were those, friends and family, who knew I'd had a serious boyfriend. They worried about me. They still do. They wanted me to forget. To forgive. To get on with my life."

It became difficult for her to speak. She stood and moved closer to the water. Jordan leaned forward to hear better. "But I did get on with my life. I compartmentalized my private life—you. And I gave myself to my work. I don't know if you care, but if you do, you might be proud to know that the kid you used to hang around with is the only Interpol employee of either sex to win two personnel citations in the same year." Jordan nodded. He *was* impressed. She shrugged and laughed. "What can I say? They love me."

Jordan smiled. He knew her. He knew she was not boasting. "I'm impressed. I really am."

"So, you see, I didn't just sit pining for you."

He sensed she was fishing for an apology, something, anything. Regardless of his reason, he had dumped her, jilted her, ignored her, rejected her, in effect made it appear that their mistake was her fault. But he wasn't ready to deal with their past, not until he was certain about her role in the present. "You said you had something to show me?"

She popped open the wallet, fat with pictures. She held one photograph up to the light and he leaned close for a better look. "That's Mother and Dad. Their hair's white now, but you'd probably recognize them anyway."

He nodded. "Sure. I remember the pictures you showed me in Indonesia. And I can see the family resemblance."

"And here's my sister and her husband and their kids."

"Good-looking kids."

"Yeah. She's at Vassar. He's working."

"Uh-huh."

She flipped to another photo. "Recognize her?"

" 'Course. It's you."

"Nope. Look again."

He took the wallet from her and held the picture up to the light. "It's you twenty years ago."

She shook her head. "We didn't wear dresses like that in the sixties, Jordan."

"A niece?"

"No."

Jordan was uncomfortable with their small talk, given the reason for their being in Ecuador. He still peered at the photograph, but he grew impatient. "I'm out of guesses. If it's not you, it's a relative, that's certain."

"Katrina."

"Pretty name."

"Pretty girl, don't you think, Jordan?"

"Beautiful girl. I said she looked just like you. How old?"

"Almost twenty-two."

"Who is she?"

"My daughter."

Jordan grimaced. He couldn't help himself. He handed the wallet back, and much as he tried to stifle the sarcasm, it escaped anyway; "You didn't marry, but you didn't waste any time bedding down with someone did you?"

He was ashamed of himself for the remark. He sensed that her mouth was open as if to speak, but he heard nothing and wouldn't look directly at her. What was the matter with him? Was it all right for him to sleep with her in a moment of passion and then run away, but not

253

all right for that to happen with anyone else? He wondered if he would ever outgrow the snap judgments, the black-and-white morality.

Cydya accepted the wallet back, but she sat with it facing Jordan, open to the beautiful young girl. Her voice was barely audible. "You kept track of the years, Jordan. But you didn't keep track of the months. She goes by Katrina LeMonde, but her real last name is Kettering."

Jordan covered his face with his hands. He knew she was still holding the photo open before him and he wanted to see it again, but he couldn't bring himself to look. "Are you sure?"

She stood and looked down on him, pressing the wallet into his hands. "Don't insult me! There was no one after you! No one! I didn't so much as date anyone else! I loved you and you loved me, but when we made a mistake, you ran. Look what you missed."

"Why didn't you tell me?"

"I wrote you about missing two months, but you weren't opening my letters."

"I opened them! I just said I wouldn't. Which letter?"

"The third, but who's counting? You didn't answer any of them."

"Cydya, I never got a third letter!"

He had silenced her, but only momentarily. "And what if you had?"

"I'd have done the right thing."

"The right thing? What would have been the right thing?"

"I would have married you."

She nodded knowingly. "Because I was in trouble."

Jordan blinked back his tears and looked again at his daughter's face. "No!" He was shouting and he didn't care if the sound carried out to the islands. "Because I loved you! God, forgive me, I never stopped loving you!"

Cydya LeMonde gently took the wallet and put it on

the bench next to her bag. Then she embraced the sobbing father of her child and laid her head on his shoulder.

"I'm sorry, Cydya! I was young and scared, but that
was no excuse. And I didn't know. Forgive me, I didn't
know."

She caressed the back of his head and pulled him
closer.

Nineteen

Until midnight, Jordan and Cydya sat by the little lighthouse, interrupting each other with questions. Jordan was compelled to explain himself, to tell her every emotion he had felt about her from the moment he awoke in Jakarta with remorse over their intimacy until a week before when Harley raised the possibility of her involvement in the terrorism.

He found himself curious about the daughter he had never known. He wanted to know everything about her, her tastes, her interests, what she knew of him, what she thought about him. "I want to meet her. Does she want to meet me?"

Cydya shifted uncomfortably. "That's our biggest conflict. We've gotten on so well together, but she's angry with me beyond reason because I will not tell her who you are. I told her that we once loved each other very much and that she was a product of that love, but I also told her that you were now married and that I had no idea whether you had ever told your wife about us. It's been a very, very difficult thing for her, Jordan, yet I just felt I could not do that to you."

"To me?"

"When you get to know her, you'll realize that with the first solid lead, she would have immediately tracked you down and introduced herself."

He was still in shock. "One glimpse of her face and I would have known she was telling the truth. I'd have died." A low whistle escaped his lips. "What would I have done?" It nearly made him smile. *What will Judy and Ken think?*

Cydya told Jordan that she had surprised herself with her reaction to his rejection. "I had dated before, you knew that. I'd even had disappointments. But somehow, even before that night in Jakarta, I believed we were meant for each other."

"I never knew that."

"I wasn't hiding my feelings, but you know that wasn't something a young woman was supposed to say back then. The thing is, Jordan, I felt it so deeply, was so certain, that learning I was pregnant only confirmed it for me. I'm not saying that what we did was right, but after Katrina was born, I never even considered having anyone but you help raise her as her father."

"You have reason to hate me, Cydya."

She smiled. "I know. But I don't. Did for a while. It was a strange, mixed-up emotion. Talk about love/hate. I loved you so deeply I could hardly live without you, and I hated you so much I wanted to punish you. I made Mr. Rollins swear he would never say a word about Katrina."

Jordan shot her a double take. "You're not saying he knew!" She nodded. "I can't believe it!"

"Apparently he's a man of his word, Jordan. I'm moved to learn that he really didn't tell you."

"If he had told me, I'd, I'd—."

"Done what?"

"I don't know what I would have done. I mean, once I was married, what could I have done? I'd have had to tell Rosemary. I would have helped support Katrina." Saying her name stopped him. It sounded so strange, and yet already he felt the tug toward her. "Cydya, I feel I owe you so much. I just want you to believe I didn't know."

"Oh, Jordan, I know. At first I thought you knew and that's why you had dropped me. But Mr. Rollins assured me. He said if you knew, he would know, because he could read you like a book."

Jordan nodded, staring into the distance. "I can't

explain it, Cydya. I actually believed for a while that God was judging me. I had failed so miserably that I just knew we shouldn't see each other again and should try to forget each other."

"I tried that, too, Jordan. It never worked."

"It was my fault. I see that clearly. Even if it hadn't been for the fact that you were, you know, that you had Katrina, I can see that I was wrong. I've known that for a long time, but I didn't trust myself to admit it to you. What if I had made just one contact to apologize, to see how you were doing, to make sure you were married and happy? For all I knew, you were. But my love for you had been so overwhelming, I was afraid it would rush in on me again. And what if I found you had been married several times and didn't even remember me?"

Cydya laughed. "It's not funny, Jordan, except when you contrast it with what my life has really been like. You, through that gorgeous daughter of ours, have dominated my life, probably more than you would have if we'd been married and you'd been gone all the time."

"I wish you could find it within yourself to forgive me, Cydya. I know nothing can repay you for what you have endured, but I would like to help you with Katrina's education, or whatever else she needs."

Cydya looked offended. "Oh, Jordan! This has nothing to do with money or support."

"I know, but I *want* to help. I really do."

She shrugged. "It never crossed my mind. But listen, there were trade-offs. You suffered, too, though you may not have known it. It'll bother you now, the more you think about it, that you had a daughter all these years you never knew."

"It bothers me already. But even without knowing about her, I was drawn to you, Cydya. You'll never know how close I came to looking you up." He touched her shoulder as if she were a fragile, china doll. "We're parents. I can hardly believe that."

She put her hand over his. "You'll love her."

"I do already and I've only seen the picture. Let me see it again."

He lifted the photo to the light. Cydya chuckled. "Jordan, you'll be proud of me. She's devout."

"What do you mean?"

"Just what I said. What do *you* mean when *you* say someone is devout?"

"Tell me."

"You made an impact on me, what can I tell you? I started taking her to church from the beginning. She grew up just like you, Jordan. She's a believer."

"And you, Cydya?"

"Me too, Jordan. I told you all about it in the third letter and promised to raise our child as a Christian."

He shook his head. "I want so badly to meet her, I could leave for Paris tonight."

"We've got a little work to do first, wouldn't you say?"

He nodded. "And I'm tired. Man, am I tired. We'd better get back."

When they reached the sand, he stopped her. "Tell me you believe me. I didn't know."

"I believe you, Jordan."

"And forgive me. Either way, I was wrong."

She avoided his eyes. "You owe me one first."

"What, anything."

"Tell me you believe *me*. Would the mother of your own daughter come to kill you?"

"I believe you."

He interpreted her embrace as forgiveness.

When they picked up their keys at the front desk, the night clerk spoke to Jordan. "Señor Blanc?"

"*Oui?*"

"Your brother-in-law is here."

His eyes met Cydya's and he froze. "I beg your pardon, sir?"

"Your brother-in-law, señor, or another relative. He said you were expecting him."

"Did you—?"

"*Sí*, I gave him an extra key."

"What did he look like?"

"I'm sorry, señor. I didn't notice too much. Average. Dark hair maybe. Middle age."

"American?"

"*Sí*, I believe so."

"Alone?"

"*Sí*."

"He went upstairs?"

"*Sí*."

"Ring my room, please." The clerk dialed his number and handed Jordan the receiver. No answer. "Thank you, sir."

"I am sorry, señor."

Jordan hurried to the elevator, with Cydya right behind him. "Jordan! What are you going to do?"

He didn't answer. If anyone trailed him here, Harley had to be in trouble. "Who knew I was here, Cydya?"

"Only Mr. Rollins. He made the arrangements before he left France. He even wrote the cable for me."

"And no one else saw it?"

"No one but the telegraph office. What are you going to do, Jordan?"

They reached Jordan's floor. "Cydya, does Interpol know you're here?"

She hesitated. "Yes, but Harley cleared that, so they know none of the details."

"Then you are here with diplomatic privileges?"

"After a fashion, yes, but—."

260

"All I want to know is whether you have a weapon."

She hesitated again and Jordan didn't hide his impatience. "Well, yes, I do, Jordan, but don't you? You didn't come through customs. I didn't bring mine to dinner because I thought it would make you suspicious."

"Good thinking." He pulled his gun from his pocket so she could see it, then hid it inside his jacket. "We need to get your gun."

She pushed another button. "I'm on seven, but Jordan, you know Interpol can't be involved in anything political."

"Cydya! This isn't Interpol *or* political. This is someone in my room or waiting somewhere with a key until I'm in bed. Now unless you'd like me to go in there alone, I'd appreciate it if you were with me, and armed. When this whole case blows sky high, you're not going to get in trouble for acting a little outside the bounds of your own agency."

It didn't seem she was gone long enough to change, but within minutes she returned wearing a top and slacks with a bulge in the right front pocket. She was apologetic. "It's just a .22."

"Better than nothing." They stepped out at his floor again. "Stay back about ten feet and let me know if anybody else comes along, other guests, whatever. I'm going to knock a couple of times. If I get no answer, I'll use the key. If the door isn't bolted or chained, I'll move in quickly, weapon up. You want to follow or wait and listen?"

She didn't hesitate. "I'll follow."

"Good. If we go in, I'll pass the bathroom, which is immediately on your left, and cover the room. You've got the bathroom."

She nodded and they headed down the hall. When they were ten feet from the door, she dropped back. He reached the door and knocked. No answer. He put his ear to the door. No sound. He knocked again. Nothing. He glanced back at Cydya. She moved in closer. He moved away from the door to the left and reached out with his right hand to unlock it. It opened a half inch. No bolt, no chain.

He nodded to her and crouched before the door. She stepped directly behind him. No one was in the hall. He pushed off with his left foot and kicked the door open with his right. The door smacked the wall and flew back, forcing Cydya to fend it off with her gun hand. Jordan bounced past the bathroom in a crouch, his .45 in front of him. Cydya pushed open the bathroom door and saw the room was empty. Then she heard Jordan shout:

"Harley, you dog! I could have killed you!"

Rollins was sitting on the bed with his back against the headboard, hands behind his head. He wore street clothes and was barefoot. "I knew you wouldn't do that. I'm an unarmed man." He smiled at Cydya. "Hello, dear."

She collapsed in a chair. "Hi, Mr. Rollins."

Jordan pocketed his weapon. "Why didn't you answer the phone or the door, you scoundrel? Liked to scare me to death."

"Gotta keep my troops in shape. Not too many of you left." Harley had stopped smiling and Jordan knew he wasn't kidding anymore. "So you know about Roscoe and Pauly?"

Rollins sounded tired. "I know, Jordan. Machala Diego and his multinational task force celebrated those hits. He ordered them personally and there wasn't a thing I could do. I was worried to death about you until I talked to Cydya."

"I want Diego, Harley."

"Jordan, you know if we can get by without any firing—."

"I know, but if he does us the favor of resisting—."

262

"Shut the door, Jordie. We've got work to do. I'm bunkin' with you, but we've got an early wake-up call tomorrow."

Jordan looked at Cydya. "We're beat, Harley. She traveled most of the day and I've been up since before dawn. I caught an hour siesta early this evening, but that's it."

"I know. This won't take long. Let me spread some stuff out on the table here." Jordan and Cydya joined him. "I know you didn't expect to see me, but we were wrong about Stu's message. Or maybe he was wrong. Anyway, the twentieth is no meeting date. That's the day Diego and his people truck warheads from a ship to an airport for the flight into the States."

"Why? What happened?"

"The Maldonado meeting was today. Everything's set for . . . well, we're after midnight now, so everything's set for tomorrow. About twenty-eight, twenty-nine hours from now."

Jordan was amazed. "How do you know all this?"

Harley sat back with a self-satisfied look. "Wasn't easy. I staked out Diego's place in Frankfurt a few days ago and recognized one of his security men. He's been loyal to Diego for two years and apparently has won his trust. His name is Ricardo Sanchez. That should ring a bell with you, Cydya."

"Sure does. One of the FBI's ten most wanted. We thought he was in the Far East."

"So did I, but it was him all right, and in Frankfurt. I followed him home, knowing he would notice me. He's one of the best, very elusive. I employed a couple of local contacts to bring him back to the States, and we made a deal."

"You and Sanchez?"

"Yup. He's got a twenty-year sentence hanging over his head for international flight to avoid prosecution. It's automatic. When he sets foot in the U.S., twenty years is minimum, no parole."

"So he jumped you?"

Harley nodded. "Probably would have killed me if I hadn't had help. This is a strong boy. The three of us wrestled him to the ground and dragged him to his room, where we came to an amicable settlement. I told him I'd see to it that he served no more than seven years if he told Diego he had to get home to his father's funeral and that he recommended his oldest and most trusted bodyguard as his replacement. Yours truly. It worked perfectly. It was risky, because there are a lot of ways for him to warn Diego now. But he'll be incommunicado for a few weeks anyway."

"You used an alias?"

"Oh, yeah. Sure. Charlie Epson. An old standby. Good thing I did, too. I wasn't with Diego a day and a half before he spat out his contempt for the NSA and Stanley Stuart, who tried to pawn Harley Rollins off on him. 'Do you know who that is?' he asks me. 'Who?' I say. He says, 'Only the best friend of the guy who met with Stuart, the one we tried to kill in London.' He blamed that screw-up on Felix. Doesn't have much good to say about him. A couple of days later, he informed the group happily that 'Felix got Rollins.' I had wondered how long it would take that news to get to him."

Cydya leaned forward. "So he's convinced you're dead?"

"Yeah, while I'm actually one of his three body-guards. Don't you love it? We rotate, forty-eight hours on, forty-eight off. Since I'm off, he sent me on ahead to the port city in the Yucatán Peninsula to make sure everything is in place. I have to be there when he arrives at midnight tomorrow night to assure him that every-thing is on schedule."

Harley smoothed out a hand-drawn map and turned it right side up for Jordan and Cydya. "A Government of

Mexico ship is expected before dawn on the twentieth. The ship is bringing warheads for the MiG-23s from Las Martinas, Cuba. It will dock at the harbor in Progreso on the Campeche Bank of the Yucatán Peninsula. Then just before sunrise, a truck will leave the ship—."

"Wait a second, the truck is coming with the ship?"

"Right. From there it's about thirty miles to Mérida where there's an airport with a runway long enough to get a jet off the ground toward Alabama. Look at this, Jordan." He pulled another map from his pile. "See how short that flight will be, straight into the United States from the peninsula? We're farther than that from Yucatán right now."

"How are we supposed to get there and what are we supposed to do when we get there?"

"Well, I got here the same way you did, but we're going to have to fly to Mérida. Basically, our job is to stall them, Jordan. I'd like to see that ship stay right in the harbor, but if they get to the airport, the plane must not take off. I'm in touch with the only man from the Pentagon who trusts me implicitly, and he has the power to dispatch military aid at a moment's notice. I want to wait to give him all the details until we're certain that ship is on its way to Progreso. You know by the time we get there, Felix could have found out that I'm with Diego. Or Diego could find out who I really am."

"Then what?"

"Diego would kill me in a minute. Felix would too, but as long as I'm inaccessible to him, he'll try to stifle me by spreading stories around the NSA and all of Washington that I've gone crazy and used you without permission and whatever else he can think of. All he needs to do is to keep us from interfering until they can get that plane in the air. If for any reason I have trouble getting military help in time, that plane has to stay on the ground. Once it's airborne, it's as good as in the U.S. We can have the Air Force combing Alabama, but my guess is that Felix will hurry things along by telling the Soviets that I've infiltrated. Once those MiGs are nuclear equipped, the Soviets have the proverbial gun to our heads."

"You basically don't want the truck to come off the ship before the Air Force gets there, assuming the Navy doesn't have a battleship close enough to help."

"You got it."

"If they do get the truck off the plane, how are they going to get nuclear warheads on board a plane in a major airport?"

"You forget, the Mexican government is in on this plan."

"What's in it for them?"

"That I don't know, but I'd hate to guess. No doubt there's a territorial prize waiting for them, just like Hitler offered in World War II."

"It didn't work then. Backfired."

"Mexico didn't want any part of it then, Jordan. For some reason, they're in this one up to their elbows."

"So, what's your plan? How do we keep the truck from getting off the ship?"

"Well, Jordan, it's a surprisingly small operation because the Mexican government wants no attention drawn to it. It's supposed to look like a routine dock, unloading, and transport, from the ship to the road to the airport to the jet and into the air. But the route is right through our soft underbelly, as Felix himself used to call it. Right through the radar gap. So plans? Yeah, I've got a few. None of them pleasant. Because even though Diego and his buddies total only a half dozen, including me, there are Mexican military and governmental support and backup people all along the route. We have to strike quickly and effectively to stall the whole process.

"There are only three of us, but it'll be my turn to stick close to Diego. He likes me. I have suggested to him that I be alone with him in the cab of the truck. My thought is that I would wait until he's maneuvering the vehicle into position to leave the ship, then disarm him and, in effect, hold him hostage."

Cydya squinted. "He carries a piece?"

"Always. An automatic and sometimes a smaller handgun. But I'm counting on his being nervous about driving a rig loaded with that many warheads. At first no one will understand the delay, but as they approach, I'll threaten to kill him or detonate the warheads. That should keep everyone at bay."

Jordan walked to the window. He parted the curtains and looked down on the quiet city. "I don't like this plan."

"That's what we're here for, Jordie. To poke holes in it. Tell me where it's faulty."

"Too risky. You don't know how long you'll have to hold him hostage. What if it turns out to be hours?"

"I can handle hours."

"What if it turns out to be twelve hours?"

"Twelve would not be fun. That's where you come in. I'll be in command if I have his weapons and control of the truck. I can make demands. You two will constitute my demands. We can spell each other."

It was Cydya's turn to take issue. "I don't know either, Mr. Rollins. It goes against all traditional strategy to try to take control of a situation from the middle rather than from the outside. Just imagining the situation makes me feel vulnerable. You know you'll be immediately sur-rounded by military and by the multinational force."

"True enough, but if I have enough fire power at my disposal to wipe the Yucatán Peninsula off the map, I don't mind going against conventional wisdom. Besides, how do we take control of this situation from the periph-ery when there are only three of us and they have the nuclear power?"

Jordan's hands were thrust deep into his pockets. "I assume you're going to show us where to station ourselves."

Harley nodded. "That's another obstacle, of course. I

don't know how carefully the area will be sealed off. It's such a hush-hush operation, I think the military is counting on Diego and his people to handle it so as to not be too visible."

"That would work to our advantage. But I have a bigger question for you, Harley. It's one you've asked me for years, so let me turn it around. Are you prepared to die?"

Harley cocked his head. "It's not on my things-to-do-tomorrow list, if that's what you mean."

"I mean this: what if someone from the Mexican military or one of Diego's people calls your bluff."

"My bluff? I wouldn't be bluffing."

"That's my point. Suppose that someone who knows they can't shoot at you without risking a nuclear explosion comes toward the truck. What do you do? Kill Diego?"

"If necessary."

"And suppose they keep coming? I mean now that Diego is dead, who else can you kill without killing yourself?"

"With Diego eliminated, I would shoot to kill them, yes."

"And if there are more of them than you have ammunition for?"

"I would expect help from my associates, you."

"But now suppose there are dozens of them, and they are rushing the truck, and you have threatened to detonate the warheads. How would you do that?"

"With a grenade into the truck bed."

"That would do it?"

"You betcha."

"Then, Harley, only the simplest base of my question is left: *would* you do it? Would you sacrifice your own life for this cause?"

"For the cause of the security of the United States, yessir, I would."

Cydya spoke. "Even if it means having to sacrifice who knows how many innocent lives in Mexico?"

"I've thought about that, and it seems to me the Mexican government is responsible for those citizens. They put their heads on the block when they agreed to help the Soviets invade the United States. The Soviets would not hesitate to sacrifice innocent civilians for their unjust cause. Otherwise, why equip the MiGs with warheads in the first place?" Harley stood and stretched. "These are big, important questions, and I don't want to be glib. But you realize that all three of us have to agree on this. Because if we are going to rotate, if we are forced to spell each other, any one of us could wind up with fate in our hands. If we're not ready to follow through on the threat to detonate, we'd better back out now and be prepared to salute whoever is running the U.S. this time next year."

Jordan looked at the floor. "Are there no options in the scenario I described?"

"Oh, some, sure. There's always the chance you might run the truck off the ship into the water, likely drowning in the process and risking explosion that way, too. But if the warheads did sink to the bottom of the harbor, at least we'd have bought time for the U.S. military to intervene. But not having seen the ship or the truck, my fear is that trying to crash the truck over the side would be akin to tossing a grenade into the cargo."

Jordan noticed the anxiety in Cydya's tired eyes. "I'd better walk her to her room, Harley."

He nodded. "Before you go, Jordan, I want to know: could *you* detonate? Given that was your last, worst, and only option?"

Jordan started to speak, but his mind was flooded. Yes, he would give his life and make the difficult decision to sacrifice the lives of others for his country, his family. But in his mind's eye were the friends and acquaintances with whom he had never pursued the great mysteries of life and God and the hereafter. He had definite beliefs, real fears about their welfare.

And there was the daughter he had never met. He didn't want to die before he saw her. And yet, what kind of world would she live in if the Soviets controlled North America?

Jordan spoke quietly. "Detonate."

Harley turned to Cydya. "How about you?"

Her voice was a monotone. "I could detonate. But don't ask me to sleep well tonight."

Twenty

The next morning at breakfast, Harley sketched the Progreso harbor for Jordan and Cydya and recommended that when they arrive, they split up but stay within sight of each other. "It will likely be impossible for me to communicate with either of you, even through signals. So you'll want to be close when Diego starts bringing the truck into position for off-loading."

Cydya was scribbling notes. "And you say that'll be just before dawn."

"Right. And I don't anticipate a change of plans because there are checkpoints along the way where he is expected. If he doesn't arrive, military personnel will start heading for Progreso to investigate. If he had to tell them all in advance of a new schedule, it would introduce a new element that might make them scrap the plan."

Jordan shrugged. "That would be all right. It would give you more time to make your Pentagon contact."

"But it's not likely, Jordan. That's my point. Probably the best thing we've got going for us now is that there is a tight, precise schedule. If they can stay on it, they'll all feel much more comfortable. And maybe a little overconfident."

Cydya drummed her pencil on the table. "I still have a lot of questions, Mr. Rollins. I hope you don't mind."

"Are you kidding? Right now, the odds are against us. If there was a choice, I'd back away from this one. Too many variables. Too many people lost already. Too much evidence that these people will crush anyone who gets in their way. By all means, let's hear your questions."

"When do you make your Pentagon contact?"

"Well, I've already made preliminary contact and have convinced my man that I have information on a crisis situation that is a threat to the security of the United States. We have agreed on a code system that is fairly new and has been used without detection, as far as we can tell. It's quick and brief and can be used orally by phone. He's given me a special number so I'll reach him on a scrambler phone. After I check on everything for Diego, and just before he arrives, I'll call the Pentagon."

Jordan raised his eyebrows. "And they'll send in the cavalry?"

Harley smiled. "I *can* tell you the code name for the operation, in the event the cavalry shows up and would otherwise mistake you for the enemy. 'Crimson Tide.'"

Cydya ran a hand through her hair. "If there's a crimson tide tomorrow on the Campeche Bank, it'll be our blood."

Wiping his mouth with a napkin, Harley shifted in his seat and crossed his legs. "If you wonder where that name came from, just ask yourself what the late Bear Bryant and his boys would have done if they'd known the Russians were in their backyard."

Cydya doodled on the paper. "What if Diego arrives early and you can't get away to make your call? Should you give one of us the information so we can make it?"

"The problem is, it's memorized, and I'm reluctant to put it on paper. If you were caught with it—."

She nodded. "We want to look out for your welfare."

Harley pulled plane tickets from his pocket. "I've booked you on a late morning flight. I'm going earlier. Both your weapons should be in Cydya's luggage, Jordan, just in case. I booked you under your Blanc alias, but you don't have any Blanc identification, do you?"

"No. That reminds me, Harley. You wouldn't have an extra clip or two for a .45 automatic?"

"Matter of fact, I do. How many do you need?"

"Better give me two. I've got seven rounds left."

"Hope you don't need any of them. When you get there, you might want to see if you can find clothes that will allow you to blend into the streets. If you look like foreigners nosing around the harbor this evening and in the middle of the night, you may spend the night in jail."

Cydya stood. "Will we see you between the time we get there and when you're in the truck with Diego?"

"Not likely."

"So we won't know if you made your call, or if everything is all right with you."

"Nobody said it was going to be easy."

She shook her head. "It looks like suicide."

"It may be, dear. Got any better ideas?"

When she didn't respond immediately, Jordan glanced at her. He thought he saw fear in her eyes, but it didn't concern him. He assumed his eyes gave him away, too. If she'd had the look of bravado to go along with her unhesitating assertion the night before that she was willing to die for this cause, then he would have been worried. Finally, she spoke. "I do get the feeling, Harley, that we're going to be doing a lot of hanging around, waiting for some action."

"That's right."

Jordan pursed his lips. "And when that action comes, we can only hope it's orchestrated by you. If it isn't, what are we supposed to do?"

Harley sighed. "Jordan, we worked together how many years? You know by now that not everything can go by the book. If this thing falls apart, if I can't call the Pentagon, if my cover is blown, someone still has to stop those warheads from leaving the ground in Mérida. That someone is you and how you do it is up to you. It won't be easy, it won't be sophisticated. We have no more inside help, and we have no time for any grand schemes."

"What would *you* do, Harley?"

"If the truck left the dock and headed toward the airport? I'd do whatever seemed necessary. Everything's out the window at that point, folks. Shoot at it, jump in front of it, kill the driver, threaten to blow it up, blow it up, whatever. I can't emphasize enough: once that truck pulls into the cargo bay of the jet and gets out over the Gulf of Mexico, the Soviets as good as have a beachhead on American soil."

Just before Harley left for the airport, he raised another issue with Jordan and Cydya. "There's a related problem almost as big as the operation, and, Jordan, you should know what it is from your poly sci background."

"I know. The U.S. may have to take overt military action, which they won't be able to hide from the press and the public."

"Exactly. But they must do it without exposing the fact that the MiGs are already in the States. Our government blockading a Mexican harbor where they've found nuclear warheads is one thing. Think of the ramifications for U.S.-Mexico relations—our border agreements will never be the same. But none of us will ever be able to tell a soul about the MiGs."

Jordan thought back to the many cases he'd worked on with Harley. None came close to this one in danger or importance. "Frankly, the whole thing gives me a headache."

Harley snorted. "If we pull this off, it'll be the quietest, most anonymous thing we've ever done."

"I'm used to that."

"People in four countries will disavow any knowledge of it."

Three hours later, as Cydya and Jordan waited to board their flight, she was pensive. "There's a terrible irony here, Jordan. You realize that by this time tomorrow, they could be shipping us home in boxes?"

He felt strange and uncomfortable around her. Despite her youthfulness, she had a depth and maturity that was not part of his memories. Now it was if he were talking to the aunt or the mother of the girl of his dreams. He wondered if he would feel more comfortable with Katrina.

"Cydya, if this mission fails, they won't find enough pieces to identify either of us."

"That's comforting."

In fact, this venture was the purest embodiment of the do-or-die cliché Jordan could think of.

"*Your* speculation wasn't much more pleasant."

"But you see the irony, Jordan?"

"Sure."

Her eyes followed the landing of a plane. "More than twenty years of separation. A few hours to mend fences, and we exit as kamikazes."

There were things Jordan wanted to say, but he wasn't a sentimentalist. Never had been. But she was right. The odds were fifty-fifty at best that they were living out the last day of their lives. There was some delicious aspect to that somewhere deep inside him. Jordan had lost Rosemary and seen three friends die, all because a veteran agent trusted Harley enough to tell his protégé the darkest secret in American history. Now death seemed a haven.

And yet, there was Katrina. Judy. Ken. Cydya. Whether he'd ever get an opportunity to say what needed to be said to his children was a matter of chance now. But if he died without somehow impressing upon Cydya what she had meant to him, it would be no one's fault but his own.

"You know, when I worshiped you in Indonesia, I thought you were too good for me."

"Oh, Jordan."

"No, really. You were twenty already, remember? And you would turn twenty-one while I was still nineteen. You'd been around." She laughed. "At least compared to me, you had. I saw you as a grown-up, an adult woman. And I was feeling very much the overgrown child. Still a teenager."

She stared out the window, watching baggage handlers. "You make me feel so old."

"That's my point, Cydya. It's seeing you now, in the light of day, that's such an education. In the early sixties, I hoped one day to grow up the way you had. But seeing you last night in the lounge and on the pier, I realized that you have grown up. You're a beautiful, beautiful woman, Cydya, and at twenty, in spite of your beauty, you were still a young girl."

She turned to face him, an embarrassed smile on her lips. "And now that you've seen me in the light of day, I suppose there's nothing like the morning sun on the equator to expose every flaw."

He shook his head. "Now act your age. Don't deflect compliments. You were better at taking them when you were twenty."

"Sorry, and thank you. I suppose people tell you this a lot, but you haven't changed a bit. Of course, I'd like to see all your blond hair, not just the roots. And either your eyes have changed color or you're wearing brown contacts."

"Right. They're still blue."

"No lines on the face. Wish I could say the same."

He sat looking into her eyes for several seconds. "I only got into that because I think it's interesting how perspectives change. You know, for years, you were in my mind as a twenty-year-old. I didn't want to think of your growing older. And now, to see you in the prime of your life and to realize that at twenty you were not yet grown up—."

She interrupted him. "I knew you wouldn't age. You were a youthful nineteen, and you look just as I imagined you would."

Jordan felt foolish for emphasizing the externals after so many years, but maybe they had exhausted all the rest the night before. "Cydya, do you think you could ever trust me again?"

She didn't answer immediately, which cut him deeply. "That's a fair question. There are those who say what I went through clouded my view of all men. But I don't think so. I think my decision to avoid getting involved with anyone else had more to do with my feelings for you than with any general anger or bitterness. As I told you last night, I believed we were meant for each other, and I lost out. I was not meant for someone else."

"But I was so cold, so cruel. I broke it off in the worst way."

"You were nineteen years old, Jordan. Eventually I came to realize that. It took a while, a few years, but I knew that the same earnestness, the same simplistic approach to life and work and the world, the same wonder you brought to our relationship was what made you react the way you did. You didn't have a choice. You were made that way, shaped that way."

"A scoundrel?"

"No! It was just that to you everything was black and white. Either we were in love or we weren't. Either I was interested in you or I wasn't. Something was either right or wrong. And if someone did something wrong, he paid for it."

"But you see—don't you, Cydya?—that by running from you I was punishing myself? I didn't mean to punish you. I know it must have looked that way, but I felt responsible. I had taken advantage of you. And the only appropriate penalty was to lose you."

Their flight was announced and they stood in line, whispering now. "Don't misunderstand me, Jordan, but I want to clarify something, especially in light of the fact that you are still mourning your wife. When I said that I believed we were meant for each other, that I was meant for you, and that I never stopped loving you, I'm fully aware that the 'you' I'm referring to does not exist anymore."

"What do you mean?"

"I mean I believed all that about the nineteen-year-old I was in love with. I still believe it was true about *that* Jordan Kettering. But I want to be careful not to complicate your life by implying that those feelings therefore apply to the current Jordan Kettering." She tapped his chest with her forefinger. "You've lived longer since I saw you last than you had lived up till then. So despite the fact that you're the father of my child and that I feel a certain kinship for you due to that, I don't even really know you, do I?"

He shook his head, unable to speak. It was the kindest put-down he'd ever heard. He knew she was right, and he also knew that she had said what he had been trying to say, only infinitely better. Finally he managed to respond. "I guess I wasn't bargaining for all that. My question was whether you thought you could ever trust me again."

She took a deep breath and let it out. "If the forty-one-year-old Jordan Kettering is the same man he was at nineteen, then I confess I'd be pretty wary."

The line was hardly moving. The attendant at the gate was carefully checking everyone's ticket.

"I'd like to prove myself worthy of your trust, Cydya."

"Well, Jordan, I'm trusting you with my life tomorrow morning. Antiterrorist activity isn't exactly my thing."

"Not into weapons?"

"Oh, yes. And I've fired three times in the line of duty."

"Ever kill anyone?"

278

She shook her head. "Almost, once. Wouldn't have made much difference. He was murdered later in prison anyway."

"Yes, it would have."

"Hm?"

"It would have made a difference. To you."

Jordan realized he had just come closer to telling her that he'd killed someone than he had ever come to telling Rosemary.

Finally, they reached the gate. "Ma'am, your name is LeMonde?"

"Yes."

"Would you step aside, please?" She called for a security guard. "Is Mr. Blanc traveling with you?"

Cydya hesitated. Jordan jumped in. "*Oui*. Problem?"

The guard appeared. "Come with me, please."

Jordan and Cydya were led to a small room off the main corridor where a chunky, dark man in a skinny tie leaned over the table and stared at Cydya with tiny, black eyes. He was pleasant enough, but all business.

"Miss LeMonde, is this your suitcase?"

"Yes, sir."

"In your suitcase we found a loaded .22-caliber Smith and Wesson and a box of forty rounds of ammunition. We also found a Colt .45-caliber automatic loaded with a partial clip of seven rounds and two additional full clips containing nine rounds each. Are these your weapons, ma'am?"

"I am responsible for those weapons, yes."

"You have a license to carry them?" She nodded and produced a document from her bag. He studied it. "Interpol. Then customarily, you would have diplomatic immunity." She nodded again. "And you, sir, Mister Blanc, are you also with Interpol?"

Cydya raised a hand and interrupted. "Excuse me, sir. Was there a problem with Mister Blanc's luggage?"

"No, ma'am."

"Then I suggest we concentrate on the problem at hand. I am in your country on official business and prefer to exercise my right to transport those weapons to Yucatán. I'll be happy to unload them if you prefer."

"Ma'am, what I prefer is irrelevant, as is your diplomatic privilege in this case. The government of Ecuador is cooperating with Mexico in not allowing any weapons to be flown out of our country into Mexico until further notice, and there are no exceptions."

"But—."

"I am sorry, ma'am. You may file a grievance, or we will be happy to refund the cost of your flight. It leaves shortly. What is your choice?"

"How will the weapons be returned to me?"

"When we are given clearance, we will ship them to whatever address you provide."

She snapped a business card on the table. "At your expense, I presume."

"I'm sorry, no."

On the plane Cydya worried aloud about Harley's guns. Jordan discounted the problem. "Harley will have access to Diego's arsenal. The question is what you and I can find on the black market. Anything reliable will be hundreds of dollars."

"Pesos?"

"No, American dollars. That's talkin' money on the black market. And I only have a few hundred left. How are you fixed?"

"I have francs and pesos, Jordan. A couple of hundred dollars worth."

"Any credit cards?"

"American Express."

"Perfect. What's the limit?"

"Ten thousand francs."

"Which translates to what in American dollars?"

"Depends on the exchange rate. A couple of thousand, I guess."

"A thousand in cash should be plenty, but we aren't going to have a lot of time to shop."

They both slept during the flight and awoke sweaty to a blistering day in Mérida. Jordan felt gamy as he walked down the steps and onto the runway. "Let's hope the next time we see this place, it's for a ride home."

They took a taxi all the way north to Progreso, and Jordan figured it cost him about a dollar a mile. They were deposited about six blocks south of the harbor in front of a cheap hotel. "Cheap and within walking distance of the water" was just what Jordan had asked for.

The place smelled like it looked. Drunks loitered in the lobby where a black-and-white television set carried a soundless soccer match. "Two rooms, top floor if you have them. Two nights. How much in American dollars?"

The clerk, who had been leering at Cydya, lit up at the prospect of dollars. "Two room. Two night. Twenty dollar."

As if they'd choreographed it, Jordan and Cydya turned to leave. The clerk chirped. "Fifteen! Ten!" Jordan turned and slapped a ten on the counter.

He chuckled on the way up the stairs. "Probably still got ripped off."

Jordan was impressed with how adaptable Cydya seemed. She had to be tired from all the traveling and the short nights, not to mention the tension. The weather was oppressive, not unlike what they had endured in Indonesia half their lives ago. Her hair was moist and matted, her blouse wet in back.

As the highest ranking woman in the history of Interpol, she was used to nice things, comfortable accommodations, even luxuries. Yet Jordan didn't hear a hint of complaint. In fact, it was she who urged that they not wait on replacing their weapons. He agreed. "You go class, I'll go trash."

A few minutes later, Jordan shut and locked his door and met her in the hall. If anything, she looked too good to be coming out of that dive. She drew a lot of stares on the way out, too. Jordan looked right and left. "Some modern buildings, maybe a hotel or two, to the west. Best bet for a bank. Get a thousand, if you can. I'm going the other way, looking for a sombrero and some grubbies. Need any?"

"What're you getting?"

"Secondhand stuff so it looks like we've lived in it."

"You decide, Jordan. Anything close will be fine. Get a fix on my size."

He stepped back and measured her with his eyes. "Don't mind if I do." That elicited a smile, and he wondered if he would ever see one from her again. "See you back here in an hour. If you're late, I'll come lookin' for you. If I'm late, stay put."

She strode off purposefully with a look that dared anyone to say or try anything. He watched until she was three blocks away, then he turned and jogged east. Within a block, he was drenched with sweat. To the north it appeared that the shops were nicer. He turned south.

He found a place that sold clothes so old and shabby that the prices were mere pesos each. Fat women in faded dresses and thongs milled about, children scampering around them. They picked through the stuff and haggled with the lone clerk. There was no cash register, just an oversized shoe box stuffed with bills and coins. Security came in the form of a German shepherd who slept at the foot of the counter that contained the box.

Jordan started with shoes, trying a couple of pairs of all-fabric slip-ons. He picked through the women's shoes, not knowing where to begin. They were so cheap he chose three of different sizes, figuring he'd get lucky. He found a khaki slacks and top outfit for Cydya that would probably be the best buy in the place. A deep burgundy corduroy beret topped it off.

For himself he picked up work pants, a boxy, plain, oversized pullover shirt, and a sombrero that rode low on his forehead. He also grabbed two cloth shoulder bags and piled the stuff on the counter, causing the dog to stir and open one eye. The clerk poked through the merchandise. He spoke only in Spanish and said something about pesos.

Jordan held up one dollar. The clerk managed, "Ah, American dollar," and held up ten fingers. Jordan shook his head. Nine. He shook again. Eight. No. Seven. No. Six. Jordan shook his head more slowly each time so as not to insult the man by not even considering his offer. Finally the clerk was left with just one hand up. He thrust it out vehemently. Jordan gave him six dollars, which brought a grateful grin. The man tossed in a cardboard box, and Jordan was off, his booty under his arm.

He hurried back to his room and changed. He didn't have enough money for weapons yet, but he wanted to scout out the possibilities anyway. He realized his walk was a little jaunty for his outfit and slowed down. It was near siesta time anyway, and he would be conspicuous, bounding about the neighborhood looking for bargains.

He walked a mile south into a section where more drunks and malcontents hung out. When he saw the store, he knew he had found at least the entrée to the type of weapons he wanted. In the window were a hundred knives of different sizes, beginning with the smallest on the left and crescendoing to the largest on the right.

The smallest was a novelty, a miniature dagger. Next was a tiny jack knife, and on up they went to hunting knives, skinning knives, Bowie knives, stilettos, switchblades, and even a bayonet. An old Mexican with thick, black, horn-rimmed glasses smiled at Jordan as he admired the display.

Jordan stepped inside and looked at small-bore rifles and cheap handguns. Horn Rims spoke only Spanish, so Jordan made clear to him through hand signals that he was looking for two much bigger, much better handguns. The man shrugged. Jordan smiled. "American dollars."

The man smiled, too. He handed Jordan a piece of paper and a pencil. Jordan drew a .45, a .38, and a .357 magnum, carefully printing the numbers and brand names. For good measure, he also drew a hand grenade, but wrote nothing next to it. The man went in the back and came out a few minutes later. He had crossed out the .45 and had written a dollar sign and 600 next to the other two guns. Next to the grenade he wrote a dollar sign and seventy-five.

Jordan crossed out the numbers and cut the prices in half and the grenade by two thirds. The man went in the back and returned, nodding and smiling. Jordan totaled the figures and wrote $625 on the sheet. He took the man's wrist and pointed to five o'clock on his watch.

The man nodded, led him back to the door, and pointed upstairs, then back at his watch. Jordan wondered if it was just his imagination or did he attract more stares on his way back to the hotel this time? He knocked at Cydya's door. She answered from inside.

"It's Jordan. Got somethin' for ya. Be right back." He returned with her "new" clothes. "How'd it go?" She fanned out ten fifties and twenty-five twenties. "Good work. Give me six and a half. I don't want to take much more than I need. You get your choice, a .357 magnum or a .38."

She shrugged. "Both heavy and ugly. Guess I've practiced more with a .38."

He told her the arrangement he had at five and that he didn't want her to go with him when he went back to purchase the guns. "Bad neighborhood."

"Oh, I'm safer near the harbor and a couple of dozen nuclear warheads?" She looked through the clothes. "Lovely."

"Thought you'd like 'em. Just $400 at Saks. I'll be back."

"Jordan?"

"Yeah."

"I don't need to tell you that going upstairs at that place could be playing right into their hands. They know you're coming back with money. If they play their cards right, they could wind up with your money without coming across with the guns."

"Good point. I was so worried about the quality of the merchandise, I might not have thought about that. I don't make a habit of using underground weapons."

"Be careful."

He skipped down the stairs, feeling in his element, doing what he was born to do. No one in twenty years of such work had ever told him to be careful on his way out. It was a good thing she did.

Twenty One

At the door of the knife shop, Jordan stood in the shadows, waiting. He was not going upstairs alone, even if the owner accompanied him. He sensed he was being watched and wondered how many on the street were aware of a gringo with hundreds of American dollars who ventured into this neighbor thinking he would be trading his money for hot pistols.

Many were sleeping in doorways, or were they sleeping? The shop was closed for siesta, but Horn Rims himself had made the appointment. Jordan kept an elbow clamped tightly over his shoulder bag and the money.

Five minutes. Then ten. He would give Horn Rims three more minutes, then he'd take his business elsewhere. Two men came up the street on the other side. Strange. One was drunk, weaving, nearly falling. The other was cold sober, walking straight. Yet they appeared to be together.

They crossed in midblock. Jordan tensed. Neither looked at him, but the sober one fell in behind the drunk. As they passed, the drunk stumbled into him, grabbing the strap of the shoulder bag as if to steady himself. As the loop slipped from Jordan's shoulder, the sober one joined the fracas.

Jordan ran his thumb up the strap and over his head so his neck was between the loop and the bag. With a shout he shot his fist past the face of the phony drunk and drew it back, elbowing him just above the nose, between the eyes. He went down and didn't move.

Jordan saw terror in the eyes of the other man and didn't want to disappoint him. He backed away, so Jordan rushed him and drove his right foot into the man's knee. He hurried away, limping. Jordan leaped around to face any surprise attackers from the rear. But there were none. Just dozens of pairs of sleepy, curious eyes. Within seconds, Horn Rims appeared from upstairs.

He waved Jordan up, but Jordan shook his head and pointed to the ground, as if to say, "Right here, right now." Horn Rims held out his hand and rubbed his fingers with his thumb. No way Jordan would give him money before seeing the merchandise. He shook his head again and shaped his thumbs and forefingers like guns. Horn Rims went back inside.

While Jordan waited, the "drunk" groaned, rolled over, and wobbled to his feet. He stared at Jordan through bloodshot eyes. Jordan feigned a move toward him and he hobbled off. Horn Rims returned with a bulging paper bag and held it open. Jordan turned the bag toward the sun and peeked in to confirm the two pistols and the grenade. He pulled the .38 out just far enough to point into the chamber, signaling that he needed ammunition. Horn Rims made the money sign again. Jordan showed him the $650. The man jogged upstairs a final time and returned with two boxes of bullets, one for each gun. After they traded, the man extended his hand. Jordan ignored it. He pushed the paper bag into his shoulder bag and the weight strained against his shoulder all the way back to the hotel.

Jordan warned Cydya about the food as they went for a walk just before dark. "Eat light and safe."

"I'm not even hungry. I won't sleep tonight either."

Jordan agreed. "Sleep in your clothes and be ready to move. If we get any visitors tonight, you can bet they won't be anybody but the lechers in our own lovely establishment."

She looked out over the gulf. "Yeah. Or somebody

who followed me from the bank or you from the gun buy."

"That's all we need."

They were within one street of the harbor. She stopped and looked between buildings. "It's really quite lovely, isn't it?" To their left, the setting sun sent orange and pink streaks across the water. The temperature dropped, but the weather was still humid and uncomfortable. He took her arm and led her north to the far right end of the harbor.

"I'll be up here. You'll be to the west about three hundred yards at the other end of where the ship will dock, Harley's guessing sometime between four and five in the morning. Just before dawn, whatever that means, Diego will pull the truck to the ramp."

He sensed Cydya had picked up the pace and he wondered if she was too tense. "They wouldn't lower the ramp until just before they were ready to go, would they, Jordan?"

"Probably not, for security's sake."

"And they're definitely driving the truck off, not craning it?"

"That's the plan. I wouldn't crane a truck with that cargo, would you?"

She shook her head. "The lowering of the ramp should be our cue, then?"

They were getting closer to the site where the ship would dock, both trying not to appear new and nosy.

"Frankly, Cydya, I don't know if a cue can be predetermined. We'll have to play it by ear. I doubt we'll be able to see Diego or Harley in the truck while it's onboard. The ramp will probably be lowered as Diego is getting the truck in position, and that's when Harley will make his move."

"How will we know, Jordan?"

"That he's done it? There will be a delay, of course.

The ramp will come down, but the truck won't. That'll be the first clue. Then I would expect some announcement from either Diego or Harley with instructions for the ship's crew and the others. We'll be innocent bystanders until he needs us."

They strolled within two hundred feet of the dock. "Jordan, have you thought of the possibility that Mr. Rollins wasn't able to get his call made for some reason?"

He nodded. "I have. That phone call is the one weakest link in this admittedly thin plan to thwart the invasion. You were right when you suggested that Harley give us enough info to make the call for him, if necessary. Because if he didn't make it, the rest of this is meaningless. We can slow, stall, stop the truck. We can kill ourselves in the process of making sure the warheads are detonated here instead of in the States. However, unless the Pentagon is notified, the only people who knew what was in the works will be gone. If he didn't make the call, it would almost make more sense for him to abort his plan to make a hostage of Diego and just get to the Pentagon whenever he can."

"You're confusing me, Jordan. I see what you're saying, but if for some reason the truck pulls off that ship and up the street through town toward the airport road, what are we supposed to assume? That you and Mr. Rollins think alike and that he has dumped the plan because we have no U.S. military backup?"

"No! The way the plan stands now, if the truck makes the ramp, our job is to stop it at all costs."

She stopped and turned to face him. "Then we'd better quit trying to second-guess Mr. Rollins. We'll have to assume he made the call. If he didn't, we're dead anyway."

They walked in silence toward the setting sun, then strolled south to head back to the hotel. Jordan stopped at a food cart and watched a man handmaking flour and corn tortillas with meat sauce. "If he'll let me, I can put together a couple of those that would be safe to eat."

Jordan put the man at ease by paying him in American dollars first and smiling as he reached for his own tortilla. He held the tortilla directly over the flames for as long as he could stand it. That would take care of any bacteria. He dipped the steaming dough into the meat sauce and handed it to Cydya.

She loved it. "Just what I needed."

Jordan licked his fingers and prayed this wasn't their last supper. At her door he told her to try to sleep and that he would knock at three-thirty. He looked at his watch. "That should give us about six hours of rest, if not sleep. You ready?"

She cocked her head and gave him a closed-mouth smile. "No. I'm not. But I'll be there." He reached out with both hands and squeezed her shoulders. Then he waited until he heard her lock and chain the door before he headed for his own room, two doors down.

Jordan arranged his room precisely so he could simply rise at three twenty-five, fill his shoulder bag and pockets, and head to the communal bathroom. He stretched out on his back and put his hands behind his head. Looking at his watch, he told himself when to get up, then shut his eyes.

He hadn't realized until that instant how bone-weary he was. His elbow ached from where he had cold-cocked the drunk, but otherwise he felt fit. He ran the plan over and over in his mind, sending Cydya up the street at the west end of the harbor, making his approach from the east. He wondered how many people would be out and about that early in the morning besides the small group who knew what was happening.

He hadn't expected to sleep well, but as he felt himself drift, he reminded himself of the number of hours he could doze. In fact, his sleep was not peaceful. He didn't dream as much as mix and match the images of the day. The breakfast meeting with Harley had been troubling because the job seemed so big and their resources so limited. But Cydya's questions had been good. The flight had been crowded and hot, but at least he had not been alone. The black market purchase was sloppier than he liked, but Cydya's reminder had probably saved his life.

At two o'clock he bolted upright. What had awakened him? He'd heard something. He stood and staggered to the door. There it was again! A shout, a thud, a door banging. He ripped at the chain and the lock and grabbed a pistol as he lunged into the hall.

Under the faint light of a single bulb he saw Cydya's follow-through as she karate-kicked a man over the railing. Her face was flushed with the effort. The man landed with a hard flop halfway down the stairs and rolled slowly to the landing. Jordan bounded after him and held the cold barrel of the .357 to his temple. But he was just a drunk. Bleary-eyed and reeking, he repeated a Spanish phrase over and over.

Jordan looked up to Cydya who stood at the rail. Spanish was one of her languages. "He's saying, 'Wrong floor, wrong floor.' " Jordan helped him up and guided him to the floor below. Indeed, he had a room on that floor in the same spot as Cydya's.

When Jordan returned, Cydya was standing with her back to the wall, one hand across her stomach, the other cradling her head. He touched her shoulder. "You all right?"

She nodded. "Scared me, that's all. Kept trying the doorknob and the key, and when they didn't work, he banged and hollered. At first I thought it was you and that there was trouble. When I peeked out with the chain still attached, he yanked the door and the casing broke. My eyes hadn't adjusted to the light yet, so I reacted instinctively."

"And wonderfully."

She shrugged. "You do what you have to do. The poor man, if he hadn't been drunk, that tumble over the bannister would have killed him."

"He won't even remember it in the morning."

"What time is it, Jordan?"

"Just after two."

"I won't sleep now. And look at this door." With the casing ripped off, it wouldn't lock.

"Put your valuables in my room. I'll stretch out in here with my gun, and pity the next drunk who gets the wrong room."

"Don't be silly, Jordan. You're not going to sleep either, are you?" He shook his head. "Then let's just talk. It may be the last chance we get."

He thought of the stark truth of that as he went back and gathered up his money and munitions. In her tiny room, she sat on the bed with her back to the wall and he sat on the floor, his back to the door. Neither spoke for several minutes.

Cydya made a clicking sound with her mouth. "Do you remember one of the first things you ever said to me?"

He thought. "You mean the very first?"

"Um-hm."

"At the airport in Jakarta?"

"Yup."

"No. I was overwhelmed, I remember that. Thought your name was unusual, of course. What?"

"C'mon, think!"

"I really don't know, Cydya."

"You said you felt grundy!" That made her laugh aloud. "Do you remember that?" He nodded, smiling, and she laughed more, until her laughing turned to crying. At first she still smiled through her tears, but then she covered her face with her hands and great sobs wracked her body.

Jordan stood awkwardly, not knowing if she wanted

to be comforted or left alone. She cried and cried. He sat next to her and put his arm around her. He held her for half an hour until she seemed to doze. Then he stood carefully, laid her down, and returned to his place on the floor by the door. He glanced at his watch before lowering his head to his chest and closing his eyes.

At three twenty-five his head popped up as if automated. He licked his lips and stretched. Standing, he folded his arms and leaned over, touching his elbows to the floor with his legs straight. One in a thousand men could do it.

He bent over Cydya, put one hand on her head and the other on her shoulder. She stirred.

"Zero hour, Cydya. I'm gonna run down the hall. Be right back."

On his way back he passed her. Her eyes were puffy and dark, but she forced a smile as their eyes met briefly. Five minutes later, weapons loaded and hidden in their shoulder bags, they tiptoed down the stairs.

They walked in silence four blocks north to the place where they would part. He turned to her. "Remember, we're just moseying by the harbor, lost, drunk, on our way to work, whatever. Just hangin' around. Not tense, not interested, the type of person no one even notices. We'll be able to see each other, but let's not get closer than a hundred yards to each other unless something's going down."

He could barely see her in the predawn darkness. She turned toward her route to the harbor. Jordan caught the elbow of her khaki top. "Cydya. I've loved you all my life. I want you to know that."

She wrapped her arms tightly around his neck and whispered in his ear. "The next place we see each other might be in heaven. I have you to thank for that."

He chuckled as she pulled away. "For making you sure of heaven or for helping you to get there early?"

But she said nothing as she turned and walked west.

He watched her until she turned north. She didn't look back. He walked east two blocks and turned north. No one else was on the street. He wandered, forcing himself to relax, though every sense was raw, every fiber on fire.

He was glad they had come out early. What a nightmare it would have been if the ship had been docked when they arrived. He pictured it, the ramp down, the truck already gone. He meandered up to the harbor road and casually looked west. Cydya sat on a bench along the bus route, almost as if napping. She looked small and fragile, but he smiled, thinking of how she had booted that drunk over the railing.

At four o'clock Jordan imagined the sky was lighter in the east, but he knew it was only wishful thinking. He also thought he saw lights on the far horizon. He walked a quarter mile over the next several minutes, trying to will the clock to move. Another part of him wanted it to stop.

He hated inaction. And this assignment had death written all over it. He had never felt so alone. His wife was gone. His house was gone. His uncle's house, his refuge since he was a child, was gone. And what had he done to the only other woman he had ever loved? Run from her when she needed him the most. Now he might be leading her to her death.

Those *were* lights on the horizon. Faint, tiny, still distant, but red and green and white against the sky. A great, ponderous ship, larger than usual for this part of the harbor, crept higher on the gray horizon, still miles from shore. The sky *was* grayer than it had been minutes before. Soon the horizon would glow in the lightest of pastels.

Jordan wanted to signal Cydya, but they had agreed not to do that. What would he tell her anyway? *Our ship has come in.* She'd see it soon enough, and he wondered if she would share his excitement.

He didn't know how to judge the speed and estimated

time of arrival of the ship or he would have tried to wander along a route that would bring him near the harbor at the same time. As it was, he reached the harbor road again while the ship was still at least a mile out, and he noticed a jeep pulling in near the dock. From his vantage point, he could see a driver and three passengers. The driver emerged and began working at the gangplank, swinging it far over the dock, but leaving it suspended. Apparently he would lower it to the deck when the ship docked. He had some trouble with the gangplank, but received neither help nor seemingly even any interest from the other three in the jeep.

Jordan walked south three blocks and looked west at every intersection. As far as he could tell, there were no police or military personnel in place anywhere to escort the truck. Obviously, Machala Diego thought this operation was the best kept secret in Mexico.

The next time he looked out to the gulf, Jordan saw the ship, big and clear against the dawn sky. He heard the great engines and watched as the craft began maneuvering to dock in the harbor. The machinations took several minutes, during which he averted his eyes several times to keep track of the men in the jeep. All four were now in the vehicle, two in the front and two in the back.

Finally, the ship was in the harbor, within a hundred feet of the dock. Jordan wanted to head west on the harbor road, but he waited to make sure the attention of the men in the jeep was fully directed toward the craft. He hoped Cydya had the same idea. He couldn't see her, so he assumed she did.

As the ship neared the moorings, a small crew appeared on the deck and began securing lines. Four men emerged from the jeep. One was Harley. All had their eyes on the ship. Jordan transferred the .357 from his bag to his right pocket and turned west on the harbor road.

Harley was walking strangely, hands behind his back.

And Jordan suddenly recognized one of the other men. He was tall and dark and gangly—Felix! It couldn't be! Harley had thought Felix would be waiting on the other end, in Alabama, protecting his identity. What a shock it must have been for both of them when Felix showed up and they saw each other!

Jordan's mind was racing. Had Harley made his Pentagon contact? If he had, did Diego and Felix know? What would they do with Harley? No way would they spare him after eliminating all the others. Felix must have really believed in Machala Diego to think he could brazenly show up for the delivery without risking his NSA cover.

The crew was on the bridge, their eyes on the foursome nearing the gangplank. Jordan didn't see any weapons out, yet he knew all but Harley had to be armed. He found himself hurrying toward the dock, against his own will. The plan was out the window, and he had no way of knowing whether Harley had made Pentagon connections. Jordan's first goal now was to protect Harley. If only he could communicate to Harley that he was there.

Jordan came within a hundred feet of the dock. He could hear the truck engine starting. Someone from the crew drove the truck around from the cargo hold and left it idling in the middle of the ship near the ramp. The foursome from the gangplank boarded the ship, but only the short, slim, dark-haired one peeled off. That had to be Diego. He slid behind the wheel of the truck and slammed the door.

The other three—the driver of the jeep, Felix, and Harley—walked past the truck and continued around the other side of the ship. Jordan had to get there. He wouldn't worry about the truck until the wide, metal ramp was lowered to the dock.

He had to take the chance. With Diego in the truck and no one else in sight on the deck, he broke into a sprint across the gangplank, trying to stay low. The ship's engines and the idling truck covered the sound of his steps, but halfway across he felt the ships engines shut down and the vibration of someone behind him. Cydya!

He pointed to the right, intending to send her around the other side of the ship. He would go left and directly in front of the truck. He wouldn't deal with Diego unless forced to. He couldn't risk a shot at the truck. His best hope was that Diego would not see him until he passed directly in front of him. By then it would be too late to stop Jordan from getting around the other side to Harley. If he and Cydya arrived at about the same time, they'd have a good chance of saving Harley's life.

From the bridge above him he heard the first cry. Military. Two Mexicans, both quickly removing weapons snapped in holsters at their sides. Jordan held out a hand to stop Cydya as she approached from behind. They stared up at the Mexicans, but now there was only one. He held his weapon in both hands, aiming for Jordan's head.

Jordan's voice was hoarse. "Amigo!"

But before the one on the bridge could answer, the second appeared at the ship end of the gangplank. Cydya whispered. "Should we jump over the side?" Jordan shook his head as the Mexican approached with his weapon trained on them as well.

He stole a glance at her. "Your weapon hidden?"

"They'll find it easily enough."

"Draw it."

"Are you crazy?"

"Draw it! Do it easy, as if you're going to surrender it."

The cry from the bridge had stopped all activity on the ship. Diego was in the truck, engine warming. With the ramp up, there was nowhere for him to go.

297

The jeep driver, Felix, and Harley had disappeared around the other side of the deck. Jordan was certain they wouldn't hesitate to use Harley to get rid of him and Cydya.

The Mexican in front of them barked orders. Cydya translated. "He wants us to back slowly off the gangplank to shore."

"We can't do that. Play dumb. Draw your gun now. Carefully."

They shrugged and tried to look puzzled in the faint light of dawn, but as their weapons came into view, both Mexicans shouted and raised their own, ready to fire. Cydya and Jordan dangled their handguns over their heads by their little fingers, making them impossible to fire.

"Pray he moves forward to take them. I'll break his neck."

But the uniformed Mexican at the end of the gangplank wasn't buying. He signaled with his head that they should throw their weapons overboard. Jordan talked calmly to Cydya. "Somehow we've got to get the one up there to come down here. It's hopeless with him up there."

The other man was growing impatient. He moved out onto the gangplank, twenty feet from them. He spit as he talked and looked ready to fire at the first provocation. Jordan called to him.

"You know what's on this ship?"

He answered in Spanish. Cydya touched Jordan's arm with her free hand. "He doesn't speak English."

The one above hollered down in a thick accent. "What is on this ship does not concern us. What concerns us is that you are trying to get on. Throw your weapons overboard."

"We can't do that, amigo. What if they discharge? We know what is on this ship."

The door of the truck opened and Diego stuck his head out, screaming at the man in uniform above him. "Shoot them! Shoot them and be done with it!"

Jordan lowered his weapon and slid it down the gangplank to the soldier. Cydya, moving much more slowly, did the same. "We are unarmed now! Let us go!"

Diego was maniacal. "Shoot! Shoot!"

Jordan's eyes shifted between the two soldiers. Diego had no good line to them. If he and Cydya were to be dropped, the soldiers would have to do it. He spoke under his breath. "Time to find out whether or not the soldiers know what's in the truck." In one motion he reached for his grenade and pulled the pin. He held it out before the soldier, then waved it over his head so Diego could see it, too.

"Shoot me and the whole ship and harbor go up. The whole peninsula! Is that what you want? You want to go with it?"

The soldier below immediately dropped his weapon. Cydya started toward him. Jordan stuck his foot out to block her. "Wait! You, up there! Throw your weapon down." The gun clattered to the deck. "Now you come down." The soldier ran down to join his partner. "I want you and the crew off this ship. Round 'em up and get 'em off. Now!"

As Jordan stood with the grenade live, the pin in his left hand and the lever tight in his right palm, he felt the cramping in his wrist. Cydya retrieved the four weapons on the deck. There was no movement in the truck. Jordan began to shout instructions. "Diego! Shut that truck off or I blow the ship!"

The engine sputtered and died. Jordan was surprised. He thought Diego would call his bluff. Letting go of the grenade was his last option. "Granger! If I hear a shot, a yell, a splash, anything, we're all going out together, you got it? Answer me!"

No answer. "You'd better grunt or something, Felix, or you'll regret it!"

He heard a mutter from the southerner. "We're here."

"I want Harley safe, and I want you and Diego and your people to surrender! Nothing less!"

The soldiers appeared at the end of the gangplank with six crewmen, all with terror in their eyes. The eight turned sideways and slowly crept past Jordan on the narrow gangplank. If Harley had been freed, he might have tried to lock them away somewhere. But for now, he simply had to improve the odds.

He handed the grenade to Cydya. "Jordan! I've never used one of these."

"Don't use it now. Just squeeze it tight."

Now that his hands were free again, Jordan manually raised the gangplank. He knew the soldiers and crewmen onshore would immediately go for help, but an army wouldn't dare do any more than the two soldiers had done. Not as long as he and Cydya had a live grenade on board.

Jordan's bag was full of pistols now, and he followed Cydya toward the truck where a menacing Diego sat behind the wheel.

"If any of them is suicidal, it's this one. We have to start with him." Then he spoke directly to Diego. "Weapon first, amigo! Then let's go find Granger and Rollins."

Diego tossed out a small pistol. Jordan wasn't convinced. "More!" An Uzi clattered out. "Now you! Move!" Diego stepped from the truck and spit in Jordan's face. Jordan could have dropped him where he stood, but controlling the boss until Harley was safe was more important.

Diego slowly led them around the other side of the ship to where Harley stood between the jeep driver and Felix Granger. They had bound Harley's feet and were forcing him to lie on the deck.

"Tell them to cut him loose, Diego."

Diego cursed him in Spanish. Jordan turned to Cydya. "This man wants to die." At that instant, a door burst open behind Cydya, slamming into her back and popping the grenade from her hand. Diego and his people screamed and covered their heads, as did the one crewman who had stayed behind the door, waiting for the opportunity to ambush the intruders.

Jordan rushed the skittering grenade and kicked it overboard, soccer style. Its explosion was a dull thud that barely rippled the water, and he knew Horn Rims had ripped him off. Diego leaped to his feet and raced around to the other side of the ship. Gunfire from Felix and the jeep driver drove Jordan and Cydya to cover.

They followed Diego, and the brave crewman followed them until a stray shot felled him. Jordan tossed a weapon to Cydya. She looked at him pleadingly. "Jordan! Harley!"

"Diego's first!" He ran on alone.

Jordan saw flashing lights on the shore and heard the hydraulic ramp lowering as he sprinted toward the truck. Diego had set the lever in motion and was already behind the wheel again. The engine roared, the horn blared, and the headlights came on. Still on the dead run, Jordan raised his weapon and pointed it at Diego. Ten feet from the vehicle and running at top speed, he saw the driver's door open and heard Diego screaming. "Don't shoot! Nuclear!"

Jordan veered off course and ran directly at the door. He leaped, throwing his feet out in front of him and smashing the door on Diego's body as he attempted to jump out. The door pinned Diego vertically, starting with his face and the back of his head. Jordan scrambled to his feet and charged the door again, this time giving it a flying kick with his left foot. He felt and heard tissue give way before Diego slid to the deck. Crushed ribs had torn through his heart.

Jordan ran so swiftly around to the other side of the ship that he slipped making the turn, tumbled and rolled twice before bouncing back to his feet. The jeep driver held a gun to Harley's head as Felix tugged at his feet. Finally, the driver holstered his weapon and they bent over him, one at each end. They carried him toward the side of the ship.

Cydya crouched at the other end of the deck, both hands around her gun. Jordan pointed at her, then at the jeep driver. He raised his weapon toward Felix and they shot simultaneously. The driver grabbed for his gun as he went down. Cydya fired twice more.

Harley had been dropped hard on the deck and was perilously close to the edge. Felix, down and wounded, kicked at him, pushing him closer to the water. Cydya screamed as Harley flopped overboard. "Jordan!"

Jordan skidded to the side of the ship and put a final shot through Felix's heart. He hollered to Cydya. "Radio a mayday and the code word!" He dove overboard.

Harley struggled in the water and Jordan had nothing with which to cut the ropes. He yanked the big man's head above the surface. Harley sputtered. "Is Diego in the truck?"

"More likely, he's in hell. Are we in this thing alone or did you make your contact?"

They went under again, Jordan fighting to hang onto his friend. He yanked at the knots, but the rope was thick and slippery. Harley stiffened and Jordan pushed him above the surface again.

Harley sucked for air. "Hands first!"

Jordan knew that was the best idea, because then Harley could use his hands to paddle and stay afloat while Jordan worked on the rope at his ankles. But the rope at his wrists was so tight it cut into his flesh.

Jordan bobbed him up so they could both get one more breath before he dived under to work the ropes off

Harley's feet. He pulled Harley's shoes off, but the rope was still so tight that his socks came off when the rope did.

Now Harley was able to kick, at least, but keeping him upright with his hands behind his back was a chore. Jordan kicked his feet and guided Harley to the side of the ship. There he was able to pin him while working in earnest on the knots. Harley kept shaking his head to clear the water from his face. "Those were good shoes!"

Finally, he was loose and they rested, pressing against the side of the ship. There were sirens on shore and someone shouted through a bullhorn in Spanish.

"Cydya went looking for the radio, Harley. She gonna be able to raise any help or not?"

Harley stared into the distance. "That a good enough answer?"

Jordan turned to see a submarine surface and hear the scream of two jet fighters crisscrossing above the ship. A helicopter hovered, its searchlight scanning the gulf. The two of them waved and shouted: "Operation Crimson Tide!"

Cydya LeMonde was flown courtesy of the United States Air Force to Paris, where she was met at the airport by her daughter, Katrina.

Jordan Kettering and Harley Rollins were flown to Washington, where they were met at the airport by Jordan's daughter Judith.

Judy offered to help her father look for a new home. He thanked her. "I appreciate the help, honey, and I'll take you up on it when I get back. I'm going to France for a few days."

59607